WRITING THE YUGOSLAV WARS

WRITING THE YUGOSLAV WARS

Literature, Postmodernism, and the Ethics of Representation

DRAGANA OBRADOVIĆ

UNIVERSITY OF TORONTO PRESS
Toronto Buffalo London

ISBN 978-1-4426-2954-7 (cloth)

∞ Printed on acid-free, 100% post-consumer recycled paper with vegetable-based inks.

Library and Archives Canada Cataloguing in Publication

Obradović, Dragana, author
Writing the Yugoslav wars : literature, postmodernism, and the ethics of representation / Dragana Obradović.

Includes bibliographical references and index.
ISBN 978-1-4426-2954-7 (cloth)

1. Yugoslav literature – 20th century – History and criticism. 2. Yugoslav War, 1991–1995 – Literature and the war. 3. War and literature – Yugoslavia – History – 20th century. 4. Postmodernism – Yugoslavia. I. Title.

PG567.O27   2016   891.8'2609006   C2016-903912-9

This book has been published with the help of a grant from the Federation for the Humanities and Social Sciences, through the Awards to Scholarly Publications Program, using funds provided by the Social Sciences and Humanities Research Council of Canada.

University of Toronto Press acknowledges the financial assistance to its publishing program of the Canada Council for the Arts and the Ontario Arts Council, an agency of the Government of Ontario.

Contents

Acknowledgments

Most of this work was written while I was working at the Department of Slavic Languages and Literatures at the University of Toronto – a supportive and intellectually stimulating environment. Thank you to my colleagues who provided me with important feedback on my work in formal and informal ways. Manda Vrkljan, librarian at St Michael's College at the University of Toronto, was formidable in assisting me with endless queries. I have benefited greatly from the University of Toronto's New Researcher Award, which enabled me to finish this manuscript and undertake essential research trips to Sarajevo and Belgrade.

My doctoral research at University College London was the beginning of this project. I would like to thank Zoran Milutinović, my supervisor, for his mentorship and assured guidance during my time there. He was essential in forming my intellectual sensibilities in ways that are only just becoming apparent to me. The university provided me with a graduate research stipend that was essential to my existence and the Department of Comparative Literature was an exceptional place to expand my knowledge of literature.

It was also at University College London that I formed truly meaningful friendships with a group of talented and exceptional individuals. My life would be unthinkable without the sage advice and reason of Delphine Grass, someone I can rely on for both criticism and support. The memory of our many conversations about literature, art, and life sustain me when we don't have the luxury of time to speak at great length. Zbigniew Wojnowski supported me by responding to even the smallest concerns and anxieties with a unique combination of humour and seriousness. Moreover, he was always ready to challenge whatever idea I put forward, which was frustrating but also illuminating. Gesche Ipsen was such an enthusiastic supporter of my project and tirelessly read every draft of this book. Alex Nice always managed to talk to me about difficult and impossible themes in ways that were inspirational and influential. Most importantly, to these friends, thank you for the many adventures we have shared together.

I would also like to thank the wonderful Jessica Copley and Rosa Van Den Beemt, who listened patiently and kindly to me ramble on about the book throughout endless evenings in Toronto. Very warm thanks also to Kate Holland and Christina Kramer, who are, first and foremost, close friends but also my unofficial mentors. Their advice will benefit me for many years to come. As this book project drew to a close, Naomi Nattrass Moses and Zev Moses read various drafts with a keen editorial eye for infelicitous mistakes in expression and tone. They're an incomparable and uncompromising linguistic duo who deserve my thanks not only for their editing but also for making me enjoy the search for the right expression.

The team at the University of Toronto Press has been incredible to work with. Special thanks to Richard Ratzlaff, my editor at the press, who was always incredibly generous with his time and counsel. I am very grateful for the serious work done by the anonymous reviewers whose criticism helped me think through individual sections. I would also like to extend my gratitude to Charles Stuart, whose copy editing truly helped polish the manuscript at its final stages of preparation.

Finally, my sister Jelena and my parents Ljuba and Dragan have provided endless support and enthusiasm – and a good dose of pragmatism – to every single endeavour I have ever attempted. To them, I owe everything.

WRITING THE YUGOSLAV WARS

Introduction

"The city seemed to me – and I described it so in the book – like a post-modern work, an object of art, a photograph or piece of cloth."[1] What is surprising about this sentence is that it describes a city under siege – broken, razed, and ruined – as possessing the mask of artistic creation. In Semezdin Mehmedinović's *Sarajevo blues*, a volume of war writing that is at its core a work of testimony of survival during the modern-day siege of Sarajevo, there is a strong concern with the idea of the art of destruction. This collection expresses a conscious conflict between the pursuit of truthfulness as an ethical matter and the pursuit of an aestheticized representation of a besieged city. The ambiguity and tension exposed by the demands of the witness genre in the hands of an author with a propensity for figurative language point towards a fruitful line of analysis: how does war, either despite or because of its tragedy, become literary?

Beginning in 1991, the Socialist Federal Republic of Yugoslavia was torn apart by a series of violent conflicts. The long years of war resulted in many records of the tragic events produced by diverse observers and participants, but none are as discordant as the prose and poetry by literary authors who, in critiquing the war as a political and ideological cataclysm, also approached the event as an aesthetically constructive force. War literature in general confirms the radical power of violence to harness the human imagination and to enable artistic creation when so much of social, physical, and psychological existence is being destroyed. On the whole, war writing thrives on the contradiction that war is an event demanding trenchant assessment *and* an opportunity to suspend (or re-evaluate) commonly shared artistic values. In subsequent chapters,

I focus on the following query: what does the production of literature during war communicate about the values presumed to reside in art and aesthetics? To put it more directly: working with the assumption that violence is correlated to aesthetic transformation insofar as it shatters the known world and ways of perceiving it, what challenges are presented to literary forms of expression in the case of Yugoslavia's dissolution? The assumption that historical rupture and social crisis beget formal innovation is a commonly accepted view, frequently foregrounded by scholars of war literature, and theorized most thoroughly in trauma discourses. The literary and artistic debates surrounding the two world wars – the two most devastating and widespread modern conflicts – exemplify this strongly:

> In the early twentieth century, art responded to a great war so shattering that it required new forms of expression and engendered theoretical and institutional controversies over the priorities of aesthetics and pity. But when combat targeted civilians in World War II and regimes murdered entire populations of cities and communities, art – like the world itself – stood aghast. Bafflement over *how* to speak this magnitude of manmade violence was overtaken by bafflement over *if* one can speak, or should speak, the unspeakable at all. The artistic challenges posed by World War II were recognized as foundational ethical challenges to the functions and prerogatives of art itself.[2]

The implicit statement is that new aesthetic forms are coeval with new wars. But worth noting here is Margot Norris's insight (given fuller articulation in her book) that the structure of each particular war – its technological prowess, its organization, its rationality – generates problems of form in the subsequent human articulation of its ethical and social repercussions. In the twentieth century, the magnitude of mass death demanded revised philosophical and aesthetic systems. In the later decades of the last century, one distinct quality that characterized the experience and awareness of distant wars was the immediately mediated knowledge of them. It is not the novelty of the mediation that matters here, but rather its processes, framing, and formatting. I frequently return to some of the implications that this accelerated media landscape has for the literary text.

Literary matters – whether of crisis or evolution – were just as central to writers experiencing the violent, tragic dissolution of Yugoslavia as were matters of testifying to the experience of war. This book is an investigation into how aesthetic and ethical factors – and the interdependence between them – are crystallized by the tension between creativity and severity of war in the literary writings of three authors from the former Yugoslavia. The study considers questions of the amorality (or immorality) of producing art in a war zone, the consequences of aestheticizing horror or ruin, the banality of political aesthetics, the gross misappropriations of historical themes, and the solipsism of intellectual engagement. The authors discussed in this study – Semezdin Mehmedinović, Dubravka Ugrešić, and David Albahari – are all critical of the mechanisms of warfare, the economies it supports, and the ideological manipulations it enables. Their aesthetic challenge lies in confronting the war through the dimension of physical devastation and human casualties and in grappling with the symbolic logic – the suspension and deligitmization of pre-war values, customs, and behaviours – that maintains the military mechanism. The parenthesis of war was concomitantly a process (and the initiation) of nation-building that in large part involved discontinuity with the ideological values of communism and a discrediting of the very same.[3] Yet the break between socialist Yugoslavia and its successor ethnonational states was by no means a clean, surgical cut. The early 1990s proved to be, above all, profoundly confusing in the grafting of communist legacies, styles of governance, and political structures onto the ostensibly democratic sovereign nations.[4]

While examining these issues, this study reinstates the importance of literary form, style, and rhetoric in war literature – structures that are often sidelined by the ethical urgency of addressing and listening to a text's social content, an urgency for the real that values literary expression that is factual, informative, and inflected by historical verisimilitude. Without diminishing the contributions of literary genres of witness, and without denying that some of the texts in this study function as such, the subsequent chapters consider how three writers from the former Yugoslavia – all of whom faced a metastasizing conflict and an entrenched collective crisis – end up discussing poetics, systems of representation, and technical-formal approaches. Their ruminations are by no means complacent or solipsistic exercises, relevant only to dynamics operating exclusively within literature. Rather, I read their reassessment of literary language, forms, and aesthetics as answering to the demands of social problems – a reading that is inspired by the ideas of literary creation as articulated by the Serbian-Jewish writer Danilo Kiš (1935–89). Literary form, writes Kiš, is

a discovery not just of literature as such but also a discovery of reality: reality is equally as unknown, equally a secret, as the literary form with which we attempt to decode and fix it. More concisely: when an author discovers and conquers one of the possible forms of approach to reality, he has, it seems to me, discovered a new layer of reality, a new angle of observation. It is through these very formal endeavours that reality itself is widened and deepened.[5]

Kiš argues that writers give a frame and structure to reality rather than mimetically reproducing an "objective" external world. The act of creation – the engagement with form – raises its own theoretical questions about what constitutes reality and social conflict. Thus a contextual reading of literature – where an external, agreed-upon history sheds light on the text – is reductive because it leaves the representation of social reality unexamined. Kiš suggests that in the pursuit of a resolution to an aesthetic problem, the text processes other conflicts – whether ideological, social, or historic. Equally, I would add, these broader conflicts subsequently raise aesthetic concerns across different levels of the text, a relay that is then repeated. This book traces precisely these interactions between the aesthetic and the non-aesthetic in Mehmedinović, Ugrešić, and Albahari's prose and poetry. I focus on their distinct interpretations and images of social reality that present the war as a mediator between the divisive particularist logic of essentialized nationalisms and the globalist enterprises of late capitalism. Within this discussion, the study outlines possible ways of situating these literary responses to a national conflict within the international reverberations of postmodernism.

This brings us to something of an impasse between the demands of history and the dominant aesthetic paradigm of postmodernism. The wars in Yugoslavia reinstated the "real" through the destruction of bodies and places – but also injuring, maiming, exploiting of the very same. In *Sarajevo blues*, Mehmedinović writes about the obsession with materiality of the city and people's bodies: the physical is an index of the real during the siege as much as the testimony of the survivor. Theoretically and academically speaking, the past few decades have also been characterized by a rise in the "aggressive desire for the real" in artistic practices, correlated to the rise in theoretical exegeses of trauma.[6] Postmodernism, on the other hand, is marked by self-reflexive, pluralistic, hybrid aesthetic playfulness and – this is especially true of late socialist Yugoslav fiction – by its non-referential function. Thus, against this new horizon of war, writers with a poetic sensibility characterized by simulation and self-reflexivity have to heed the pressing matter of the "real," in its various manifestations, and the politics and ethics with which they are entangled.

My study is in dialogue with some of the main arguments put forward by Michael Rothberg in *Traumatic Realism: The Demands of Holocaust Representation* (2000). Rothberg's investigation covers non-contemporaeous theoretical and creative works that, he argues, demonstrate "the persistence of the question of realism ... as one of the central problematics forced back into view" after the Holocaust.[7] Realism, he contends, is a particulary thorny dimension in the post-war period because of the rise of post-structuralist theories and their discrediting of mimetic representation. "Traumatic realism" is the term he proposes for the aesthetic practice of texts that challenge "the narrative form of realism as well as its conventional indexical function."[8] The focus of my study is less on identifying a literary-poetic paradigm of this kind. Rather, where our studies come into encounter is over the idea, as put forward by Rothberg, that "the analysis of literary, philosophical, and artistic responses to the Holocaust sheds new light on many familiar debates of the recent 'theory wars' about the status of postmodernism and the political implications of poststructuralist theories."[9] My study examines how this reckoning with aesthetic postmodernism occurs against a conflict taking place on the ruins of Yugoslav late socialism – a social, political, and economic system of particular references and histories.

When Rothberg writes of the post-war period and its "suspicion of questions of reference and a flight from the links between discourse and the materiality of history,"[10] this claim has an entirely different resonance in the post–Second World War Yugoslav context. How and why those non-referential characteristics played out in the sphere of cultural and intellectual discourse in Yugoslavia has more to do with a prohibitive public sphere and a conservative, dogmatic model of literature than with a wholesale acceptance of post-structuralism. Furthermore, even though postmodernism is a theory of the global with international dissemination, it emerges from a specific centre of production, and its integration into a "peripheral" European, socialist space requires some explanation. As Rafael Peréz-Torres writes, "the postmodern valuation of difference – informed by poststructuralist thought – must come under scrutiny by 'minority' discourses."[11] The identity of postmodern poetics across the Yugoslav republics is shaped by distinct political, historical, and social relations that are not duplicates of Western capitalist democracies.

Another qualification about the relationship between the local and global must be addressed. In Rothberg's study, "the postmodern engagement with the demands of Holocaust representation ... focuses on a recognition of the power of the image and the commodity."[12]

Television, for Rothberg, is "the medium most indicative of postmodernity" in its capacity to popularize knowledge, in production of copies of the real, and in its compression of spatio-temporal dimensions that allow a relativization of worlds.[13] What is interesting about the break-up of Yugoslavia is that a local conflict was globally present because of technologies of mass communication. Yet these very same mediums often wrongly framed the conflicts as a civil war of "ethnic hatreds." The perception of the region as populated by irrational, bloodthirsty peoples was part of the centuries-long problem of othering the Balkans in historical and cultural representation.[14] The local is permitted to circulate globally but only within a very specific narrative that says more about the demands of Western political power – and the colonialism of representation – than it does about the conflict.

Another aspect of this tale is the role played by the silent, nameless victim – the counterpart to the image of the warmongering ethnic group (who are, in most cases, the Serbs). The figure of the victim, who is often portrayed as passive, female, or vulnerable, is the subject not just of media representation but of humanitarian aid discourses. Silent victimhood is constructed by using images of the body in pain as the index of the "real" with its markers of suffering and wounding. The medium instrumentalizes the local population without even letting them speak, thereby discounting or obscuring their political or social agency.[15]

Importantly, however, the first order witness (and survivor) who writes about the war is also, in my study, a postmodernist. The postmodern aesthetic dimension is the present during the Yugoslav wars and not the mode of postmemory. This contrasts with Rothberg's mapping of traumatic realist texts in which the postmodernist overwhelmingly tends to be the one who "attempts to negotiate between the demands of memory and the omnipresence of mediation and commodification."[16] Conversely, in witnessing and narrating the wars in Bosnia and Croatia, testimony happens under the sign of the postmodern and the sign of modern mass communications, complicating the relationship with the real event as the referent is often obscured by its almost immediate media simulations.[17]

II.

The appearance of postmodern artistic practices in Yugoslavia was coterminous with late socialism – a rather complex and contradictory period of the country's existence that was also, at times, its most depressing.

Parallel to declining material and social conditions, the 1970s and 1980s saw the rise of what is now referred to as populist literature whose aesthetic logic was easily transposed onto the national-ideological paradigm of the 1990s.[18] Yet it was also a time when artistic manifestations of the postmodern became more riotous and extensive, impacting all mediums of cultural production even as Yugoslavia was hurtling towards its demise.[19]

What are the particular features of this condition referred to as late socialism? In a poetry collection titled *Emigrant* (published in 1990), Mehmedinović writes: "No one knew what anyone was doing / which is usually the case/in a country of real-socialism. / Except, maybe, for that smuggler / With a golden watch on the bridge."[20] A description of endemic nothingness, of lives undirected and only purposed in between the lines of the law, somewhere beyond the pale of institutionalized socialism, the resigned tone of this poem matches the characterization of late socialism by Aleš Erjavec as an "ideological, political, and social vacuity of the ruling utopian doctrine ... [that] held in its grasp the whole of the social field."[21] A key component of this vacuity, notes Miško Šuvaković, is that "the sign from the epoch of Realsozialismus, 'actually existing socialism,' has declined into a signified that has disappeared and a signifier that continues to exist as an institutional order, a historical trace, and a mimesis of a mimesis of a lost social phantasm."[22] That is to say, while the official language of utopia, of an equal and progressive society, was maintained institutionally and publicly, the forms of everyday experience – such as material conditions and social hierarchies – did not reflect the stated aims of the socialist project.

Social disenchantment and disaffection had been articulated as public dissent long before the Yugoslav union officially collapsed so destructively and spectacularly in the 1990s. That was the external, visible threshold of systemic failure that had been unspooling for decades. Short-lived protests and politicized cultural movements in the years of Yugoslav socialism had revealed the transformation of Tito's revolutionary project into a stagnant bureaucracy. The iconic year for observing the root of the revolt, for a number of observers and critics, is 1968, when student protests in Belgrade, Zagreb, and Sarajevo dovetailed with their international counterparts – though how scholars interpret this period (it also saw the suppression of the Prague Spring) is rather different and dependent on political inclinations and sympathies.[23] The rupture in the social landscape engendered by the student uprisings – that, broadly speaking, criticized from a Marxist position, the class bifurcations within what should have been a classless society– pointed at structural inequalities and hierarchies that had become entrenched in Yugoslav real socialism.[24] From that point on, multiple disappointments gathered pace over the years: the Communist Party's staunch measures of repression that paralysed the student protests; immobilization of experimental and critical cultural production (ending the activities of Yugoslav "black wave" filmmakers); punishment of nationalist intellectuals affiliated with the Croatian Spring in 1971 (demotions, expulsions from the Communist Party); media censorship; and fiscal corruption that tainted the operations of large enterprises.[25] The party's repressive measures targeted both those with liberal and nationalist standpoints – both sides were voices of dissent. By the 1980s, the last decade of Tito's Yugoslavia, "[t]he monolith of socialist ideologies fragmented on a daily basis," writes Bosnian literary critic Enver Kazaz, adding that "the communal horizon was dominated by depression, melancholy, and decadence of the social system of values."[26] And so when Mehmedinović writes of a "poor poet" sleeping "in the fetal position" while "wrapped up in the national flag," this image of a nascent birth (of the nation) is heavily ironic, written as it was in August 1989, the waning year of Yugoslavia – knowledge that transforms the flag into a shroud.[27]

It is striking that in such a depressed climate, the dominant strain of postmodernism to gain ground was an aestheticized or ludic kind, manifest in metatextual, non-referential texts that had little connection with social discourses and commentary. Given the urgency of the social and historical circumstances of the 1990s, these poetic strategies and tendencies are predictably disrupted, ceding way to a literature that was more ethically oriented. What interests me about this moment is how ambiguities about postmodern textual practices themselves are thrown into relief as a result of the war order. Principal features of postmodern art, it turned out, could be linked to the methods by which political machinations were performed, by which war was waged, and by which it further promulgated itself (for instance, the ruse of simulacra and its power to insinuate truth). This is part and parcel of a broader problem: instrumentalization of culture by political and military factors that, at times, reveals culture's own collusion with and perpetuation of discourses of power. I consider how postmodern poetics are not a route to be bypassed (in favour of other alternative stylistic avenues) but precisely the problem to be worked through, as compromised and as problematic as postmodern poetics might be.

The postmodern is a mode of representation of the local in global terms and not just a peripheral subset of artistic tendencies that are randomized through cultural production. The experience of the war makes the shift to the postmodern as a social condition palpable – though this is not to say that the war is when the transfer occurred but more when it is foregrounded. My view dovetails with Erjavec's proposition that "the socialist countries had actually entered the 'hypperreal' postmodern world" expressed through the over-ideologized social fabric of simulated ideals and values that bore no link to social and material experiences.[28] Contrary to the essays in Erjavec's edited volume *Postmodernism and the Postsocialist Condition* that zone in on the visual arts of "politicized postmodernism," I explore a sample of practitioners of predominantly "uncritical postmodernism."[29] The spectre of the uncritical – uncharitably called by one scholar "self-absorbed literature" – is fascinating to study precisely because it does not have easy recourse to a grammar of critique to inhabit.[30] Engagement through ethical poetics cannot be easily claimed by literary practices that had suppressed referential mechanisms, that had eschewed historical dimensions or depth, that had a delegitimized authorial (subject) status – all while propagating intertextual and citational models. Uncritical postmodernism does not position literature as entitled, in Dragan Bošković's words, to "a redemptive power" that "solves the riddle of history" – all penned by an author who can "therapeutically prescribe adequate literary ideas, because the symptoms of our illness are self-evident."[31] Rather, at the meeting point of postmodern poetics and war, literature that relied on the ostensibly uncritical strategies does not assume the position of being the *end result* of critical and poetic thinking but problematizes itself anew. This is what I tease out in in the works of Mehmedinović, Albahari, and Ugrešić. Moreover, I also raise the possibility in the following chapter that the labels that circumscribe this type of cultural production (the playful, aesthetic, and apolitical) are produced in part by the academic reception of the postmodern – a discourse that did not meditate on how this literature landed ideologically.

III.

Though the wars in Yugoslavia confirm the end of the collective era constitutionally and systematically, late socialism is nonetheless present in the war writing. The texts I submit to scrutiny are zones where non-contemporaneous realities collide: the writers are immersed in treating, analysing, and absorbing the defunct signs of the (late) socialist period as much as they are attempting to interpret the war and to apply themselves to the aesthetic challenge of the conflict. Importantly, war time does not displace the experience of socialism nor does it entirely supplant the authors' concerns with the political utopia that is expiring right in front of them. There is something of a synchronous nature between the temporalities of late socialism, post-socialism, and wartime in the works under examination even though they are chronologically distinct.

In *Sarajevo blues*, a text I analyse in the second chapter, Mehmedinović writes of the many archival remnants of the socialist bureaucracy – undigested moments of political disappointment – that come to the surface in the debris of a destroyed city, a collision of contexts that is the source of some absurdity in the collection. By comparison, in Ugrešić's essays the rhetorical gesture is more chiasmus than peristalsis of archival fragments. For her, political systems have the capacity to become inversions of one another and exist as outgrowths of past forms rather than embody newness and change. In Albahari's post-socialist prose (novels and essays alike), there is a muted but deep sense of loss for a time that is utopian, forward looking, coherent in its outlook on the world: "The future is no longer what it used to be."[32] In a sense, this is a reading of socialist temporal organization after it disappears. Albahari's established rhythms of family time – the prosaics of domestic ritual – expand so as to discover a relationship to the past and through this relationship access the well of historical and trans-generational trauma.

Very often these non-synchronous temporalities are present together, but they are not to be subsumed into one another. There are crucial differences between them: time of the political project and ideology versus time of suspension jostles with the time of the eternal present of military destruction. I do not wish to suggest that wartime is a non-politicized concept and outside of ideology, but I do suggest that it possesses a specific organization and scale (its actual formal principles are specific). Wartime, on the whole, tends towards the unending horizon. The duration of war is a distinct entity that cannot "turn to pre-war for self-definition as pre-war ... is too ineffably other," writes Kate McLoughlin, with the consequence that conflict is rendered "an extended present."[33] Conventional means for measuring time in war are often irrelevant, whether they be the calendar of labour and rest or the academic year. Those artificial ends are exposed – why does it matter that a new year is beginning if life is still organized by the logic of military destruction? This notion of a continuous present, as I explore in the second chapter, conveys poignancy and melancholy given that what exists beyond this present is probable death.[34] Considered on a different scale, my book as a whole brackets a fleeting moment that I call the amorphous historical present: there is an explicit lack of certainty and a lack of knowingness of ends in the literature I examine.

Important here is the conceit that these writers are of an era of certain global and aesthetic practices and united through it in diverse constellations that are not visible simply through content or even form. This approach helps me foreground the extension and development of aesthetic conversations and override the privileging of discontinuity and rupture (peace time vs wartime; socialism vs post-socialism). It accommodates porous boundaries in which one period bleeds into another, allowing my readings to focus on the interplay between late socialism and wartime. A tension is implicit in this interplay. On the one hand, responding to the challenge of representing violence, the authors register an immobilization of the mind in the face of stupefying and grotesque acts, the qualities of which are on (or beyond) the threshold of comprehension and inscription. On the other, the writers push back against this categorical response to violence – a response that is in close affinity with the effects of the sublime – because it suppresses the knowledge of the political event that preceded or structurally enabled the violence. To lose sight of this is to treat conflict and the violence as aberrations.

Overall, my study bucks the dominant trend of the post-war division of literary nationalisms in the post-Yugoslav context that has, in turn, led scholars to retrench behind new state borders for which there are theoretical, pedagogic, institutional, and political justifications.[35] What we can often read about in popular and scholarly criticism are symptoms of the new, post-socialist national alignment in which literary history has become a contested terrain, rewritten in order to accommodate explicitly national (at times nationalist) agendas, and to give the new fledgling states cultural legitimacy.[36] Approaches that prioritize political currents over and above scholarly measures of evaluation (e.g., literary analysis) have no doubt delayed a lucid assessment of literary production during the war.

Over the past two decades, the divisive political situation has also indirectly influenced attempts to establish a field of research of post-Yugoslav war literature or, more broadly, studies in culture and war. The classification of "war writing" has gained some currency, but only within Croatian and Bosnian literary conversations. Attempts by Croatian literary scholars to introduce the genre of "war writing" (*ratno pismo*) tend to perpetuate ethnic boundaries and promulgate singular visions of the war narrative, a step that can only end with an isolationist, monologic model devoid of polysemy.[37] Yet while this cluster excludes on the basis of national and cultural identity, it is inclusive in its embrace of all registers, such as high literature, serialized newspaper columns, war diaries, soldiers' autobiographies, propaganda tracts, and non-fiction essays. In other words, this category suppresses function and affect, and flattens out distinctions between ideological perspectives. Thus this version of "war writing" is limited to an archival rather than an evaluative role, since it forecloses the possibility of understanding literary genealogies, influences, and typologies.

More noteworthy is the explanation and use put forward by Enver Kazaz. He positions "the phenomenon of war writing" of the 1990s as the continuation of a deeper literary history of Bosnian-Herzegovinian storytelling that has its roots in the Bosnian short story tradition of the early twentieth century.[38] The practitioners of "war writing" during the disintegration of Yugoslavia produce material that, at its core, promulgates an anti-war stance: this literature is "ethically engaged, unambiguously oriented towards ... the frame of the victim who suffers or who has suffered the horror of war and war crimes.[39] This genre, however, can only exist within the parameters of the Bosnian-Herzegovinian literary genealogy since it foregrounds a very specific experience of the war that is direct and visceral. Indeed, this is reflected in Kazaz's own definition of the poetics of "war writing" as the "poetics of testament."[40]

This concept has been taken up by Mirnes Sokolović, whose argument that the post-Yugoslav anti-war writing is a genre evolved out of the ethical demands of Danilo Kiš's poetics is indebted to Kazaz's work on the same theme. This version of anti-war writing is restrictive in its own way since it insists on the factional, testimonial, and autobiographical aspects of this genre to the exclusion of "pure poetry, [and] literature as a fictional and non-binding game."[41] While Sokolović does not define quite what he means by factional, it is possible to deduce that the qualities within its parameters are in opposition to aesthetic values. But if engaged, anti-war literature is one way to ensure the "deconstruction of the national-realist writer" – any writer who, in Sokolović's article, participated in the "cruel national projects" of the 1990s – is this deconstruction only possible through the power of the factional?[42] This critical approach forecloses on other literary strategies that do not come with the explicit treatment of the real. My position is that "reality" does not necessarily have to appear in a recognizable form in literature for that novel or poem to be about a relevant social event.

Yet these prevailing definitions of "war writing" are shot through with blindspots and exclusions, argues literary critic Nirman Moranjak-Bamburać, that then help reproduce the values of a dominant, but mostly unconscious, masculinist discourse. This "quasi-natural masculine monopoly" of post-war Bosnia and Herzegovina, she argues, defines and regulates social and gender practices within religious, national, and ethnic spheres.[43] "War writing" can thus only be read, she adds, as the continuation of a literary history dominated by criteria that have been authorized by male critics.[44] Ironically, however, "war writing" attempts to position itself as an alternative current, both politically and literarily. The genre, notes Moranjak-Bamburać, "vampirically" feeds on the premise of *écriture feminin* that it subsequently pushes into oblivion: it seeks to embody a marginal form of writing and to impersonate its values of deconstruction and decentring.[45] Yet "war writing" cannot be seen as a form of difference since its existence is only enabled by unexamined and prevailing assumptions and norms.

By focusing on an overarching, supranational literary frame, this study does not favour one national literature over another; though, importantly, I try to avoid ahistoricizing the conditions of production, depoliticizing the implicit or explicit ideological convictions in the texts, and leaving unexamined the category of the postmodern itself. Yet I do open myself up to the critique that while I examine three writers from Bosnia, Croatia, and Serbia this is to the exclusion of Slovenian, Macedonian, and Kosovar literature – a frequent problem in overviews of (post-)Yugoslav cultural production. The process of selection, as mentioned earlier, is fraught with duplicities that are both motivated (produced by political exigencies) and unintentional (each act of selection displaces other texts, authors, literary currents). Even if I were to avoid such omissions, no book could be definitely representative of the linguistic, national, ethnic, and cultural complexity of the war narrative in Yugoslavia. Ultimately, my criteria rest predominantly on how a text's engagement with aesthetic issues is transformed into an ethical concern of representation, or of politics. I sought to include texts whose complexity towards issues of war and the culture of war exceeded the matter of the conflict itself and involved an examination of the literary-poetic dimension as it was responding to external circumstances (at times without direct reference to them).

IV.

Before delving into close literary reading of the texts in question, the first chapter lays out the significance of the postmodern for my project by contextualizing its appearances across discourses (theoretical and literary) within the former Yugoslavia. Specifically, I discuss the dominance of ludic and apolitical postmodern strategies that prove, at first glance, ambivalent at best against a landscape of war. My intent here is not to chronicle the breadth of scholarly activity of the 1980s and early 1990s that contributed to the habituation of the postmodern. Rather, I scrutinize tendencies that are evident in the interpretation and dissemination of postmodern literature (in the region) and the consequences and aporias of these readings, which, I argue, overlap with the ambiguities raised by the literary works themselves. A case is made for the conceptual perceptiveness of prose and poetry ahead of the theoretical expositions.

The second chapter concerns the Sarajevo siege and Mehmedinović's aesthetic of surfaces, which informs his wartime prose-and-poetry collection. I examine how the spectacle of warfare – from the ruins of destroyed buildings to pictures of bodily horror – becomes a source of creative pleasure and even inspiration for authors who transformed the destruction into verbal lyricism. I argue that this witness literature is primarily concerned with the ethical tensions faced by artists, for whom war represents both devastating trauma and artistic fulfilment. While military force was responsible for the widespread destruction of the city and its population, this force is the provenance of a fragile beauty in Mehmedinović's collection. Such haunting and aesthetically pleasing scenes, as Mehmedinović is aware, actually suppress the trauma of loss. I read *Sarajevo blues* as an examination of the morality or amorality of art when faced with the value of human life in wartime.

The closing section of the chapter explores the concern with spectacle and aesthetics that is part of Mehmedinović's broader obsession with visual modes of representation. The supremacy of sight is evident in the collection's mimicry of a cinematic mise-en-scène. Yet a complication emerges for Mehmedinović as the Sarajevo siege grew into a global spectacle, visually documented by the international media in excruciating detail. In turn, the spectacle became commodified and therefore was transformed into a perversion of the plight it wished to communicate. I work through an anti-ocular critique put forward in *Sarajevo blues* by examining the limits of visual representation and its lack of credibility as a frame for knowledge of contemporary conflicts.

While the second chapter concentrates on vision and image, the third focuses on texts, speeches, and sloganeering – or more broadly, the language of popular politics that Ugrešić gathers under the category of kitsch. Examining her essay collection *Kultura laži* (*Culture of Lies*), I argue that the trope of kitsch, typically associated with the criteria of taste, can actually become part of a political strategy within the context of war. For the author, state politics is a textual game based on the principles of "postmodern chaos in which all manner of citations are mixed" including

> citations from the museum of totalitarian regimes, citations from the broken Yugo-project, citations from the rubbish heap of fascism, citations from national history (which with each passing day become more ancient and celebrated), citations from the European dream … citations from the dusty ethno-museum.[46]

Politics, Ugrešić suggests, no longer has any substance or depth, no unifying ethics or ideals. Her essays work hard to convey the dismal ends of transposing aesthetic strategies to a political arena for the purposes of consolidating a nationalist ideology – even when the aesthetic in question is the debased aesthetic of kitsch. Why should the presence of aesthetics be so troubling in the political arena? Ugrešić claims that sentiment, passion, and illusion have no place in the system of political values because they sanitize a frightful power. Ugrešić's *Culture of Lies* highlights the frequency of the phenomenon of aestheticized politics in Croatia during the early 1990s (with kitsch being her principal and most common example). In developing my argument, I trace the historical evolution of kitsch as a category of both mass consumerism and propaganda. In doing so, I draw on theories linking banality and political ideology that developed from studies on fascist and Nazi aesthetics and their socialist counterparts. I undertake an analysis of the very properties of kitsch that are crucial to its functioning, such as authenticity and synecdoche. I conclude that Ugrešić's essays ultimately collapse the distinction between commodified and politicized kitsch. For her, this means that the possibility for irony in popular culture has been obliterated.

In the fourth chapter, I turn to the role of history in the works of Albahari, a self-confessed sceptic who "had developed a persistent denial of the meaning of historical writing and even history itself."[47] Yet his 1990s prose includes cryptic and oblique references to the war, couched in the conceptual register of disaster and chaos, rather than the historical specificity of ethnicities, politicians, and republics. These changes are accommodated not through a shift in Albahari's poetics but a change in the temporal order. His prose no longer exhibits the constant present of daily routine but begins to layer other temporalities within the boundaries of the text. The bulk of the analysis is focused on two novels that are diametrically opposed to each other: *Snežni čovek* (*Snow Man*) and *Gec i Majer*

(*Götz and Meyer*). The first of these is a rather abstract narrative following a self-conscious narrator who has to face up to the fallacy of the post-modernist "end of history" thesis. By contrast, *Götz and Meyer* is a novel immersed in the archive of an episode of the Holocaust in Serbia. I focus on the radical differences between these two books in order to demonstrate the challenge to Albahari's dehistoricized prose brought on by systemic upheaval and rupture.[48]

The book closes with a consideration of the revived landscape of intellectual engagement during Bosnia's years in the international spotlight and as the focus of charitable fundraising, crisis reporting, and public moral concern. While international writers used the mass media as a form of self-publicity that further propagated the newsworthiness of both themselves and the war, many public figures across the former Yugoslavia metamorphosed into apologists of nationalism and engineers of the conflict. Others became voices of opposition, dissent, criticism. This was certainly how much of Ugrešić's career was framed in the decade after her departure from Croatia: her consecration in the international literary market came from her anti-nationalist, liberal, pro-European messages. A number of scholars – and Ugrešić herself – have subjected this circulation of her authorial persona to critique, foregrounding its cynical marketing strategies that bypass any actual reading of her work. The trajectories of Albahari and Mehmedinović are less public and less publicly touted as exemplary, but I foreground the ambivalences that are implicit in their work about the social, public role of a writer. This is particularly interesting in light of Albahari's insistence on a model of writing in which speech begets speech without recourse to an originating voice (an author). In this final chapter, I am less interested in what they had to say politically than in how their ideas of authorship, together with reigning cultural myths of the author, reveal tensions and contradictions when read against the aesthetic-ethic engagement of their literary works. In developing my argument, I scrutinize their articulations of public engagement and the social role of the author as expressed within their literary works as well as in interviews, articles, and author's notes.

This chapter also includes a discussion of how these writers responded to the ethical and moral obligations of the Western world as framed and justified by numerous intellectuals, from Susan Sontag and Bernard-Henri Lévy to Jean Baudrillard. As I do so, I draw on scholarship that has conceptualized intellectualist terms in recent decades, including Edward Said and Pierre Bourdieu. Yet the impression that this book ends with – the lasting impressions of the work of Mehmedinović, Ugrešić, and

Albahari – is the sense of being watched, the sense of being collectively maligned or collectively perceived as victims. The discerning observations of the authors transform their work into a (literary) conversation with the global unseen, exceeding their local landscape of nationalist politics and internecine warfare.

As I was working on the first version of this manuscript in 2012, Bosnia observed the twentieth anniversary of the beginning of the war – an occasion of extensive official remembrance and much private reflection – against a background of profound disappointment with processes of transitional justice, neoliberal policies, endemic institutional corruption, economic stagnation and recession. It served as a reminder of my early obstacles in tackling the literary production of the Yugoslav wars of secession. In pragmatic terms, academic discourse did not offer a stream of past works with which my work could dovetail, particularly with regard to fiction (the cinema of the war years was much better served). But more important was the challenge and, admittedly, the intrigue of academically approaching a conflict – a civil war – still in the living memory of a significant part of the population. The signifiers of trauma and suffering episodically punctuate the veil placed over these post-transition countries. While the commemorations of 2012 did memorialize the events of the war – in the sense of marking the passage of time – later in the year, events at the International Crimes Tribunal for the former Yugoslavia at The Hague underscored anew the vitality of the war's afterlife. This book internalizes this precarious and unsettled moment: the temporal distance from the conflict and the inevitability of its ongoing hold on people's lives. I write with the awareness that future anniversaries may produce new conversations and new optics that will survey this ruined landscape of war differently.

1 War, Postmodernism, and Literary Immanence

I

Postmodernist art can be summarized through its features of ironic, self-reflexive playfulness, formal inventiveness, and heterogeneity of genres. In certain currents, it can be especially hermetic, closed off from outside influences and concerns. Add to this the combustive power of social and physical violence, and postmodernist poetics can appear somewhat ambivalent against a horizon of warfare and conflict. Literature that frolicked "in a palace of mirrors and literary codes and intertexts" became "terribly unsympathetic," writes Jurica Pavičić, "at a time when [people] placed sand bags around their homes and taped their windows [to safeguard them after explosions]."[1] In the subsequent chapters, I focus not on the change in postmodern poetics but rather how a refunctioning of similar aesthetic coordinates produces tension, anxiety, and disappointment – but also delight – in the literary works under examination. I posit that while the texts might not integrate into their form a specific set of political critiques – by using the language of ideology, a political-rhetorical warfare – other properties contribute flashes of insight that contain socio-historic resonance. This is not simply to state that what may appear ludic and trivial is immediately consequential and disturbing in its social implications, but it is to insist instead that these features require contemplation of *how* they may be relevant as a commentary on the environment beyond the literary field.

I evoke the idea of postmodernism and flatness as a Lacanian *point de capiton*, an anchoring point, for three writers who belong to a cultural model that was, in the words of art critic Ješa Denegri, "polycentric and decentralized, yet at the same time unified and shared ... polycentric and decentralized because it comprised several cultural environments and their capital cities … unified and shared because it was interlinked by numerous personal and institutional ties."[2] My concern lies with poetics that falls within a configuration of the postmodern as understood and elaborated by three writers, though the narrow idea of postmodernism as a solely cultural attribute (which is how it is implicitly and at times explicitly understood by the writers) is challenged against the new horizon of warfare. In order to elaborate on my main task – namely, how war demands an articulation of the dynamic between aesthetics and ideology in postmodern poetics – I first characterize what postmodernist sensibility these writers articulated. I contextualize the migration of predominantly Western critiques and theories on the postmodern to a geopolitical and economically distinct terrain (i.e., late socialist Yugoslavia) and the implications of such a theoretical displacement. Subsequently, I explore how this first wave of reception delayed the arrival of more social or politicized postmodernisms.[3]

Even though postmodernism often circulates as a disparate and nebulous term, even though it functions interchangeably as the indicator of the times *and* a designator for certain discursive forms, it is Western European and American thinkers (in the majority) who advanced postmodernity "as a condition specific to (late) capitalism and its consumerist, simulacral cultural forms."[4] While Frederic Jameson was the first to periodize the development of postmodernism as commensurate with late capitalism, the economic dimension was present in almost all expositions: Jean-François Lyotard's version of the postmodern condition, for instance, relied on the upsurge of a system of technoscience in the First World.[5] Even those who depart from Jameson's configuration of late capitalism as the presupposition for postmodernism at the very least agree with the diagnosis that postmodern culture involves the degradation of modernism in the wake of post–Second World War commodified culture.[6] Consequently, in this formulation, cultural production cannot be divorced from the material conditions of late capitalism, meaning, as Terry Eagleton puts it, that "the very autonomy and brute self-identity of the postmodernist artefact is the effect of its thorough integration into an economic system."[7] Bearing in mind the popular reception of postmodern artistic strategies in Yugoslavia from the late 1960s, how do postmodern strategies get repurposed at the site of late socialism – aesthetically, socially, politically? I pose this question with the following in mind: while the provenance of postmodernism lies within a particular ideological and cultural space, these origins are not a contractual obligation that must be honoured in subsequent applications. To quote R. Radhakrishnan: while core concepts of postmodernism do possess "binding gestures" that position it as a First World phenomenon, the idea that these origins privilege all subsequent "meaning[s] and valence[s] of the theory" should be challenged.[8] In fact, I intend to give a glimpse of precisely these other valences as they are delineated both by literary texts and academic reception.

Despite socio-economic discontinuities between socialist Eastern Europe and the late capitalist West, the artistic experimentation with postmodern techniques in Yugoslavia was more or less contemporaneous with its counterparts further afield. Metafictional, self-referential gestures were appropriated; fiction and critical theory translated; fragmentary and intertextual techniques duplicated – and quite enthusiastically at that. "In practically all instances," writes Slovenian critic Aleš Erjavec, "postmodernism in the former and present socialist countries was apprehended as a positive phenomenon" signifying "the most recent trends emanating from the West and its cultural capitals."[9] Some of these particular influences include the demystification of the writer's authority; a tendency towards metatextual gestures (ones that were also intertextual, intermedial, intergeneric); the rejection of mimetic literary practices; the interrogation of the ontological status of reality; the exploration of non-referential properties of language; the destabilization of messages and codes; and negotiation between – as well as synthesis of – low and high cultural forms.

One of the constitutive features of postmodernism is "a new kind of flatness or depthlessness" in which "depth is replaced by surface, or by multiple surfaces (what is often called intertextuality in that sense is no longer a matter of depth)."[10] In the pre-war writing of Mehmedinović, Albahari, and Ugrešić, the idea of depthlessness is communicated through the masterful use of citations, the dominance of ocular discourses (vision, spectacle, image), and the suspension of historicity in which language becomes a world system unsure of its own signification. Perception is limited by surfaces of the material world, of which language is one such surface. But this limitation brings forth its own insights: in Albahari's prose, for instance, the quality of depthlessness leads to a constant deferral of the reader's expectations that behind language lies a world of real relations and not simply another deferral. This is what Jameson calls the disappearance of "interpretative depth": we can no longer approach a text with the idea "that the object is fascinating because of the density of its secrets."[11] The critic-reader has to forgo their sleuthing. This goes for Ugrešić's prose, too, though she explores this position through diverse media: her writing synthesizes advertising, journalism, and other forms of commodity culture with high literature, creating a relay of information without levels or hierarchies. This amalgam produces a writing that is purposefully banal and trivial, though it is ultimately functionalized in her writing as a form of commentary. Mehmedinović, for his part, advances a poetics of a world-as-image, in which a camera lens takes on perception and shapes its projection as an invariable flatness. The poet organizes his images according to this optical device, suggesting either that this mode of vision is expressly distinct from the human experience of sight, or that it is exactly like the human eye in that both are mechanical and material ways of seeing.

As I alluded to in the introduction, an important distinction must be acknowledged here between, on the one hand, a poetic style that functions as a symptom of the most pressing problems of late socialism (Mehmedinović), and, on the other, metafictional prose experiments inspired by literary-theoretical premises, written against mimicry of everyday life, against conventional realism (Ugrešić, Albahari). The 1970s in Zagreb – the centre from which Ugrešić was writing – saw the appearance of the "young Borgesians" who experimented with the fantastic as well as those who manipulated genre literature (trivial literary forms) and the national cultural canon.[12] Her own prose is emblematic of that "literary in-betweenness" characterized by critic Aleksander Flaker as a new literature for an urbane young audience that carved out a position for itself between traditional, elitist forms of culture and truly commercial and trivial literary genres (such as crime novels).[13] In Belgrade, prose writers affiliated with the journal *Književna reč* (*Literary Word*) – edited among others by David Albahari – championed the short story, pushing the limits of the genre to its extremes through an obsession with form, diction, and syntax. The work by Ugrešić and Albahari from this period exhibits such depth of interest in the literary-conceptual transformations of fiction that it lends to their writing an internationalist dimension whereby a distant reading can take place without much knowledge of the local context. Broadly speaking, for writers like Ugrešić and Albahari, the conceptual promises of postmodernism – and its implications for prose form – trumped any discussion of a possible political ground emerging from deconstructive strategies.[14] As I explore in chapter 4, Albahari explained this position by casting postmodern strategies as the defence against the ideologization of culture in socialist Yugoslavia. There is room to theorize the phenomenon of literary abstraction as connected to collective and cultural change (rather than exclusively as a genealogical outcome of literary processes.)

In the 1970s, flourishing formal and technical styles were catalysed by a politically prohibitive culture, marked by a plethora of taboos and sensitivities.[15] Literary historians and critics have argued that in the post-1968 era, and specifically in the aftermath of the suppression of the Croatian Spring in 1971, public discourse could not be overtly oppositional to mainstream state politics as writers were susceptible to various punitive measures that – in the absence of official state censorship – were random but effective (censorship of publications, imprisonment). In removing from public life an entire generation of Croatian writers who supported national (linguistic) separateness, argues Dubravko Jelčić in his history of Croatian literature, a platform opened for a new aesthetic to emerge for younger writers whose plan for literature was to avoid "explicit engagement."[16] Their solution was to "resort to the fantastic" (after Borges).[17] Radical formal innovation in the arts, then, could be practised and developed just as long as it was thematically benign, as long as it did not destabilize the projected ideal of the state. In light of such arguments, it is interesting to read the description Velimir Visković gives of the young Croatian prosaists of this period who insisted that "literature could not be made equal with reality."[18] Visković does not clarify what reality is being rejected here: whether it is a social or political reality or literature's task towards inscribing that reality. It is moreover possible that his own critical-literary vocabulary is gesturing to a context that cannot be spoken of directly. In any case, pushing boundaries in conceptual or theoretical ways is itself hardly neutral. Svetlana Slapšak posits that "the argument[s] of arbitrariness, of an open work, and a postmodern decentering had political significance" precisely because they eschewed the dominant, ideologized model of reading that foregrounded a direct link between an author's thought and work.[19] The idea that a writer's responsibility for a text's utterance was "proven" by the notion that it came from the mind of that individual easily justified the gestures of "protean Yugoslav censorship."[20] In this context, the deployment of postmodern and deconstructive tendencies in the late socialist context can be read as a way of (consciously or not) politically engaging the rigid, repressive milieu. In contributing to literary evolution, the postmodern poetic was useful as a response to Yugoslav cultural politics and as a means of circumventing repression.

We can observe a twofold trajectory of this literary experimentation. In severing itself from the representation of socialist everyday phenomena, literature developed an autonomous domain within whose parameters it grew formally, theoretically, aesthetically (and eventually became institutionally recognized), whether according to principles of high modernism or postmodernism. In articulating the idea that literature should be liberated from its social and national duties, Silvija Novak Bajcar argues that early Serbian postmodern writers were essentially trying "to create a space of freedom before that space was created within society itself."[21] Yet there were consequences to that freedom: in creating this niche for itself, Kazaz argues, literature became a discourse excluded from "shaping social consciousness."[22] The consequences of this trajectory became acute in the 1990s when the idea of literary autonomy revealed itself in its alter ego of the "prison house" of language.[23] From this perspective, autonomy forecloses both state ideologization and the potential for ethical-aesthetic responsibility.

A counterpoint to this type of metatextual, theoretically oriented literature is offered in Mehmedinović's poeticization of the experience of life in a decaying Yugoslav union. Contrary to Ugrešić and Albahari, he came to maturity as a writer in a different literary context, which has consequences for how he approaches the representation of socialist Yugoslavia and his own position vis-à-vis postmodernism. *Modrac,* a short collection of minimalist poems, launched his career in 1984: it is a contemplation of everyday life, infused both with eros towards and eroticism of nature and people. A critic at the time of its publication characterized the collection as the output of a poet who was like "a young boy in love with beauty."[24] This aesthetic bliss dissipates in his second collection of poetry, *Emigrant* (1990), which, Mehmedinović stated in an interview, represents "a symbolic departure from Yugoslavia" through a depiction of the economically depressed environment of 1980s Bosnia and Herzegovina.[25] Though one critic interpreted the title as signifying movement from life to poetry (from routine to otherness, from necessity to choice, to internal escape in the face of life's crudeness), the content of *Emigrant* is much more politically determined.[26] By recording Sarajevo's dark streets and its marginal characters gathered in suburban cafés, bus stations, and railway hotels, his poetry is infused with images of stasis and dissatisfaction and an ambivalence towards socialism, an ideology stripped of its ethical and moral compass and hurtling towards its own implosion.

The bulk of the critical work on Mehmedinović came in the late 1990s, and it declared *Sarajevo blues* the culmination of his earlier forays into "postmodern lyrical minimalism."[27] Yet his war writing is overtly despairing in its view of the postmodern both as an aesthetic and as a theoretical paradigm that has shaped the social order. In this dialectic of being both the product of a postmodern aesthetic and a text critical towards those very same foundations, the case of *Sarajevo blues* is emblematic of the evolution in discussions of postmodernism in Bosnia. Consciousness about literary postmodernism was only externalized and explicitly articulated in the Bosnian critical sphere in the post-war period, on the ruins of Yugoslavia, even though these processes were gaining momentum in the 1980s. The conversation about postmodernism was inseparable from two other currents: discussions of war writing and the formation of the country's literary canon.[28] That is to say, the periodization of postmodern tendencies in literature from Bosnia is coeval with the socially and ethically engaged war writing. This war writing exhibits decentred and pluralistic artistic experiments alongside the presence of testimony and witnessing (in themselves modes of realism).

Viewed against the narrative of postmodern conversations across (the former) Yugoslavia, a certain non-synchronicity is seen here. Bosnian postmodernism flourished slightly later and emerged from distinctly engaged genres – unlike its Croatian and Serbian counterparts, which were explicitly non-referential and not socially oriented. Yet in the mid-1990s, these different approaches dovetail – a convergence I account for in the third section of this chapter.

II.

On the whole, the institutional response to postmodernism in Yugoslavia trailed behind its artistic practitioners. Even the most basic consideration of chronology reveals the academic as the rearguard. Nonetheless, "the sleepy critical thought"[29] showed an upswing by the mid-1980s in its engagement with the postmodern through an array of activities that included translations of the major works of postmodernism (Frederic Jameson, Jean-François Lyotard), conferences, workshops, and special issues of journals.[30] The spectre of postmodernism was debated in both the literary-aesthetic and philosophical scholarly quarters across Yugoslavia as a condition, era, or term of classification.[31] Priority is given in such scholarly treatments to understanding the fundamental as well as transcultural parameters of postmodernism that might usher in a new form of society or philosophy.[32] However, at this stage of reckoning with postmodern thought, it is difficult to ascertain exactly what position on postmodern theory and what position within the theory academics and critics across Yugoslavia occupy. There is hardly any regard for the difference in material conditions and little historicization – not of the term itself (indeed, this is well served), but of the broader disciplinary and linguistic context in which it now circulates (Slovenian, Croatian, and Serbian publications, departments, institutes, etc.). Potential ideological incompatibility started to surface towards the end of the 1980s – as is recorded of the October 1990 Dubrovnik conference, which brought together pre-eminent thinkers from the United States, France, Russia, Bulgaria, and Yugoslavia who came to recognize each other's misunderstanding over theoretical propositions that might have previously seemed an indisputable commonality.[33] To sum up: the central tension revolved around the discord in the expectations of Western Marxists, who were philosophically and politically attracted to forms of socialist collectivity, and the hopes of those from the East who saw themselves as living already in a post-utopian state, where the failure and disappearance of the Marxist social project had been experienced if not officially declared.[34] One could say that the acknowledgment of incommensurability is in itself what Jameson calls in an interview for the Croatian journal *Quorum* "the development of consciousness of those paradoxes" that exist between the intellectual positions of those separated by their geopolitical contexts.[35] Material conditions, too, are floated as a distinction between these two spaces: as one of the *Quorum* interviewers puts it to Jameson, critiques based on the dissatisfaction "with the social system [and] excessive spending" are "unattainable dreams" for an intellectual from the Soviet Union.[36] It would not be amiss to suggest that tackling difference and mutation in the traffic between Western, metropolitan postmodernist theory and its application elsewhere became more pressing in the post-socialist era, a wave led by a new critical Left in the Balkans as well as post-colonial and feminist scholars.

Much as in conversations about American cultural production after the Second World War, the treatment of postmodernism in Yugoslavia within "special, concrete, and empirical fields – architecture, art, and literature" was less likely "to be lost in a fog" than attempts to redefine philosophical systems, terminology, and teleological tenets.[37] By the late 1980s, literary histories (of the biographic-bibliographic variety) in Serbia and Croatia started to integrate postmodern classifications into their order, which were then followed by theoretical-critical expositions that attempted a genealogy of poetics.[38] The lag in response time to poetics of postmodernism as represented by cultural production – with its elasticity towards external influences – and the rigid, closed nature of the literary establishment was typified by Ugrešić in the following way:

> [Postmodernism] broke into the local literary milieu from randomly translated foreign articles. For the domestic literate public, postmodernism was like *gossip* from a distant literary world, so that *gossip* about a concept was adopted instead of the concept itself. Using my *author's notes* as the only relevant source, critics concluded that the collection of stories was a typical postmodern product, which was a polite synonym for plagiarism.[39]

Plagiarism, suspicion, gossip: Ugrešić's serious-minded critique of the domestic literary scene takes on the very same playful characteristics typically associated with postmodernism. Here, she demotes literary criticism from its status as a high-minded intellectual endeavour to the rank of unprogressive activity: its response to foreign and strange elements is to reject them, to present them as inadmissible into the designated sphere of art and discourses of art.[40]

Once postmodernism had received partial accreditation within institutional and academic quarters (the early 1990s) and once the Western theoretical corpus had been assimilated, a particular feature seems common across the scholarly contributions on literary postmodernism by intellectuals and academics across the former Yugoslavia. This scholarship is marked by a particular neutrality towards ideological, historical, and political circumstance; by features that rest outside the literary system, which itself tends to be portrayed as autonomous from other social processes and dynamics.[41] There is very little in this literary criticism that probes the complicated intersections between ideology and aesthetics – an examination which seems pertinent even in postmodernist fiction that is hermetic and apolitical (such as Albahari's) since all texts are implicated in a broader web of institutions and do not emerge from an inherently blank cultural space. Social and historical phenomena that might be relevant for considering the postmodern in its many guises are frequently characterized by vague references to a world of the commodity form and mass culture.[42]

However, recent critical assessment has attempted to bring to light what some of this early scholarship foreclosed. Aligning himself with the view that postmodernism concerns primarily politics and not poetics, Dragan B. Bošković argues that early literary criticism in Serbia observes postmodernism exclusively as a "poetic and immanently literary break leaving the meaning of the ideological identity of Serbian literature ... poorly visible."[43] This results in scholarship that is based on "deductive copying" of Western theoretical postulates.[44] Furthermore, these early "importers" of postmodernism in the Serbian context, asserts Jasmina Ahmetagić, consecrated particular authors into the postmodern canon – an irregular gesture given that canon formation runs counter to the central premise of postmodernism to decentre and break homogenizing dominant narratives.[45]

One can trace this preference in academic-critical discourse for understanding the evolution of postmodernist literary assessment as a process immanent to literature in other cultural communities across Yugoslavia. Theoretical exegeses – such as Dubravka Oraić Tolić's update of her seminal theory on citationality – are also not detained for any length of time by social relations that inform the poetic and aesthetic rupture in the first place. In her reworking, the caesurae that propel the development of postmodernist strategies involve "the consequences of totalitarian regimes (such as the Soviet Union) [or] from the appearance of mass-media culture (such as in the West)" that date from the late 1960s.[46] This is a rather homogenizing gesture since it does not probe the connection between what Oraić Tolić characterizes as a post-utopian historical moment and the surge of playful, aesthetic postmodernism that emerges in its wake. It is not obvious why the historical moment during which "European civilization does not have a conception of its future ... nor its present nor past" – namely, the loss of belief in international communism – should translate into the proliferation of metafictional postmodernism.[47] The sense of impact upon the aesthetic sensibility is there, but the relationship is not deeply probed. On the other hand, the periodization that is offered does not account for the spaces in between, for the possibility of a society of a softer regime that is nonetheless steeped in mass media communication.[48] Even when we examine recently published literary histories (of the post-Yugoslav period) or histories of genre of those who are actively engaged in teaching postmodernism, this type of reading of postmodernism as a phenomenon immanent to literature is still privileged.[49]

The implication of a critical thought that leaves unarticulated the complex relations between aesthetic (creative, poetic) expression and ideological conditions (narratives of dominance and power) is that its own politics of interpretation circumscribes the type of critical position that is accepted as valid. This politics of interpretation neutralizes postmodern rhetoric and domesticates certain appearances that shape subsequent readings. It is interesting, for instance, that while Ugrešić's work has been praised for its mastery of pastiche, parody, and the poetics of camp, an analysis of her prose as an examination of the woman question in socialist Yugoslavia was significantly delayed.[50] In praising Ugrešić's appropriation of trivial textual forms – typically affiliated with female consumers-readers – her early critics did not examine what her fiction illuminated about gendered literary positions that were thematized by the stories themselves.[51]

In sum, this early criticism is instrumental in consecrating writers into more elite, respected positions. Nonetheless, these critical texts do sideline important questions about the dynamic between postmodern theory and the content of the specific, pre-war cultural systems of Yugoslavia as well as its signs and values.

III.

With the onset of the Yugoslav wars, talk of postmodernism changed emphasis. "If anyone was to mention the foolish word postmodernism [during the siege of Sarajevo]," writes Tvrtko Kulenović in his 1994 novel *Istorija bolesti* (*The History of Illness*),

> its tendency towards the concrete ... is here manifest in the shape of the word bread, water, electricity, sniper, grenade and the visual captured in scenes of women gathering water from dirty puddles in the middle of the street while cars pass them by and spray them with water – something not yet seen in a single war film.[52]

In this passage, metafictional strategy is called in to assist in the depiction of the real: namely, the everyday of the siege. It is an experience that itself resists coherent modeling, though, as Kulenović's passage makes clear, it finds refuge in the dispersive character of postmodern writing. A problem nonetheless remains with this solution: the perpetual enclosure of that real experience through another lens (the cinematic reference) hermetically seals the description and keeps it within the game of mirrors (constant deferral and play). The criticism in the first sentence of the quotation – that the consideration of lofty or intellectual distractions such as postmodernism in war is irrelevant – is complicated at the very moment of writing. With this in mind, I contend that the literary works of the 1990s by Mehmedinović, Ugrešić, and Albahari start to raise questions about the dimensions of postmodernism that exceed the operations of a literary text. In a sense, they reject the habits of reading embraced by academic discourses. They do not necessarily do so in explicit, direct ways (i.e., commentary) but by using poetic form itself. Responding to exterior motifs and social phenomena, the authors undertake an immanent critique of their own texts, questioning whether strategies that were essential to their poetics have the capacity to ethically address what Linda Hutcheon calls "the problem of the relation of the aesthetic to a world of significance external to itself … to ideology and history."[53] To give this claim more detail, the authors observe a world where the postmodern textual depthlessness was transformed into a reactionary (political) force: the public arena became a textual game of postmodern citations offering revisionist history as a discourse of truth, while the ubiquitous images of war and terror reproduced nameless and abject content with no density or affect.

Suddenly, strategies of national mythmaking become formalized as postmodern: in the words of theorist and art critic Šuvaković, "[a] post-socialist nation state of the 1990s and of the first decade of the twenty-first century looks like an 'unexpected' simulated *monstrum* of historical copies without a real source in reality."[54] Yet, even as the newly independent republics sought legitimacy for their claims to nationhood through postmodern characteristics, they did so through the logic of modernity of the state (which took inspiration from a model of nineteenth-century national romanticism). As Tatjana Aleksić puts it, this "multiplicity of national narratives," which goes back to the "retrograde 'movement'" of 1980s Yugoslavia, was

> internally interpreted as a *return* to the traditional European civic values of nationhood, citizenship, respect for the law and private property, and even a rise in religious consciousness that had apparently been undermined by Communist ideology. At the time, it was defined as a veritable *rapprochement* with Europe and the legacy of the Enlightenment.[55]

However, in the projection of these ideals, in their simulations, the post-socialist republics, observes Šuvaković, mimicked Western postmodernism but with a crucial transformation in its application. Unlike Western postmodernism with its "uncontrolled multiplication" of commodity culture that packages free-market ideology into spectacle, the post-Yugoslav sphere exhibits "the uncontrolled and unscrupulous emptying out of political concepts and ideological apparatuses as well as religious identities."[56] The point Šuvaković is making here is that certain decontextualized and dehistoricized postmodern gestures formally account for political machinations (read: spectacles) in which traditional codes (of the nation, homeland, heroism) were used to mobilize popular support while simultaneously disguising the extent of depoliticization and disenfranchisement of the civic subject. Similarly, "postmodern reflexivity" has been referred to in the Bosnian cultural context as "the retraditionalization of a necrophilic postmodern state" in which the valorization of micro-narratives fulfilled not radical or alternative trajectories but developed "degeneration and an aggressive particularism, the privileging of nationalist narratives."[57]

The practices of mythmaking as constituent of collective identity and narrative of the nation state are not distinctly postmodern. But observers like Šuvaković are pointing to the reactionary dimension of postmodern application that was not prescient or anticipated in the earlier, "radical" and predominantly artistic experiments with postmodernism in Yugoslavia. It is only during and after the years of war that Terry Eagleton's claim about postmodernist culture made full sense: it is "both radical and conservative, iconoclastic and incorporated, in the same breath."[58] The "conservative" and "incorporated" qualities are manifest in the post-socialist world on the back of political rather than economic orchestration.

This insight crystallizes how the relevance of postmodernism moves from the domain of immanent literary poetics to the field of political and social practice. There was some urgency as to how postmodern writers, with their distinctly disengaged literary identities, would respond to what Tihomir Brajović calls "the 'vampiric' return of history," which incorporated the regional waging of war and ensuing collective trauma as well as continental and global changes (the end of the Cold War, the dissolution of the Eastern Bloc, the fall of the Berlin Wall).[59] This phrase "return of history" is an echo of Francis Fukuyama's 1989 declaration about the "end of history" in which he proposed that, given liberalism's triumph over communism, history would cease to be an ideological problem.[60] For the (post-)Yugoslav context, dramatic developments in the political and economic fields that culminated in military campaigns made addressing the historical chaos imperative. One form of engagement was seen in the rise of the "new historical novel," as Brajović calls it, which was concerned with a revalorization of national history that had been artificially disrupted by Yugoslav socialism and served a "utilitarian and pragmatic function as well as one that sought to enlighten the collective."[61] These novels, common in both Serbia and Croatia, slotted into the nationalist-patriotic paradigm that had its forebears in writers of the 1970s and 1980s but was fully present in the literary marketplace in the 1990s.[62]

In a sense, such writers had an easy task: their aesthetic response was determined by the model of history and political project they sought to promulgate. However, self-declared postmodernists whose work was marked by characteristics of self-reflexivity, irony, and auto-criticism, including Albahari and others of his generation, found their poetic sensibilities vulnerable and myopic with regard to these social and political realities. Their literature functioned in dialogue only with other literature: it had committed itself to self-exclusion from social relevance. A fundamental dilemma in these writings that were focused on pure form was the lack of access to the language of the historical. And so, the qualities of neutrality and disengagement could no longer hold out as the lynchpin of such literary strategies as external exigencies brought to the surface certain aporias of their poetic sensibility, particularly with regard to the status of history or ideology. This quandary deepens to become articulated as a concern with what I call the undeclared ideological positions of postmodernism articulated both in critical discourse but also, as my book demonstrates, in fictional and essayistic writing that articulated this problem under the "sign of auto-demystification."[63]

This disclosure of blind spots in postmodern approaches within the post-socialist context has the primary effect of confirming the absence of a depth model of postmodernism that is typified, as Dick Hebdige puts it, "by a rejection of the vocabulary of intellectual 'penetration'" that cannot "[trawl] for hidden truths" and go "behind appearances or 'against the grain' of the visible and the obvious."[64] This then leads to a certain negotiation of its relevance, of its currency: Albahari even goes so far as to say, in a recent publication, that "postmodernism [has] definitely become history."[65] Yet a second-wave response that interprets postmodernism as a critical movement has been forthcoming by critics keen to assert and locate the progressive potential of postmodernism both as a paradigm and an aesthetic apparatus in a way that resonates with the parameters of the local in the context of the post-conflict years. One approach attempts to reconfigure postmodernism by appealing, broadly speaking, to the discourse of victimhood, which, in my reading, is revealed as a politicized and instrumentalized critical position. The second example is an attempt to recover blind spots of (more localized) literary scholarly practices that inform my methodological approach in chapter 5.

Oraić Tolić's *Paradigme dvadesetog stoljeća* (*Paradigms of the Twentieth Century*) is a work that attempts to theoretically establish the grounds for postmodernism's moral turn. "Light, aesthetic, playful" postmodernism ends, in her account, with the Yugoslav wars that also officially confirm the death of the socialist utopia (of both real existing communism and international Marxism).[66] This anticipates the second postmodern period: in the post-1991 era, she argues, global postmodernism has found its paradigmatic cultural constellation in the artistic milieu of Central Europe – specifically Croatia and Bosnia and Herzegovina, two nations that were the first to experience what Oraić Tolić calls "postmodern war."[67] The exceptional historical events experienced by these borderland countries (between East and West) come to define the implosion that takes place within postmodernism itself: namely, the change from "ontological ludism" towards "ontological moralism."[68] Vukovar, a city that was destroyed by Serbian forces in November 1991 and that also sustained thousands of civilian deaths, becomes the trope (for Oraić Tolić) that makes explicit the demand for ethical writing. Srebrenica, one can extrapolate, would possess the same status; the status of return to the "real" (*zbilja*). The "real" here corresponds to the visceral and physical environment of war, the loss of lives, but also more explicitly the trauma of the victim.[69] The "real," however, also seems circumscribed in this case as the extraordinary event that seizes the imagination on the grounds that it is without comparison.

It is not clear for what purposes, so to speak, the "real" takes prominence here. On the one hand, I see Oraić Tolić's approach as an attempt to introduce into the global postmodern a new set of coordinates that cohere with discourses on human rights and that further attribute immanent value to certain categories from which it becomes possible to ethically assert postmodern strategies. Large-scale destruction of human life from a peripheral geopolitical locale at the end of the twentieth century becomes, for Oraić Tolić, the year zero that facilitates this type of thinking. On the other hand – and this is my critique of her position – we should not overdetermine the "real" as exclusively related to the extreme, to the almost apocalyptic destruction of the body and life, because this distracts from the banal, everyday forms of life and war, and life in war, that require as much theoretical understanding as these overwhelming and undeniable physical crises. Perhaps the point here is to suppress the crises of ordinariness in the valorization of the catastrophe as the only "real" in a simulated world.[70] Furthermore, one of the fundamental tensions that Oraić Tolić leaves out here is the postmodern rejection of normativity and universality. Indeed, Oraić Tolić argues that a theory of moral postmodernism is possible by overdetermining the role of the victim as the ethical position; that is to say, universalizing the position of the victim, offering the victim identity as a default for all subsequent relations. Moreover, if postmodern cultural forms or scholarly readings of the postmodern assume the protection or defence of the victim – a category that can only be associated with specific identities (ethnic, gendered, etc.) – it is to already instrumentalize and politicize the critical position. This is not to deny the plausibility of such projects but to highlight that they themselves are influenced by concepts and factors that might appear, from some perspectives neutral but are not. Overall, the insistence on the potentially universalizing victimhood narrative in Oraić Tolić's text, however, seems to be nothing but a smokescreen behind which lies her attempt to further inscribe stories of Croatian collective victimhood into the national narrative vis-à-vis a global postmodern matrix.

The second – and undoubtedly crucial – intervention into debates on postmodernism's sociocultural significance in the post-socialist era lies in the approaches where it has been most absent, including critiques informed by feminist and gender theories. The recent work of Tatjana Rosić tackles not so much the aesthetic and literary qualities of postmodern fiction but rather focuses its critical gaze on the reception of this literature and the cultivation of a particular kind of canon that, in her reading, betrays some of the fundamental principles of postmodernism. Rosić begins her argument by asserting that the dominant literary model in Serbia is premised on a male author(ity) who sanctions the existence of a particular aesthetic and legitimizes subsequent poetic developments. This structure of an "author-father" is supported further by the "expressly patriarchal matrix of Serbian culture that has always continued to reproduce the myth of the exceptional writer as a male mythical figure."[71] She goes on to say that the "postmodern critical-poetic platform" has been consolidated under the auspices of the same "symbolic capital."[72] The subsequent step in her argument is to posit that the persistence of this model of authorial myth has left unexamined certain postmodern perspectives (and their promulgation) thereby preventing social postmodernisms, such as discourses of gender and postcolonialism, "long ignored [and] loudly silenced," from gaining traction in the (literary) critical establishment.[73] It is, to say the least, an ironic outcome for postmodern poetics: the "fragmented, associative and richly referential postmodern literary paradigm which would like to bring into question actual principles of a logocentric and phallocentric Western metaphysical tradition of writing and reading" had been assimilated into a literary tradition that has left intact this logocentrism.[74] In addition,

Rosić points out that the type of self-quizzical and self-referential nature that postmodernism assumes (at least aesthetically) is missing from the interpretation of the sign of the author: "postmodern Serbian literature does not want to seriously bring itself into question," even though it could do that, she seems to imply, through pastiche and parody.[75]

Her argument is simultaneously an explicit appeal for a more knowing and critical approach to the authorial function (after Foucault) that I take up in the final chapter. My central question there is: if the subject of representation is in crisis in postmodern poetics, what implications does this have in the arena of authorship, particularly at a moment when the positioning of writers as social commentators and intellectuals is even more foregrounded? I examine how an authorial position and the autonomous subject are carved out, given the challenge to authority by various dimensions of the postmodern. If the authors I consider here write against a certain kind of authority of the writer, calling it illusory, then it is worth considering what happens when their own position is consolidated through the terms they reject. I consider what aporias arise between (their own) metacritical statements and interpretation of their literature by others.

In short, many of the crises of the critical establishment vis-à-vis postmodernism comport extensively with those exhibited in literary discourse. Yet literature found its grammar of historical upheaval before the critics, even though that grammar might be unknown to the author and only revealed in the act of reading or interpretation. Indeed, literature has a grammar that is necessarily absent from critical discussion since it can harness aesthetic principles to represent *the very problem* with the aesthetic.

2 The Spectacle of the Siege

War, this chapter argues, is a store of aesthetic possibility. From the spectacle of warfare to the intricate ruins of destroyed buildings, besieged Sarajevo inspires creative pleasure among authors and filmmakers who mould physical destruction into parcels of poetic or cinematic lyricism. In his prose and poetry collection *Sarajevo blues*, Semezdin Mehmedinović (born 1960) lets the war be the muse that helps him come of age as a poet – but in doing so, he questions the principles behind this symbiosis of war as art, as beauty, as artistic fulfilment. This transforms *Sarajevo blues* into a crucible in which the amorality or immorality of art is tested against the value of human life.

Mehmedinović's slim volume is first and foremost "a poetics of testament"[1] written throughout the siege. The collection's short entries are laid out in an encyclopedic manner with titles that comprise many recognizable signifiers of the siege, from the masculine romanticism of the Bosnian "Drina" cigarette to the social critique of "War profiteer" and the poignancy of "Washing the dead." This idea of inventory as chronicle is duplicated in "Letter from Sarajevo," a piece by journalist Ozren Kebo that was published towards the end of the siege: "there are concepts which will not for a while yet lose their magic: gas, electricity, water, lentils, rice, sniper, can, cigarette, grenade, firing, detonation, chetnik, cunt, sea, UN, Security Council, America, Canada, Australia, tunnel, death."[2] Whereas Kebo lists the items that are to form the lexicon of the siege, *Sarajevo blues* provides the definition to these facts of everyday life. The entries of *Sarajevo blues* are predominantly about material survival but also include those that focus on existential and spiritual concerns to which the conditions give rise (such as "Religiosity" and "Loss").

The collection does not make recourse to a broader background or narrative of the conflict – that is, the Yugoslav wars of succession – which reached their highest incidence of bloodshed in Bosnia and Herzegovina, historically the most multi-ethnic as well as the most culturally and religiously heterogeneous republic. Without delving into the anatomy of the conflict, it is sobering to consider that three and a half years of fighting between Bosnian Serbs, Croats, and Muslims claimed 95,940 civilian and military lives, the majority of whom were Bosnian Muslims, and generated a refugee crisis affecting two million displaced persons.[3] The siege of Sarajevo is probably the most iconic and enduring event of the Yugoslav wars, partly because it unfolded on global television. The siege lasted from 1992 to 1995, and over the course of these three years, Bosnian Serb forces (who occupied positions on hills surrounding Sarajevo) trapped the citizens of the city and limited their access to food, water, and aid. Civilian life involved regular encounters with violence, death, and impoverishment. It was also an existence assiduously recorded by the international media.

Through the power of the press, Bosnia quickly became "the icon of contemporary atrocity."[4] The city of Sarajevo, in particular, achieved the status of war celebrity because "it was in Europe, it was a capital city, it was relatively accessible, and it had the basic infrastructure for international media coverage."[5] Journalists also drew on the symbolic and civilizing facets of the city's cultural syncretism, religious pluralism, and ethnic diversity to further engage audience sympathy. The journalistic presence was buttressed by a rotating roster of intellectuals, politicians, and celebrities, whose appearances generated additional media events. All of these factors led to a certain asymmetry when it came to the broader knowledge and comprehension of the conflict as the "marketing of Sarajevo"[6] sidelined other sites of atrocity, particularly in provincial towns and villages.

The interest of works such as *Sarajevo blues* lies in the nature of media documentation itself. Mehmedinović is explicitly critical of the tendency of journalism to transform a "picture of a mass massacre" into "the advert for war": "[i]t is not important that those people have names, they are a bare picture; television has translated them into its cold language. The camera depletes from the image its psychological content and makes information from it."[7] Furthermore, the intrigue with the media revolves around two additional threads: 1) the media as an instrument of vision, with strategies of perception and framing that can be staged in prose and poetry, and 2) the transformation of the documentary into an artistic mode (of beauty, of pleasure) that supplants the communication of evidence and testimony. Even when questions of aesthetic effect or beauty are not overtly discussed, there is a heightened awareness of the aesthetic composition of the siege. In Aleksandar Hemon's short story "A Coin," one of the narrators disparages the style of an American cameraman because his five-minute close-ups of a massacre are "like fucking Tarkovsky."[8] A twofold critique emerges from this story. On the one hand, documentation is interpreted as a passive form of profit-making that undoes its imperative to witness, but, on the other, it forms artistic objects out of body horror and violence that communicate an ethically dubious position. This critique of the media function is an embedded critique of the artistic text itself: when Hemon's protagonist derides the "montage of death attractions" (a reworking of Eisenstein's montage of attractions), it is a perfectly apt description of Hemon's short story, which itself relies on cinematic editing. *Sarajevo blues* announces its own legacy to the lens of the camera and to ocular discourses in general, a topic to which I will return.

In general, the Sarajevo siege has been made photogenic in the presentation of ruins as artwork, in the attractive depiction of destruction, and in the stylization of death and suffering. The difficulty of this metamorphosis of violence into beauty, argues Martin Jay, lies in "the chilling way … nonaesthetic criteria are deliberately and provocatively excluded from consideration."[9] This, of course, refers to the ethical transgression in much of this material (media, art, film), a transgression that is disregarded in its pictorial or verbal articulation. Such aesthetic representations trouble us because they are marked by a certain "disinterestedness," adds Jay, which is justified in the service of art, but is "precisely what is so radically inappropriate in the case of that most basic of human interests, the preservation of life."[10]

There is a historical and theoretical precedent to this discomfiting cluster of war, politics, and aesthetics. Towards the end of his essay "The Work of Art in the Age of Mechanical Reproduction," Walter Benjamin turns his attention to the spectre of the fascistic "management" of aesthetics (first articulated in Marinetti's 1909 *Futurist Manifesto*) within the arena of waging war. He concludes, in an astute and ominous manner, that mankind's "self-alienation has reached such a degree that it can experience its own destruction as an aesthetic pleasure of the first order."[11] This degree, grounded by its own historical moment (the essay was published in 1936), has been surpassed. In this statement, Susan Buck Morss identifies salient observations for our "televisual times": "We are to assume that both alienation and aestheticized politics as the sensual conditions of modernity outlive fascism – and thus so does the enjoyment taken in viewing our own destruction."[12] Abetted by technological developments, the circulation of and exposure to the aesthetic communion between death and destruction has gathered pace throughout the century to become, in Mehmedinović's experience, simply "commonplace" (26). Within the siege of Sarajevo, the metaphysical thrust of death – that is, death as a unique event that requires contemplation – is diminished by the cumulative number of civilian losses, a figure that cannot be made, in some ways, intelligible. I later consider Mehmedinović's attempt to rekindle death as tragedy through his reading of Goethe's poem "Der Erlkönig." Commonplace, too, is the commercial distribution of an aesthetics of suffering by the contemporary media, a feature to which audiences have, to some extent, become inured. *Sarajevo blues* attempts to compensate for this state of affairs and to disrupt the ease of televised horror.

This notion of the gaze and seeing is this chapter's starting point. It is Mehmedinović's central obsession (how to avoid being seen; what it means to be seen; what happens when the poet looks) and therefore presents a plausible introduction into a disjunctive, randomly organized text. I then explore the ruined city as a source of beauty for the writer, an encounter that emphasizes the value of literary creation at a time when all social and institutional processes are suspended. It is a depiction that stands in contrast to the words of Lidia Ginzburg, author of the St Petersburg siege memoir *Blockade Diary*: "A man who is being tested to destruction by catastrophes is incapable of believing in beauty and the absolute value of the individual soul."[13] *Sarajevo blues* offers a glimpse into how the attraction of forms of destruction transcends the destruction itself, but all while being haunted, as a collection, by the question as to whether it is possible to separate the ideological and military sources from these aestheticized scenes.

The final section of this chapter analyses how spectacle becomes a commodity through a constant stream of suffering and viscera, and how this very stream, with its claims of visibility, turns the medium into a masking, a silencing. As Elizabeth Dauphinee writes, the imaging of pain renders the content of the frame "abject, nameless and humiliated – even when our goal in the use of that imagery is to oppose their condition."[14] Mehmedinović shares this view, a view that can be broadly conceived as an anti-ocular position. Throughout his collection, he does not challenge seeing per se, but rather the *dominance* of seeing, its construction of semblance, and its lack of depth. Photojournalism, he argues, makes the conflict visible through an aestheticized form of suffering deposited only on the surface of the image. In other words, the visible presence of horror conceals its other qualities – whether physical, such as its sounds and textures ("sap is like blood but easier to clean") or those that might have ethical and social repercussions (56). Is this surface an intrinsic feature of photography itself, or is it the result of veiled framing mechanisms, the control of visual modes of presentation? What ideological orchestrations are at work during this insistence on visibility? What is actually visible?

Alluding to the impotence of the camera (or that of visual communication) is no longer a novel argument, accustomed as we are to questioning, even if not fully understanding, the consequences of media formatting and its contribution to our knowledge of contemporary events. However, for the author of *Sarajevo blues*, this notion that the visual mode is ineffective and restricted is an opportunity to reappraise some of his own formal practices, to test the borders of art, and to test art's autonomy. Moreover, this frustration with forms of seeing and of representing throws into relief the author's commitment to Islamic identity and his dependence on both its cultural and religious dimensions as an alternative means of literary depiction. Describing the ritual of prayer or transcribing his conversation with a local imam draws on a tradition that restores what had been physically and spiritually shattered in Sarajevo.

II.

Sarajevo blues is concerned with particularities of vision and is equally invested in the possibilities as well as the limitations of seeing. I use the valences of ocularism as an analytic lever to identify and categorize the theoretical and conceptual core of *Sarajevo blues*, which includes debates on the amorality or the immorality of producing art in a war zone, and of aestheticizing death and ruin. These discussions do not distract from *Sarajevo blues* as a literature of witness – a literary genre, Thomas Vogler argues, that is "bound up with notions of authenticity and referentiality, a poetry that puts us in touch with raw *facts* of existence rather than effects produced by rhetorical technique."[15] While one half of *Sarajevo blues* can be read as such a catalogue of "raw facts" – the anthropology of siege survival – it is the interaction (or conflict) between direct knowledge of the siege and moments of stylization and aestheticization that elicits more profound insights from the author. The visual realm is the absolute horizon of the text's commentary on the siege because it functions as the anchoring point of wartime experience and its documentation, mediation (through journalism), and spectacle. The following section locates the thematic and structural presence of visual modes in *Sarajevo blues*, simultaneously introducing narrative features that organize this catalogue of the siege. I will also demonstrate how intricately bound the visual is with spatial, temporal, and linguistic categories.

The text abounds with adjectives and synonyms indicating degrees of "visibility": "The war cannot be seen. Sarajevo's reality does not weigh more than one newspaper photograph with a grainy structure" (11). While the narrator is an active onlooker – "I look with interest," "through my binoculars" – Sarajevo's besieged citizens are hidden, exposed, seen, blinded, detected, or lurking in shadows (52, 58). They are constantly hunted by the telescopic military gaze that, through its technological finesse, penetrates even the darkness of a city without electricity: "I pass through covert streets, hidden from the sniper's gaze gifted with infra-red rays that can detect me in the pitch black" (8). This new logic (tyranny) of the citizens' daily existence is reflected in the reorganization of urban life: "Do not be exposed: that is the only relevant law of city traffic. It is in complete contrast with demands of peacetime – to be on the main street and to be seen" (8). In its aim to seek out the vulnerable citizen as a target, as an object of death, the work of the sniper is bookended by the work of the photojournalist who is poised to capture the ensuing horror. Two optical instruments of surveillance thus intersect:

> I run across the intersection to avoid the sniper's bullet from the hill and run straight into the photographers, doing their job in the thick shade. If I was to be hit by a bullet, they would create photographs which would, with their attractiveness, exceed my life. In that moment, I did not know who to hate more: the chetnik snipers or these monkeys with Nikon cameras. For the snipers I am an ordinary target, but the photographers confirm my help-lessness and further want to use it…Life has been reduced to gestures. How touching, the comical gesture of a man who, afraid of the sniper's bullet, protects his head with an ordinary newspaper at this very same crossing. (36)

Within the established imagery of the Sarajevo siege that was "system-atically recreated in all conceivable art forms,"[16] this tableau is patently familiar to many, especially for its evocation of the informally named Sniper Alley popularized by the media. While Mehmedinović has choice words for those who profit from the business of death, his scepticism finds fuller expression on the topic of aesthetics. He understands that there is a photogenic quality, and therefore artistic profit, in the act of documenting human life in flight, and, frequently, in documenting the act of destruction itself. While by no means sympathetic to the circus of spectacle, Mehmedinović's encounter with photojournalism throws into turmoil his own poetic principles and his relationship to ocular means of representation and expression.

Sarajevo blues stands out, as the extract above demonstrates, on account of Mehmedinović's lucid understanding of his own instrumentalization (or more concisely the instrumentalization of his body) and his objectification by the lens of the weapon and the camera: "the sole purpose of the body is to occupy the space of its own mortality" (36). This body is snared: both the gun and the camera are after him, but only in death, which is the logical conclusion of their respective assignments. Yet this logical conclusion of the tyranny of war and the tyranny of spectacle is denied to the reader (our protagonist does not die), as is the relief, perhaps, at having once more delayed or avoided this outcome. Any relief is temporary, as the crossing has to be made again tomorrow and the day after. The narrative is thus poised at a moment during which it is unbearable to live – unbearable because of the torturous awareness that one's life is circumscribed, in the now famous paradigm of modern biopolitics, by "mechanisms and calculations of power."[17] In Mehmedinović's particular case, the capital behind the global media unites with the mechanisms of warfare, represented metonymically by "the chetnik snipers," who reference the ethnonationalist project of Serbian aggression in Bosnia.[18] Implicitly, they sustain one another. *Sarajevo blues* can thus be characterized as a collection in which the normally invisible and elusive lines of power that organize human violence are foregrounded in a merger between the divisive particularist logic of essentialized nationalisms and the globalist enterprises of late capitalism.

The scene at this intersection is representative of the collection in the critical insight it achieves through its access to the "inner workings" or the "digital diagram" of war (57). The collection asserts the supremacy of visual metaphors and units of description and dissection. They demonstrate the extent to which the siege is administered, as if the war was a bureaucratic process: "The city has become flat, like a military map" (149). Ekphrasis, too, is a commonly used rhetorical technique, though its relevance and connection to the context of the siege writing is not immediately apparent. Mehmedinović's descriptions of portraits and sculptures foreground a particular affective state – that of discomfort or unease (*nelagodnost*) – which functions as his shorthand for a successful encounter with works of art: "I am naturally attracted to an installation by Ademir Arapović: on a thin glass pane, standing upright, is a shallow, round dish filled to the brim with milk. Notwithstanding the laws of statics which guarantee that the glass will rest solidly on the pedestal, it seems that at any moment it could fall into pieces" (113). This ekphrastic thread opens up clues as to the provenance of Mehmedinović's artistic identity: the point when he came to understand that (as with the installation above) the knowledge of the "rational" explanation (e.g., physics) does not appease the psychological and even the physical impact of interpreting and viewing the artwork. This digression in *Sarajevo blues* is less about Mehmedinović's accounting for his own poetics as a source of this very same "stress" and more about the author's indirect exposition of the power of literary and artistic discourse (113).

Another common narrative approach in *Sarajevo blues* is the elision of an authorial voice, as if Mehmedinović was trying to "evacuate all subjectivity from literature to remove or undermine expression and feeling."[19] In this guise, his anecdotes are framed by the poetic eye (another lens, of course) that skims the surface of the enclosed frame:

> A young fretful man begs to jump the queue and fill up [his container] with water. He shows his plastic bucket. The queue in front of the cistern twists to give way. Once he finishes filling, he rushes to the end of the street where he is hit by a grenade. Only a bloody trail in the asphalt, like sap, but easier to clean. In that moment, it starts to rain and washes everything away: no trace of the young man and no trace of the bucket. Only water. (56)

It is hard to determine the narrator's spatial position and proximity to this event given the lack of intrusion on this tableau: the reader does not know if the narrator is a direct or second-order witness. The comment "like sap, but easier to clean" is an interpretation that throws into relief the lack of additional commentary or inference elsewhere in the passage. This is in keeping with a poet who was always that "young man with a video camera / filming the damp asphalt in front of him," a writer of the urban, tapping into the capital's dark streets and its marginal characters gathered in suburban cafés, bus stations, and railway hotels without the grittiness of, as one critic put it at the time, "notes from the underground"[20] (97). Either way, it is significant that while Mehmedinović favours visual communication, the overall thrust of *Sarajevo blues* discredits or at least challenges its efficacy and credibility – a point I will demonstrate later.

There is an uncompromised line of clarity and transparency in the collection, and it resides in Mehmedinović's non-lyrical language. For all its concern with aestheticizing the destroyed world, reading *Sarajevo blues* is nonetheless a prosaic experience. The import of Mehmedinović's words is delivered briskly, the tone is direct, and communication is achieved without great flourishes. It is journalistic at times: "Every morning a woman flags down cars on Malta. While on the road, I have a feeling that I am the only survivor in town. So I stop my Golf with happiness and feel that the risk of traveling is split into two" (12). Yet for all this directness of language, the book is not artless. Mehmedinović's turns of phrase are clipped: verbs are omitted in descriptions, and there is a noticeable lack of exposition, predominantly that of setting. Curiously, he also favours delaying the predicate of the sentence till its very conclusion, a feature facilitated by the fluidity of word order in Bosnian: "Twenty-four hours per day, and during hellish moments probably most intensely, people are making love in Sarajevo" (73). Or: "In the naïve belief that one should defend one's home, day and night, we guard the entrance" (52). In this example, the markers of location are subordinated to hope, feeling, and human temperament. Overall, this very transparency is a style in which expectations of poetry and poetic language are subverted. As I show in this chapter, literary discourse is at its most explosive when it is insinuated into diverse rhetorical modes rather than afforded a singular, privileged position.

The insistence on clarity is inseparable in *Sarajevo blues* from the imperative to witness: "Writing exclusively about things I saw with my own eyes, I tolerated neither censorship nor self-censorship" (142). Neither could Mehmedinović withstand speculation and imagination, refusing to contemplate events outside the parameters of the besieged city. This self-imposed myopia is all the more interesting when one considers that for all the news the author is exposed to – "on the hour we bend our heads closer to the transistor ... What do the journalists say?" – *Sarajevo blues* presents no connections to the war's other tragedies (52). For this, we have to look elsewhere: "Srebrenica, the radio announces, is on the threshold of starvation," wrote journalist Ivan Lovrenović in the winter of 1994.[21] So Mehmedinović is somewhat mistaken: he does practise self-censorship, but only as a rigorous demand of testimony. Within this function, sight is privileged (over language) because it intimates a link to irrevocable evidence.

Mehmedinović's commitment to transparency evokes scholarly definitions of testimony that draw on a relationship between sight and truth.

"In the legal, philosophical and epistemological tradition of the Western World, witnessing is based on, and is formally defined by, first-hand seeing," writes Shoshana Felman in *Testimony: Crises of Witnessing*, adding that: "'[e]yewitness testimony' is what constitutes the most decisive law of evidence in courtrooms."[22] Remarkably, *Sarajevo blues* never makes the switch from seeing to narrating beyond the initial encounter; the subject does not attempt to square his experience with a broader temporal frame of social and historical coordinates. This feature is informed, in large measure, by the lack of certainty of survival that underpins the book. There is no discernible temporal lapse between events and narration. The publication dates provide a degree of measurability to this. First published at the end of 1992, some nine months into the Sarajevo siege, the collection was fifty-two pages long and looked like a photocopied pamphlet. No doubt this latter feature reflects the compromised and impossible conditions of publication in a war zone. The booklet was subsequently taken up by a Slovenian publisher in 1993 and produced in a similar, slim version, part of a series by writers either exiled or trapped by war.[23] Throughout the 1990s, Mehmedinović's spare collection of prose and poetry grew with each edition (and translation), occasionally reaching into pre-war Sarajevo, loosening the chronological binds of war, but topographically still committed to the city.[24]

There is no definitive "edition" of this book, and there are no author's commentaries, prefaces, or epilogues. The fragments of the text are arranged to portray both simultaneity and synchronicity of experience: few of the entries possess dates and therefore cannot be pinned to a particular juncture in the siege. They share the same temporal horizon insofar as the narrator is never outside the time of the present. Time is signified by adverbs of the "current" (14). In the later editions, Mehmedinović does not rework the temporal distance between narrator and conflict, and therefore does not account for the war's aftermath. What we have instead is a unifying motif, a previously unknown form of clarity, which I call the "interval before death." *Sarajevo blues* describes a mode of existence and not an arranged narrative, a technique reminiscent of Frank Kermode's assertion that "No longer imminent, the End is immanent."[25] Within the frame of *Sarajevo blues*, the crisis of personal death displaces the arbitrary orderliness of temporality: "There is day, there is night: within them is a man who has defined himself in relation to the end of the world" (9). War thus becomes interpreted not as a consecutive gesture (implying linearity, coherence, and the possibility of relating the self to some sort of epoch or grander moment) but as the condition of being "in the middest" (*in media res*) without the possibility of concordance with imagined ends.[26] "[W]ar has buried time," we read in *Sarajevo blues*, "what day is it today?; when is Saturday?; I don't know. Dead are the daily rituals, and the annual ones: who will publish calendars for 1993 in December?" (9). Mehmedinović's declarative statement "that which exists is now" (129) puts forward what Kate McLoughlin calls a temporal "open-endedness," a "special property of wartime" within which "war is felt as an immeasurable and directionless present."[27]

Since "[t]here is no dependable measure of time," the present is given a particular role to play, and it becomes the tense of devastation (129). In a startling typographic execution, one of Mehmedinović's prose pieces (simply entitled "Children") consists of a single line: "S: Harun, get into the house, it's grenading outside!" (35). The rest of the page is left blank, a visual eternity of white noise. The effects of this extract arise from a union of content and layout. First of all, the reader encounters the incongruous linguistic element of the parent whose concerned call subverts an idiom: "it's grenading outside" is a play on words of "it's raining outside."[28] The playfulness of this inversion is jarring – the content undermines the form and makes the weight of the utterance perceptible. Further stress comes from the frame of the white page, indicative of either silence or death, which pulls the reader into the indeterminacy of a fatal scenario; a suspension which deprives childhood of all of its possible cultural and temporal dimensions. This is underscored elsewhere in Mehmedinović's simple statement: "my son and I are of the same generation" (129).

However, it is not enough to simply assert that *Sarajevo blues* is insecure about endings, whether they be death, peace, political negotiations, Western intervention. If, as a collection, it attentively inhabits a "directionless present," what is the interaction between the text and the political, social, and military conditions that constitute the present?[29] Simply put, the text has a clear sense of a historical epoch diminishing: "socialism has been thrown out on the street, just like the Yugoslav dinars, money no longer in circulation, that the wind swirls around on the asphalt" (18). What once was held in strong faith to be a way of solidarity in life, a source of "allegiance and loyalty," has transformed into ephemeral rubbish: the only items worth keeping are the good-quality frames on Tito's portraits (23, 18). This departure leaves a vacuum filled by the rhetoric of ethnonational identities but Mehmedinović's attention is engaged on an individual, spiritual level rather than the ideological terrain of politicians and their state building agenda. I examine the forging of this particular identity within the fragments of the collection at the end of this chapter.

Overall, however, *Sarajevo blues* is written in the ether of always impending tragedy: Mehmedinović's collection exhibits a relationship to temporality and succession that comes close to Maurice Blanchot's definition of a tale (*récit*): "The tale is not the narration of the event but the event itself, the approach to that event, the place where that event is made to happen – an event that is yet to come."[30] Conflicting characteristics (one liberating, the other slightly claustrophobic) emerge from this approach. On the one hand, Mehmedinović rejects the model of a literary text as "a closed universe in which all choices have been made,"[31] which means that *Sarajevo blues* does not try glibly to ingratiate itself with a political program as an interpretative framework for events. Mehmedinović writes: "A thousand false divisions are being erected in Sarajevo. The only one that makes sense is the distinction between the dead and the living" (152). At the same time, the author's style encourages an understanding of event-as-image that makes his scenes similar to those created by photojournalists and cameramen for global distribution. The media is an uncomfortable presence in *Sarajevo blues*, since its mechanisms, Mehmedinović realizes, format and restrict knowledge about the war, yet he himself employs the same strategies of framing.

The first entry point into the aesthetic dimension of the text is through the representations of the city under siege. The relationship between the poet and his urban environment collapses the distance between the singularity of his interior experience and the community. By gazing at the city, recording its cues of humanitarian distress, its broken and fractured infrastructure, and its urban transformations (park deforestations, blood donations on the street, and pedestrian paths passing through buildings), he transforms the individual anguish into a communal one. The city embodies its population. The depiction of urban destruction also gives rise to an ethically questionable pleasure in creative activity during times of conflict.

III.

Sarajevo blues is the story of a city's ruin. In this respect, the city is inserted into a broad historical lineage of civilizational symbolism that alternates between cycles of construction and destruction. As Marshall Berman writes, "from ancient times to our own times, the experience of seeing one's city in ruins has been one of the primal traumas," with ancient works giving us "most of the images and structures of feeling that we still use in our attempts to come to terms with the ruins in our lives today."[32] This longevity and potency in the image of a destroyed city stems from its representational value of civilization: the city is, according to Elaine Scarry, "the primary evidence of the capacity for self-extension."[33]

While Sarajevo's own razed and hollowed buildings were brought about by a military strategy of architectural and infrastructural demolition, this was but an abstracted strategy experienced as an attack on civic values, urbanity, community, and heterogeneity. Martin Shaw encapsulates this disconnect concisely when he writes: "People who are tortured, wounded, or killed by armed violence, or who see their homes, towns, and symbolic buildings destroyed, do not necessarily know precisely, still less care, which of the goals of political and military leaders is being worked out in their suffering. For them, the violence is often 'senseless.'"[34] The attack on Sarajevo's National Library on 25 August 1992 – in which 1.5 million volumes were destroyed[35] – is one such example. It is a destructive event that joins the pantheon of cultural heritage sites specifically targeted in warfare because it represented heterogeneity of thought and identities, and was thus a monument to a complex and layered history.[36]

Considering the manner in which Mehmedinović's collection documents the "deserted and broken" city, it seems that civilizational symbolism – and the Benjaminian ruin in which "history has physically merged into the setting" – is also to some extent an abstraction for the author (12).[37] Instead, Sarajevo is a deregulated zone in Mehmedinović's text, a site of blurred distinctions between inside or outside, licit or illicit, exception and norm:

> Now I remember the path beaten across yards that everyone uses instead of the pavement. One Sarajevo war path leads through the ruins of a movie theatre. Here the roads come into being on their own – not through urban planning or oblivious residents falling into line ... Yet, the new roads do not have the permanence of asphalt; they transform at the rate at which the grenades alter the shape of the city. (8)

The war, having exploded the constraints that regulate human behaviour and disabled the governing systems of rule, presents an opportunity for the experience of a relative semiotic freedom. The traditional map of the city thus becomes a map of the self's needs (and not imperatives that are prescribed by anonymous bureaucratic structures) because the tyranny of war shapes urban movements as times – rather than spaces – of death: "I walk imbued with consciousness of the next moment in which I might exist or in which I might not" (8). Such narration of the city is reminiscent of Franco Moretti's assertion that the spatial quality is resolved in terms of the sequential. Though Moretti's own case study is the novel, his idea that "the meaning of the city is not to be found in any particular place, but manifests itself only through a temporal trajectory" resonates in Mehmedinović's understanding of his environment.[38] Consequently, it is the waging of war (whether it consists of artillery attacks, shelling, or grenades) that marks time and imbues the city with a plasticity the urban environment cannot otherwise exhibit, given the rigidity of its sites and its organizing systems. So having a road cross through a cinema suggests a subverted model of interiority/exteriority that refers ironically to the playfulness of architectural utopias. The archness of the observation is palpable because Mehmedinović's omits, throughout most of *Sarajevo blues*, descriptions of moments of injury.

This episode also foregrounds the author's primary interest in the city as manifested in structural or formal attributes of its dissolution. Sarajevo becomes a shapeless, discontinuous landscape with no mass or volume, a site that cannot be surveyed from a privileged vantage point. In the language of cinema: the mise-en-scène is created with alternating close-ups and not a sweeping shot. The physical destruction thus speaks of the experience of war and not its meaning; Mehmedinović's eye seeks out properties of geometry and not those of symbolism in the destruction. There is very little by which to anchor oneself in the city of the collection, very little by which to navigate. It was not always like this:

> I once wrote
> how a poem about Sarajevo had to smell
> like the wrapping paper that market sellers
> used for oranges –
> with an imprinted drawing on the rustling paper
> with an accidental passerby on the drawing
> and crumpled minarets.
> Now the city has been opened; a dissolved form,
> Sarajevo reminds me of a post-modern work
> of fantastic proportions.[39]

(26)

The romanticism of this former Ottoman city is glimpsed through sensory and mnemonic stimuli, but the local colour is crudely replaced by a more conceptual vision that overwhelms the "accidental passerby" – perhaps the anonymous poet in the crowd – as the passive voice intrudes in the third-to-last line. The vagueness of "post-modern work" is less important here than the possibilities of its form and scale that transcend the spherical, perfect properties of the orange (the modernist form of Sarajevo) with its microcosm of familiarity and community. Instead, the precarious situation of the besieged city – that is to say, its reality – is "made perceptible in its wholeness only because it shatters to pieces" (30). Through its own fragmentation, the city offers features on which the author might base his own strategies of composition. Suspicious of totalities ("wholeness") that might monopolize the text using their points of view or teleological perspectives, *Sarajevo blues* replicates the fragmented state of the city. Indeed, the sentence "reality is made perceptible in its wholeness only because it shatters into pieces" is a self-description of his book that duplicates conceptually what he sees in the city around him: broken glass on the pavement and windows kept "whole" by "brown bands of tape" (30). Once again, however, Mehmedinović seems to be consciously suppressing the disquieting reason for Sarajevo's dissolution by not naming the external forces of destruction. Omitting this language of destruction demonstrates the author's willingness to inscribe the ruined city with features of aestheticization, fantasy, and defamilarization.

This hint of an aesthetic tableau is fully developed in other sections of *Sarajevo blues*. Contemplating the facade of a ruined building, Mehmedinović becomes more invested in the possibility of a private spectacle than in the idea that ruins signify a shared, large-scale devastation:

> I stand by the window and look at the broken glass of Jugobank. I could stand like that for hours. A blue glassy façade. A floor above the window I gaze from, a professor of aesthetics walks out on his balcony: he adjusts his glasses and runs his fingers through his beard. I look at his reflection in the blue façade of the Jugobank, in the shattered glass that makes out of this image a live cubist painting on a sunny day. (63)

By sublimating the formal properties under his gaze, he turns himself towards an aesthetic enjoyment of the city. Sinking into the pleasing harmony of this "live cubist painting," which is effectively a ruin, is by no means an unknown process in the history of European cities and the texts written about them. The imperative to seek out devastation and employ it for aesthetic creation has been attested to throughout the history of civilization and has been theorized by many. The general category of ruins appeals on the basis of temporal ambivalence: in the words of Julia Hell and Andreas Schönle, the ruin speaks of "the awareness of an insuperable break from the past … and the sense that some valuable trace has endured."[40] In *Sarajevo blues,* it is the latter – the ruin as mould for future use – that is dominant, calling up Georg Simmel's sentiment: "so long as we can speak of a ruin at all and not a mere heap of stones" then "there rises a new form which … is entirely meaningful, comprehensible, differentiated."[41] For Mehmedinović, the trope of recycling features prominently:

> I can't see anything but I know that to my left is a kiosk: its windows are broken, the door removed, its interior entirely stripped of furnishings. The shelves, pulled out of the walls, hang abjectly. Someone's hand has made an installation from these remains, clipping a row of coloured photographs of Sarajevo with clothes pegs on the kiosk window without glass. They've been there for days. The artist of the installation is anonymous.[42] (33)

Out of dead space, creativity rises, and out of a derelict commercial site, a proxy art gallery is produced. The extract inverts the notion of "exhibit" or "display," even though the words themselves are never used: a shop window is transfigured into an alternative artistic site, bypassing capitalist use-value. Further still, this anecdote introduces an architectural metaphor that reaches beyond this one example of guerrilla artwork. Housing art within a ruin is indicative of Mehmedinović's own writing project, writing which draws much impetus and inspiration from the destruction of war. In *Sarajevo blues,* an antithetical dynamic cleaves – divides but also intersects – art and the environment. The two adhere to each other in literary discourse, despite belonging to diametrically opposed realms in which art figures as creation and ruin as destruction. But there is much fragility in such a home: it is a site without identity or ossified meaning, a site that awaits appropriation. In that sense, it is equally functional as a place of inscription for a poet trying to find his voice and subjectivity.[43]

In the service of the writer, the ruin rises as an artefact in order to transcend the violence of the siege. Such an undertaking of the imagination comports with Hell and Schönle's assertion that the ruin, an "ill-defined" conceptual category, is defined by a beholder without whom the ruin could not exist: "as a result, the ruin is often the playground of speculative strategies that tell us more about the beholder than about the ruin or its original environment."[44] The traces help crystallize the subject's desires. Yet the appeal of destroyed Sarajevo – a place rich in the colours, shapes, and geometries of destruction – is not just found in the aesthetic topic, but also in the very impulse to create art (or literature) in such proximity to risk and death. In the following extract, taken from a prose piece titled "Fires," Mehmedinović describes how a local photographer was injured by a grenade after taking some pictures of the destroyed (and burning) national library. The quotation picks up at the point where Mehmedinović describes the photographer's experience of shock that delayed the physical pain of his injury:

> Kemo says that he didn't feel the pain while the shock lasted. The feeling of pain assumes consciousness about pain. The state of shock, while it lasts, is a unique sojourn on the other side. It is simultaneously a plunge into the world of one's own art since what else was this photographer doing, while he walked around the burning library, searching for the ideal angle, appropriate light, capturing with a wide lens the river Miljacka, what else, if not to fulfill the frightening wish of the artist, to capture the wild beauty of a horrific spectacle of death, to approach it from the other side? The need of the artist to step into the unknown is risky but it is precisely in this step that the strength of art is founded. (27)

For the photographer, the shock is both a physiological response to a wound and, more interestingly, a metaphor for the stupefaction that the photographer experienced from this mirage: his faculties are frozen, numbed, and arrested from the spectacle. The cognitive experience is thus transposed onto the body. For Mehmedinović's photographer, the attraction of the spectacle lies in the potential for distilling the quality of *otherworldliness* in art that seems to exceed certain norms (*frightening* wish, *wild* beauty). While there is a rupture between the interests of the body and the mind, there is also a constant, throbbing unease that the artist should take the step into the unknown, subsuming the mortality of the body to higher ideals. War presents an opportunity to create art that requires a willingness to risk one's life, to go beyond survival and set the immaterial values of art (whatever they might be) above material life. And so the potential of (and for) art announces itself as the possibility of life collapses – a dynamic defined by the compulsion to privilege the values of art above the ethics of survival.

This short anecdote calls to mind Kant's definition of aesthetic judgment, in which the judgment of beauty must be based on a particular feeling of pleasure. The necessary quality in the act of contemplation, according to Kant, is one of disinterestedness.[45] This distinguishes aesthetic judgment from "the interest of the senses," which defines "the agreeable" and also distinguishes it from "the interest of reason," which defines "the good."[46] In other words, a judgment of beauty must be devoid of any vested interest that would impose a moral or political function on the object. Yet witness literature is defined precisely through those goals: its status as a genre stems from its identity as a historical record. Indeed, when such literature becomes testimony, writes Hayden White, it "is at once confirmed as an index of the events about which it speaks (like a scar or a bruise) and it is pathologized as a product of a wounded consciousness which requires not so much understanding as, rather, treatment of a medical or psychological kind."[47] Such ethical (or interested) readings, Mehmedinović's collection suggests, foreclose the freedom of aesthetic judgment.

Sarajevo blues, then, is imbued with an ambiguity of sorts, one often present at sites of man-made devastation. Mehmedinović creates a literary discourse that internalizes the background actions of warfare and transforms them into atmospheric and haunting tableaux. As Hell and Schönle ask, "Does the aestheticization of the ruin belittle the human suffering that it connotes, pushing us into morally dubious territory?"[48] The traces of the ruin, after all, are also traces of the damaged or missing body. And what if this aestheticization and affect of enjoyment is also understood and given voice by those carrying out the destruction, especially where the quality of enjoyment is far more perverse?[49]

Mehmedinović also registers the loss and aporia of being in the presence of a sublime moment. This ambivalence creates two incompatible "structures of feeling" within the narrator-author of *Sarajevo blues*: one of the author as aesthete and the other of the author as man.[50] The former holds the principles of art above the general principles of morality. The latter, however, must function within the ethical realm, animated by impending mortality; this is the realm where the self, the community, and the city must be safeguarded and where that survival is maintained out of respect and concern for life. This ethical realm engages with politics, with its leaders and intellectuals: there are numerous critiques of Radovan Karadžić and his "political marketing" (38). There is also what Mehmedinović calls "the cosmos of pain,"[51] a phrase used to intimate the ontological impasse between the sentience of conflict and the total indifference of the external world to internal troubles (62). Yet, it is this external world that is a muse for the author.

This is an impossible bind to resolve, but it does crystallize the relevance of one paratextual detail of *Sarajevo blues*: the author's note on the inside cover of the book.[52] It states: "Unwillingly, he writes his own biographical note; in fact, he writes unwillingly and feels unease over what the written shows. He considers writing above all a personal task that does not make much sense unless one is writing for the *last sentence*" (no page, italics in the original). This statement summarizes all the overt and residual antagonisms of *Sarajevo blues*, with each elliptical claim cutting in two directions. For instance, the fact that Mehmedinović "feels an unease over what the written shows" suggests that he is appalled by the cumulative devastation of war in social, political, and ethical terms, but also that he is dismayed at having aestheticized those very same features. Because we are dealing with literary discourse, the latter cannot be avoided to some degree, but it can become a prominent stylistic element. The phrase "writing for the last sentence" is the statement of a man in perpetual fear for his life (a fear that he shares with others in his environment), but it is also a claim made by an artist who is willing to undertake a risk by stepping into the unknown for the sake of his art. In this case, it is the art that propels him and not morality. With this in mind, one could say that Mehmedinović's dualism corresponds to a tension between the collective and communal sphere and the subjective and anonymous artistic identity.

IV.

In the 1992–5 battle for Sarajevo, the comprehensively mediated spectacles of horror produced by global television networks provided an afterlife to the conflict in the corridors of international organizations and the cabinets of political strategists, informing the "imaginative geopolitical topography of 'Bosnia'."[53] Knowledge of the conflict was constructed alongside scripted journalistic narratives in order to render the conflict morally visible.[54] These political, diplomatic, and humanitarian actors left a deep imprint on Mehmedinović's literary vision of the war. The entirety of *Sarajevo blues* is heavily informed by the concomitant presence of local and foreign nationals (fighters, politicians, and journalists) and responds with constant ambivalence towards their professions. On the one hand, the UN soldiers are seen by Mehmedinović as indifferent or ineffective – they cannot rescue dead bodies from a stretch of no-man's-land, letting "the souls of the dead mix with the ravens of the city" (15) – while foreign intellectuals, on the other hand, exhibit the same "grandiose narcissism"

and egomania of domestic, ethnonational politicians such as Radovan
Karadžić and Nikola Koljević (55).

Moreover, the intersection between political and historical developments and the representations of violence (photographs, rolling news) that
informed the evolving conflict, Branislav Jakovljević argues, engaged a new
infrastructure of warfare that went beyond the classic union of theatre and
military strategies: the siege, through a refraction as a result of discourses
of reportage, turned military force into a veritable "media theatre."[55] David
Binder, a journalist for the *New York Times,* made the case (from which
Jakovljević takes his cue in developing a more conceptual argument) that
the televised images and news reportage of the siege of Sarajevo – and, in
particular, the massacre at the Markale market – actually instigated the
engagement of NATO for the first time since its foundation, and the first
involvement of U.S. forces in combat in Europe since the beginning of the
Cold War.[56] In no ambiguous terms, then, the international media exerted
an effect on world public opinion and policymakers. It also played its part
in modifying the experience of war for Sarajevans who were interviewed,
filmed, and photographed in their flight or their fight for survival.

Given that *Sarajevo blues,* a collection defined by its descriptions of the
external world, is essentially a cinematic montage, Mehmedinović exhibits something of an implicit communion with journalists and photographers, those foreign "monkeys with Nikons" (36). He shares their tropes
of war – the same stock of images – whether they take their cues from the
established catalogues of warfare (trenches, no-man's-land) or whether
they refer to new, untried forms arising from the evolution of "televisual
war" and the experiences they bring forth.[57] Though the topos is shared,
journalism relies on a rapid, effective transfer of meaning in its choice of
symbols. As literature of witness, however, *Sarajevo blues* has the prerogative to frustrate the facility of this communication. It needs to overcome
the rhetorical commonplaces that are endemic to the representation of
war, and make them, as Northrop Frye once remarked, "rich and varie-
gated" when used in literature.[58] At the same time, *Sarajevo blues* – in its
depiction of the destroyed city – both resists and absorbs the linguistic structures and conventions of modern communication technologies
within its own literary language, thereby addressing what role, if any,
these new accelerating types of communication play, "in the ostensibly
private language of poetry."[59]

I begin with Mehmedinović's aggressive critique of the media,
which finds resonance with the broader philosophical debates of anti-
ocularism – particularly those strands that interpret the dominance of

visual experience in the twentieth century as the direct result of technological development. The author's articulation of the image-problem expresses the Derridian notion of representation as "sendings" (*envois*),[60] which, in the words of Martin Jay, "never reach their final destination or reunite with the object of the idea they represent."[61] This is how Mehmedinović observes simulation: a picture of a massacre (such as one of the first that took place on 27 May 1992 on Sarajevo's main pedestrian thoroughfare, Ferhadija) establishes the principle of iteration for each subsequent atrocity, which is then understood as "a multiple of that same picture":

> The photograph of the large-scale massacre on Ferhadija has circulated the globe: the picture of the dead and the massacred has been transformed into an advert for the war. It is not important that those people have names: they are a bare image, translated into the cool language of television. The camera empties the scene of its psychological content and makes information out of it ... The world, then, sees what is happening here. Does anyone empathize with us in the whole wide world? No one. That's because television sees through to real human nature – which is basically the lack of empathy – until something tragic comes to concern us directly. The feeling of tragedy arrived with the coffins covered in the colourful American flag, not before that: not via television reports from Vietnam. (57)

The first point made here is that the pictures lose their status as a record of the real, despite the quality of transparency as a guarantee of the historical event. The clarity is simply a seduction of sorts. It disguises a significant failure in communicating weight and knowledge about the war: in every pixelated photograph of Sarajevo's reality, Mehmedinović writes, "a proportionate magnification of its dark corners would reveal a thousand corpses" (11). The phrase "dark corners" runs contrary to the expectation that a photograph is an immediate and complete exposure, but, moreover, the dark corners illuminate a *dis*proportionate ratio of the actual dead to the number of representations of "death." Photography, a form of mass communication with all its qualities of documentation, does not possess the ability to convey the tragedy of death or violent death. Simulations transform death into an imitable substance translated "into the cool language of television" and devoid of any "psychological content" (57). This ruptures our cultural inclination to approach death, in the words of historian Saul Friedlander, with "an *authentic* feeling of loneliness and dread," to have it be a moment which requires hesitation and restraint, a chance to be discriminating with the language used (through a language such as literature, perhaps).[62] Death should not be imitable, but it becomes so in mass communication, as it is reduced to a handful of ciphers and tropes.

Second, Mehmedinović here reveals that paradox of the news broadcast: the bare horror of human remains is powerless in eliciting compassion because it remains safely Other. The camera's exposure and disclosure of atrocity is distancing because the lives lost are not, to use Judith Butler's term, grievable. If we accept – and Mehmedinović does – that a photograph is already, in Butler's words, "a structuring scene of interpretation," then in order for life to be mourned, the population must be registered (or framed) as one manifesting precarious life.[63] Hence Mehmedinović's contrast between the image of U.S. soldiers' coffins and images of the waging of war in Vietnam: in the case of the former, the remains of life are appropriated by the state and imbued with values like valour and heroism in being covered by the symbol of that nation. Thus, the former authorizes grief only because it comports with, as Butler says, "a certain field of perceptible reality ... already ... established" – namely, American patriotism and military sacrifice against a clearly defined foe.[64] What complicates Mehmedinović's critique here – which he himself acknowledges in other sections of *Sarajevo blues* – is that the plight of Bosnian civilians receives a particular kind of compassion. Their lives are grieved to the extent that their appearance in the media is conditioned by numerous factors: they are Europeans whose civilization has been destroyed yet who remain passive, voiceless victims to be spoken for by a range of Western intellectuals.[65]

It would be misleading to identify Mehmedinović's antagonistic impression of the media as an unprecedented obstacle that eliminates the possibility of a nuanced, complex knowledge of conflict zones – and even more misleading to interpret *Sarajevo blues* as a lament for a "purer" form of communication that existed before the appearance of mass media. Knowledge of war, as well as the framing of it in subsequent historical narratives, has always been mediated and marked by ideological, contextual, and technological limitations. The mass media is simply a specific form of communication that builds its currency through ostensible elimination of indeterminacy, uncertainty, and doubt in the transmission of information. Rather, *Sarajevo blues* is in equal measure curious about and suspicious of modern communications, primarily because the media copyright over contemporary war representations complicates the status and purpose of the poetry of witness. I use the term "copyright" here figuratively to suggest that the discourse of journalism monopolizes categories of veracity and evidentiary function; shuts down alternative narratives through sheer ubiquity; and accentuates particular attributes of representation (such as the image as document) as the most valuable communicative tasks. It displaces witness literature from its central role as a genre prized for its truthfulness rather than it aesthetic contributions. Witness literature has historically occupied a particular position in the network of literary genres: its emphasis on the singularity and uniqueness of the speaker's identity paradoxically allows the writing to accrue historical and testimonial status.[66] Subjectivity and authenticity are strictly related. Words and phrases like "truth" and "raw facts" often figure in scholarly descriptions of such genres, and their authors are characterized as survivors and testifiers. However, witness literature's status as a genre is marked by a vulnerability that is arguably crucial to its existence. Mehmedinović presents this anxiety with a material dimension: "Nowhere in this city have I seen the effect of the written word" (142). The written text is also physically precarious – *Sarajevo blues* is haunted by the destruction of the national library and the loss of thousands of valuable manuscripts.

In addition to the insecurity of the text as a corporeal object, Mehmedinović's critique of media representation opens up a space for the reader to seek out in *Sarajevo blues* with particular registers and genres that make the communication of grief and its associated feelings possible. Formally speaking, the collection is overwhelmingly composed of narrative devices that stem from the strategies of technology and its associated discourses. These include applying the editing and cutting technique of a camera to literary narrative focalization, voice, and temporal and spatial relations (manipulations).[67] This literary experimentation actually corresponds to the emerging scholarly debates on the age of information technology, a field of study that was in embryonic stages at the beginning of the final decade of the last century. The active binary in these scholarly ruminations is one between the artifice of technological discourse and the perceived naturalness of literariness, a distinction that allows the quality of poetic expression to possess a claim to authenticity in the representation of experience.[68] It is further understood that this virtue was challenged by the everyday expansion of commodified language, exemplified by the development of modern communications (faxes, the Internet, and computer networks). Mehmedinović never opposed these new linguistic structures, or their formal strategies. He is not a poet who, as Marjorie Perloff has written on others, pits "the 'authentic' individual self against an impersonal, exploitative other that commodifies the consciousness of the duped masses."[69]

Instead, he finds in the tired slogans and set phrases of the media message the potential for irony through poetic intervention. In a piece titled "A Relatively Calm Day," Mehmedinović demonstrates the manner in which certain linguistic structures of media discourse become internalized and serve to subsequently rationalize, or normalize, the spectre of death. In a mocking rewrite of a weather report, he writes:

> In the daily CSB [*sic*] report, when ten grenades fall on the "narrower centre of town," when on the roads the "snipers shoot, here and there," but when there are only a few fatalities and a few wounded – then the presenters say that it has been a relatively quiet day. People are relatively normal, or relatively crazy, from the moment they accepted death as a statistical sign. (56)

The register of a news report projects the familiarity of a weather forecast that draws the reader in using recognizable idioms, but the illusion of the mimicry is dispelled with words like "grenade," "sniper," "fatalities," and "wounded." It is clear by the end of the extract that we are dealing with Mehmedinović's distancing, given his use of purely communicative language whose signs and codes dispel the possibility of expressing the tragic. In this glut of death, and in the pervasiveness of spectacle, the format of a weather report is an inadequate expression for the loss of human life, because the media takes a high quantity as a precondition for "news," and as a precondition for tragedy. "Relatively Quiet Day," however, should be read alongside (or against) "Loss," Mehmedinović's rumination on the nature of personal grief, written shortly after the death of his father. His personal loss is framed by the classical construction of Goethe's poem "Der Erlkönig," which tells the story of a child dying in his father's arms (78). The poem is meaningful for Mehmedinović in its expression of the tragic, that is, the tragic according to Michael André Bernstein's definition: "a mode of comprehending and giving form to events as a narrative … not a mode of existence as such."[70] But seeing the reality of widespread death in war through the eyes of this particular genre (in this case, a poem) does not rouse the author's consciousness.[71] Attempting to square a siege reality "choked by the presence of death" with poetic conventions rings false for Mehmedinović; more specifically, he calls it "a delusion" (78). He interprets this absence of affect as a distinction between private and collective forms of compassion, but it is equally connected to speech genres that accommodate or refigure historical events. The register of the media, while it cannot express the tragic, unexpectedly becomes valuable in its expression of absurdity: the language that is mocked becomes the language *par excellence* of representing violence, especially as it reveals "the production of people as nothing but objects of administration."[72] Death involves bureaucratic processes, from military planning to compiling lists of the dead. Moreover, the lack of pathos in this extract can be read as an honest expression of Mehmedinović's position on collective grief: the moral demand to identify with a large-scale loss of life exceeds an individual's capacity for sentiment and understanding of suffering.

Literary creation, for Mehmedinović, is not an exclusive category of elevated linguistic expression in the hierarchy of speech and writing, and *Sarajevo blues* leaves little room for doubt that aspects of intermediality are a crucial part of the author's development of narrative strategies and vision of writing. A short essay titled "Naked in the Saddle" (one that most likely pre-dates the war) hints at Mehmedinović's desire to experiment with literature in a way that implodes the sanctimonious world of art and makes it miscible with the visual clusters of documentary. He even coins a phrase for such a practice: "picture-news" (*slika-dnevnik*) (136). Mehmedinović explains that the source of this phrase (describing an intermedial medium) arose from a collision of two separate events, one artistic and the other televised. In describing the first event, he writes the self-portrait of an artist, a nude painted "with photographic precision," which contains within its frame other mimetic surfaces – a mirror, another canvas, and an artist's notepad (135). These details transform the artistic product into a process predicated on the "mixing of realities": the artist paints himself painting, looking, making, and having made (135). This image is laid out in Mehmedinović's short essay alongside the televised lovemaking of an unsuspecting young couple transmitted, due to some technical error, to their neighbours during the evening news. For Mehmedinović, these separate incidents typify the bare truth about (artistic) creation: art's potency lies in the slippage, overlap, and dissonance between the hermetic world of artistic representation and the document of the photograph or camera. Practised as such, intermediality does not reduce artistic credibility or aesthetic possiblity. Nor does Mehmedinović suffer from a fear of "low culture" or a concern that images and the screen are simply commodities of mass consumption with no creative value.

Still, the demand that one should strip bare the closed, self-referential world of art through intermediality can actually be viewed as part of the "metastasis of self-conscious watching" that typifies the metafictional literature of the second half of the twentieth century.[73] This type of verbal art, David Foster Wallace argues, resides in mediums like television, and it is not simply a response to televisual culture: it comprises a genre of "watchers and appearers."[74] Such figures proliferate throughout *Sarajevo blues*; most are professionally required to watch, like the CNN cameraman, "incredibly new and whole, with a camera on his hip," who the narrator spies as he "looks down a devastated alley in Bistrik" (57). The more this type of reflexivity surfaces in *Sarajevo blues*, the more the author holds intermediality to account because, in Susan Sontag's words, it simply "drains attention from the sobering subject and turns it toward the medium itself."[75]

This point is starkly made when the medium itself is used to protest the very news it brings to the world. Many intellectuals and humanitarians were themselves televised in action in Sarajevo; a form of self-publicity that further propagated the newsworthiness of the war and justified anew, in Keith Tester's words, "the continuation of engagement."[76] We read in *Sarajevo blues* that

> in front of the camera, while talking with the reporter, Bernard-Henri Lévy is forced to lie down and find shelter as the bullets whizz by. Sitting on the sidewalk, he continues to talk. Lévy in Sarajevo talks about what is happening in Sarajevo. The picture of that conversation will travel the world over; he saw everything, there's no illusion, he knows what is happening here – his words are addressed to Europe. If he had it his way: this city would be free tomorrow. (55)

As Lévy continues to talk "not without enjoyment amidst the bullets," the screen makes the French philosopher into a star witness of the war, as his actions are qualified by phrases such as "proof," "no illusion," "he saw it all," and "confirmed" – all expressions that assert the value of his documenting self (56). Not surprisingly, however, these words are heavily ironic considering that Lévy occupies this position from the privilege of two sources of power. One is represented by Lévy himself, whose name is a signature of European intellectual capital – he thus implies the quality that resides in his name (primarily for having brought the attention of the Soviet Gulag to "his nation").[77] The other is the world of modern communications technology which, despite its disembodied nature, is sourced from centres of capital (i.e., metropolitan cities) that, as Tester posits, propel the "narrative-making power" of the media, leaving those represented in effectively "pseudo-imperial functions."[78]

Even if intermediality enriches the literary text, it cannot be conceived or appraised in solely formal terms. The dynamism of its technical attributes – the possibility of shifting perspective, the mise-en-scène, and the montage – should not be allowed to disguise the ideological problems inherent in such artistic experimentation, or in the mediated discourses themselves.

V.

It is worth mentioning the presence of another current in *Sarajevo blues* that runs counter to the seemingly dominant downgrading of visual representation in late capitalism. This alternative tendency is found in the "objective, celestial gaze" of an otherworldly, divine presence (25). During the war, Mehmedinović "disclosed [his] religiosity," his belief in Islam.[79] While there is no explicit discussion in *Sarajevo blues* about the author's relationship to his faith during the years of socialist Yugoslavia, there is a hint of the ambivalence he held towards the state's displacement of religious belief. In the following extract from "Unease," the poet addresses his younger self:

> Throughout your childhood,
> it seemed unbelievable to you
> that the world existed before your birth
> even though
> everything that the young eyes saw
> said the opposite; everything visible –
> including Tito's portrait
> above the school blackboard
> the portrait of the one that had created that world.
> And in that world, the letter g in the noun God
> was written in small letters.[80]   (67)

The last few lines are softly ironic: while the creator of this "world," the world of Yugoslav socialism, ostracizes religion, he demanded and received the veneration of a god himself, manifest in the poem through his ubiquitous portrait. His likeness is reproduced and worshipped institutionally – a self-aggrandizing gesture of a human mortal. The reader might also juxtapose this type of veneration of the creator of the world – of a small southeast European nation – with the ban on images within certain Islamic religious practices (particularly images that depict human figures). This is not mentioned in the poem, but one cannot help but be sensitive to this particularity.

This form of political commentary is supplanted in *Sarajevo blues* by more spiritual reflections that focus on the illuminating and protective presence of God. There are two discernible roles this thread plays in the collection: one offers a means to overcome trauma, and the other offers an aesthetics of the spiritual. In the case of the former, the presence of a religious current is a discourse that rises above wholesale destruction and death. In his conversations with the Bey's Mosque imam – appropriately, a man that the author first saw on television – alternative definitions of tolerance, loneliness, and Islam emerge that rehabilitate the pain and trauma of war. This is directly alluded to in Mehmedinović's retelling of the imam's tragic losses in the war that include his wife, children, and grandchildren (59). Following his observation that some tragedies "cannot fit into the heart," the connection between his personal suffering and his religious identity is brought together by what Mehmedinović's calls the imam's "dictionary of ... loneliness" (59, 60). Here is one of the definitions: "Islam. That is a faith in expansion, but it is not imposed; it does not have its missionaries; nor an I which is prominent. But it leaves its human, noble traces everywhere. That is a characteristic of great people" (60). The dynamic of their conversation, in which a pupil follows the learned authority, is essentially about letting the limits of the self be rearranged in the encounter with religion, about letting the broader framework of belief – collective and intimate at the same time – accommodate the suffering and the fragility of the individual.

The other pole of Islamic references and insertions in the text is more aesthetic and connected to Mehmedinović's poetic project. Typified by Islamic rituals and prayers during which "the presence of God [is] in everything" (34), these moments introduce coherence and a timeless sense of order to the overwhelming chaos and ruin. Crucially, this relationship to Islamic divination and thinking is revealed as the point where identity – both of the individual and of the city – is located:

> Reader, if you walk up King Abdulah Kaukjić Street another 50 metres, when you turn around, you will see Sarajevo in fog; above the fog are the roofs of the Old Town and, above those, the minaret of Bey's Mosque, isolated from the earthly, quotidian fog, from this cosmos of pain. (62)

The transcendence of religious agency is, in some respects, a figurative restoration of the sustained fragmentation of society, but also, for Mehmedinović, a recuperation of the aesthetic and lyrical world.

VI.

With *Sarajevo blues*, Mehmedinović has produced a collection haunted by the idea that there might be no tomorrow. As this chapter has shown, his prose and poetry responds to the immediate physical danger, the new city of ruin, that day's necessity of survival, and the most recent news. These are all topics that are diffused throughout the book as a result of its rhizomatic structure. Responding to this quality, I have read the book laterally, that is, reading not just within the entries themselves but across them in order to bring certain recurring threads into focus. In this way, I have foregrounded how certain tropes form the lynchpin to entering the textual world of the siege. I started with the role of seeing and visibility: the author is himself a poet-observer but also a citizen at a precarious threshold under military and media observation. Despite this disempowering appropriation of his subjectivity – he is wanted by the media and the sniper as a victim – Mehmedinović carves out an avenue for his own poetic observation. He records the city in ruins: a city that is a shifting landscape and a work of art, moulded by the application of military force. My examination of this thread concludes that *Sarajevo blues* approaches an ethically ambiguous position with regard to aesthetic representation of war. On the one hand, pure enjoyment and beauty runs the risk of suppressing the very death and destruction that engendered the aesthetic tableau in the first place. On the other hand, Mehmedinović clearly wants to assert the autonomy of art that is otherworldly and that exceeds some of these ethical dilemmas. Subsequently, I focused on the antagonistic relationship between Mehmedinović's act of witness and that provided by the international media. Here I stress the peculiarities of what it means to testify *literarily* to an event in an age saturated with immediate circulation of photographs and news events. What complicates this discussion vis-à-vis *Sarajevo blues* is Mehmedinović's own adherence to the narrative potential of intermediality, a technique that no longer seems to him so radical and enriching.

The restorative means that attenuate not just the destructive forces of war but also the aesthetic disappointment lie in Mehmedinović's immersion in his religious belief. In the concluding section, I posit that the rupture signalled by the siege, in its existential and spiritual terms, is countered by the healing framework of his vision of Islam. His spiritual commitment is the source of hope and protection but also the potential source of poetry and symbolism.

3 The Phantasmagoria and Seduction of Kitsch

I.

In this chapter, I will explore war in the context of bad taste, through verbal and visual discourses of nationalist kitsch that justify, communicate, and disseminate the idea of conflict and that also depreciate and neutralize conditions of crisis and suffering. I analyse Dubravka Ugrešić's essay collection *Culture of Lies* (first published 1995), in some respects an expansive and annotated catalogue of nationalist curiosities, which examines how such strategies of aestheticized politics (to conceive of kitsch broadly) veil the debilitating material conditions of war through aesthetic harmony of both verbal and visual utterances. This material might not seem immediately tied to the main work of war – the expression of military violence – but as has been duly noted by Margot Norris, "nonmaterial issues (security, sovereignty, national identity)" layer the "instrumentalities of force and violence."[1] What is interesting about the premise behind *Culture of Lies*, as a whole, is that Ugrešić initiates a serious conversation – the critique of political, social, and historical mythologies propagated in Croatia in the early 1990s – through matter that is ultimately trivial and insignificant.

Very often, however, and especially in times of crisis, there is a wider social indifference towards kitsch, if we understand it broadly as a trivial, banal, and easily consumed object. To call something kitsch is, in the words of Matei Călinescu, to reject it "as distasteful, repugnant, or even disgusting."[2] Kitsch, whether manifest in commodity form or in political symbolism, is marked by what Călinescu calls "aesthetic inadequacy," given that its "formal qualities (material, shape, size, etc.) are inappropriate in relation to [its] cultural content or intention."[3] In other words, kitsch embodies very little that is formally interesting yet continuously circulates in a manner that exceeds its aesthetic value. Forms of banality have attracted very little attention from social commentators of the war years because it is often considered too banal for sustained attention. Yet it is precisely its triviality, and its supposed apolitical harmlessness, that makes kitsch such a powerful tool for nationalist discourse. *Culture of Lies* addresses what happens when the popular is used to stage populist opinions and convictions, when aesthetic properties and commodities become politicized. And on this point, Ugrešić's essays do offer an interesting insight that I think eludes the majority of commentators on kitsch. In this chapter, I argue that political kitsch and commodity kitsch need to be considered in tandem, though scholarship often divorces these two categories. I will then show how the aestheticization of politics functions through a melding of centralized propaganda produced by the state in an instrumental fashion and through commodity forms produced by the market. Ugrešić's prose, I contend, brings out how these two kinds of kitsch work together.

The chapter is organized in the following manner: first, I contextualize the publication of *Culture of Lies* and the main discussions it generated as well as the main critiques it attracted. I argue that *Culture of Lies* is often overlooked from a formal standpoint and that it is precisely the author's essayistic technique that is relevant for understanding her contributions as critical discourse. Next, I explore in more detail how Ugrešić experiences the new political reality as a text in order that I may better establish the link between culture and nationalism as an example of "aestheticized politics." I follow this with a discussion of kitsch as commodity in Ugrešić's writing that dates back to the beginning of her career, when the banality was associated with gender rather than political and nationalist manifestations. In developing my argument, I trace the historical evolution of kitsch as a category of both mass consumerism and propaganda. In doing so, I draw on theories linking banality and political ideology that developed out of studies on fascist and Nazi aesthetics and those on their socialist counterparts. I undertake an analysis of the very properties of nationalist kitsch that are crucial to its functioning, such as synecdoche and possession. On a final accounting, I argue that Ugrešić's work was so often inflammatory and offensive for the Croatian public because it attacked positive, respectable values – values represented through aestheticized politics – on the grounds that they were the most socially and morally fraudulent.

While this chapter focuses mainly on *Culture of Lies*, a collection of essays thematically connected to the Yugoslav wars, I quote from a range of Ugrešić's works, written over some thirty years. I take my cue from the author's own commitment to a constellation of concepts (such as the intersections of popular culture and gender) that recur and arrive remoulded in tandem with broader historical developments. This goes against a tendency to periodize Ugrešić's writing within two distinct moments (i.e., preceding and succeeding the break-up of Yugoslavia), thus producing an apparently splintered identity, the former personality seemingly incompatible with the latter. Such a chronology sidelines the consistency of Ugrešić's poetic and aesthetic concerns in favour of a more dramatized reading of her life. In recent decades, her competency as a writer has taken second place to her biographical legend, of which Ugrešić herself is well aware: "an identity tag is a shorthand interpretation of the text and regularly wrong."[4] At the beginning of her literary career in the early 1980s, she fashioned herself as a playful postmodernist with streaks of feminist provocation, but she became an outspoken critic of the newly established Croatian government and subsequently the war in the former Yugoslavia in the early 1990s. To some, this was a traitorous gesture, to others a valiant one. Either way, both sides viewed this turn as the politicization of the writer and her work – which ultimately suggested that her writing in the 1980s was less political, less socially urgent (or perhaps her feminist critiques were easier to ignore because her critique of social norms was dressed in trivial genres). Thus a secondary aim of my analysis is to read the "political" Ugrešić through her more "playful" alter ego, demonstrating the ongoing interactions between these seemingly disparate identities.

II.

First published as a collection in Dutch, for reasons which I will shortly outline, *Culture of Lies* comprises some twenty essays published separately in various international media between 1992 and 1995 (including *Die Zeit, Independent on Sunday, Literatur und Kritik*). This chronology is crucial for understanding the historical parameters, characteristics, and conditions of Croatian society that are critiqued in Ugrešić's essays. It is a society in formation, but also a country at war – the two are inextricably connected. Broadly, the essays respond to the early years of democratic and economic transition in Croatia under President Franjo Tuđman, whose Croatian Democratic Union (HDZ) was the victor in the first multiparty elections held in the spring of 1990. Tuđman, a former Yugoslav army general and later nationalist historian, remained president until his death in 1999. His popularity and public omniscience as the father of the nation, a recurring theme in *Culture of Lies,* is perceived by Ugrešić as modelled directly on two political leaders, Stalin and Tito: "Stalin as *batja,* Tito as *old man,* Tuđman as *papa, tata.*"[5] The core of HDZ ideology and rhetoric during the early part of the decade focused on state building through ethnonationalism – no different, really, from other republics of the former Yugoslavia at the time. The explicitly nationalist agenda of HDZ was coupled with a widespread revival of traditional values and beliefs that emerged during the splintering of the Yugoslav union. Narratives and myths of ancient origin, of both historical and literary dimension, resurfaced to validate the formation of the nation state, with scholars and writers parroting the official party line. On the literary front, for example, the writer Ivan Aralica – famous for his works of Croatian mythologizing – was at one point the vice-president of the Croatian Parliament during HDZ's time in power. Alongside these contributions from academics to nationalist ideology that fuel her antipathy, Ugrešić also depicts the seemingly petty iconography that was endlessly reproduced throughout much of this national rediscovery: she calls it the "Catholic-folkloric variant of kitsch" that mixes "Baška tablets and wattles, Catholic candles and crosses, gingerbread hearts and folk costumes"[6] (70). Curiously, there is something of an oddity to this kitsch: kitsch appears historically because of modernization, advancements in production, as well as a growing urban population for whose consumption mass culture is made. In his seminal work on kitsch written in 1939, Clement Greenberg complains that kitsch has "flowed out over the countryside, wiping out folk culture."[7] What *Culture of Lies* demonstrates is the recovery of folk culture as kitsch in reactionary political discourse precisely because dimensions of the "folk" offer a link to an untainted, premodern (and therefore authentic) historical era.[8] Ugrešić's major objection to this cacophonous grouping of iconic pieces of Croatia's material culture concerns the extensive decontextualization that results from their commodification, sale, and display. Yet she perceives that it is the very reduction, or distillation, of history to a symbolic referent that increases its value as a repository of adorned and decorated national principles.

Concurrent with the legal, economic, and cultural processes of transition, the political elites were also engaged in a military campaign, headed by the controversial general Ante Gotovina, in what has come to be known in Croatia as the Homeland war (*Domovinski rat*), which first involved territory in Slavonia and subsequently Hercegovina.[9] The war, then as now, Catherine Baker argues, "was memorialised by state and non-state actors as soon as it had begun, in order to mobilise support for the war effort and government, to homogenise the majority ethnic community around a desired narrative of the war and to attract international stakeholders to the Croatian interpretation of the conflict."[10] It is to this orchestration of the public image of war that Ugrešić responds, keenly observing the political wrangling, the official ceremonies, and the military pomp that design the narrative and spectacle of war. Pastiche and irony are the two most common modes in her writing, and frequently the two are in constant negotiation. The pastiche intensifies the irony by offering the comic relief that starkly contrasts with the serious message. Much of the material she consumes comes from the media reel, an encounter with scenes of tragedy coded into scenes of honour and pride – in other words, sober propaganda that muddles the view of "bloodily disassembl[ed] personal lives":

> I suffocate somewhat from the televised scenes where the president ceremonially hands over medals to widows and mothers of killed soldiers. And they, mothers and widows, obediently take the heap of metal and – look! – as a gesture of thanks for their fallen husband or son, some of them kiss the president's hand! (132, 131)

This neutralization of war that occurs on the home front becomes, in Ugrešić's critical discourse, ethically dubious.

It is now widely acknowledged that the early years of HDZ rule were not a legitimate democratic experience. There is the matter of rule by autocracy, the extensive corruption, the dubious privatization schemes, the state's almost total control of the media, and numerous human rights offences.[11] Questioning the legitimacy of the state is, in sum, precisely what Ugrešić sets out to do in *Culture of Lies*. She seeks to puncture the grandiloquent posturing of the political elites; to unveil the fiction of their speeches and rhetoric; and also to critique the common delusion, promoted by the years of historical revisionism, of Croatia's ethnonational superiority and excellence. Her essays were incendiary, and the personal and professional fallout for Ugrešić was not insignificant.[12] The first of her pieces, entitled "Clean Croatian Air" (which I examine later in this chapter), generated something of a controversy even though it was first published in German and was not available in a Croatian publication until 1996.[13] On the basis of hearsay, the Croatian media spurred into action with a "witch hunt" against Ugrešić and

four other writers and journalists deemed to be politically disloyal trai-
tors to the state of Croatia.[14] After months of ostracism sparked by the
media coverage, Ugrešić chose to leave the newly independent Croatia
as the fighting spread to Bosnia, and as economic and social conditions
deteriorated across the region. It was a self-imposed exile, but her decision was also made in the face of increasing hostility that included death
threats and professional antagonism.[15] Over the course of the decade, as
an East European writer abroad, her writing was received through the
lens of dissidence, a familiar shorthand for many intellectuals who came
from the geopolitical region of former communist states. The content of
her work started to focus more on the ambivalent space of exile and its
aesthetic tropes. During these years of peripatetic life, her work was not
available in Croatia until the publication of the collection in 1996 (after
its Dutch and German editions had already been released).

In summary, the polemic surrounding *Culture of Lies* ostensibly seems
to revolve around Ugrešić's patriotic betrayal, what was deemed to be her
anti-Croatian sentiment, and, by extension, her pro-Serbian sympathies.
The rage over the essays (they were not widely read at the time of their
publication) stemmed from Ugrešić's insult of the Croatian national, cultural, and political image of itself – a reminder that those in positions of
power who hold the majority view can still take offence, can still be made
to experience the threat of those who are weaker politically and socially.[16]
She construed this response to her work as an overblown reaction from a
homogeneous public of "a totalitarian mentality," steeped in conformism,
that could not even handle a "complaint made about rather obvious and
crude transgressions" (99). Time, however, has proved Ugrešić a prescient and popular social commentator on the whole, a reputation sealed
by the international success of *Culture of Lies*.[17] Despite the critical acclaim
she has received over the past two decades, the Croatian literary establishment remains to this day somewhat ambivalent about her status in the
national cultural canon: a recent study of Croatian literary history casti-
gates Ugrešić for failing to remain loyal to the country's literary tradition
at its moment of national independence, an epoch referred to by a literary historian as "a time of catharsis."[18] It is precisely this type of inflated
sense of historical importance that Ugrešić attacks in *Culture of Lies,* a
collection described by one reviewer as an ethical plea against "President
Franjo Tuđman's distorted and exaggerated nationalist mythology that
declared Croatia 'European, Catholic, and cultured.'"[19]

This polemic, which originated in the distant year of 1992 and has
marked her post-Yugoslav biography, has very little to do with her actual

writing – neither her critics nor her supporters engage at any great length with the poetic and aesthetic contributions of the essays, and at times the complaints from both camps shade into each other. The main objection concerns Ugrešić's claim to expertise that she does not possess (expertise of politics, history, anthropology, among others) and that transforms *Culture of Lies* into an indulgent and cynical exercise in journalism written, to quote Andrew Wachtel, in a "heavy-handed and untrue" prose.[20] This chimes with Antun Šoljan's review of the book that casts Ugrešić as a politically naive interventionist of literary-theoretical training, unable to find her footing "in the jaws of 'the Croatian question.'"[21] Admittedly, Wachtel (unlike Šoljan) admires the work for "being correct and courageous," though he adds that it "is not the same thing as writing a successful book."[22] Other admirers of the writer who hold some reservations about her authorial persona include Andrea Pisac, who argues that the attention Ugrešić has received (specifically after translation of her work into major European languages) stems in large part from her fashioning as "a cultural broker" of anthropological metaphors that authenticate her insider status and knowledge to Western audiences.[23] The risk of this method, Gordana Crnković has remarked, is its production of "excessive generalizations," in which an entire population is reduced to "frenzied nationalists," men into "chauvinists," and Western scholars and journalists into "self-serving careerists or else jaded observers."[24] Such mistakes, Crnković speculates, might be explained in part precisely by "the uncritical transference" of Ugrešić's literary techniques onto journalistic discourse, which is predicated on different criteria than fiction.[25] In my view, the core of their criticism stems from the general pitfalls of the essay genre, which these scholars subsume into journalism.

From a literary perspective, the essay is open to attack on a number of fronts: often written in first person, it is subjective; it lacks a formal structure and established conventions that ensure consistency among practitioners of the genre. Essays also have a tendency to come across as solipsistic exercises in writing that centre on an all-knowing self that eschews more established methodologies (such as those pursued in academic writing) to convey their knowledge. There is a tendency in *Culture of Lies* for the author to uphold a clear distinction between a homogeneous unsuspecting collective on the one hand, and the subjective, individualized experience of a knowing writer on the other. "In Croatia, which has four and a half million inhabitants," writes Ugrešić, "it has been publicly announced that there are around ten *state enemies*. The majority has conformed ... In the end, I fall among those ten" (139, original emphasis).

She constructs her narrative identity around a positive exclusion, that is, separation from the confused (conformist) mass, and the privilege of observing with acuity what is not perceptible to others.

Broadly conceived, the essay (as a genre) also lacks systematic expression: this is at the very least frustrating for those seeking reasoning and argumentation through accumulation of evidence. These instabilities of the essay actually obscure what contributions the genre makes to social commentary. Moreover, essays that are based on specific events can quickly fall out of fashion, bound as they are by their references to local events and environments. Ugrešić is well aware of the risk posed by datedness, and she actually makes it the subject of her 1997 novel *Muzej bezuvjetne predaje* (*The Museum of Unconditional Surrender*), in which she offers a lyrical portrayal of the social and historical irrelevance of communist artefacts (both large-scale official ideology and private consumerist objects) that is sliding irrevocably into obsolescence.[26] In the same vein, *Culture of Lies* could itself become a period piece, read and quoted by scholars when they need a dash of local colour to enrich their descriptions of the early Tuđman years.

These are common complaints in literary studies where essays are often read as side projects for authors who produce more serious fiction, or as evidence of the writers' ideological position(s) rather than as a distinct genre. Yet it is also true that the aforementioned critiques of Ugrešić do not address in good faith her own claim about experiencing post-independence Croatia as a *fabrication,* as a fictional representation that can only be dealt with through the demands of textual dissection. "It sometimes seems that Croatia roughly assembled its official politics from citations, inverting meanings and changing prefixes," notes Ugrešić, "and to hold it all together, it glued the elements with the strong snot of national homogenization, national myth and defensive pride" (137). So if she transposes her literary techniques onto the genre of criticism, it is because she perceives the environment around her not as objective reality but as discursive fragments of nationalist ideology. (Yet, for some, the appearance of new ways of poltical and social life in Croatia in the 1990s seems not to need require any justification and explanation.) She lets the form of her experience determine her own rhetoric, structure, and approach – a technique that Graham Good argues is a defining feature of essayism: "Instead of imposing a discursive order on experience, the essay lets its discourse take the shape of experience."[27] *Culture of Lies* is an exercise in reading the language of popular politics and commodities as a relentless text that masks and disfigures material conditions, in the process deterring sustained contemplation. The following statement, while not an explicit self-description of her own method, points to the possibility of engaging narratological, semiotic, and literary theory readings of the Yugoslav break-up: "If we read the frightening reality of war in the former Yugoslavia as a literary text, we could compile a whole repertoire of narrative strategies, a whole lexicon of stylistic devices, tropes and figures" (75). Ultimately, Ugrešić writes by reading; that is, she writes her reading. She reads by denaturalizing the social value system and its aesthetics, as a semiologist in the mould of Barthes's *Mythologies* might do. In this chapter, I argue that paying attention to the type of reading, and its subsequent aesthetic result, will elicit a new conclusion as to the reason for the offence she causes to the majority position, to the proponents of Croatian narrative of independence and nationhood.

I employ reading as the preferred term – over, say, analysis – in order to portray Ugrešić as an avid and impassioned consumer of media images, advertising, and political rhetoric. While she might repeatedly distinguish herself intellectually and positionally from the "ordinary man," she is also the target of these messages, also co-scripted into them (179). In addition, analysis is too loose a designator for the type of interpretation she undertakes, an activity better served by *parsing* and *glossing*. These two terms suggest a more targeted object of attention: noun phrases, expressions, slang and slogans. Such distinct units of language were symboli-. cally recharged in the 1990s and include both anonymous and authored sayings: "HDZ – it is known!"; "The people happened!"; "If we do not know to work, we know to fight!" (Slobodan Milošević); "Every nation is born in blood" (Tuđman); "Wherever the bones of our ancestors lie is Serbian land."[28] In addition to the language of sloganeering that provides vertically the shortest route to the core of nationalist values, Ugrešić canvasses newspapers for the underground language of criminality and the black market, exploring alternative semantic fields that are nonetheless caught up in broader social changes. Drawn to a "secretive advert for the sale of 'chickens' and 'chicks'," Ugrešić discovers "that 'chicken' was the name for a revolver and 'chicks,' logically, the name for bullets" (79). From this brief survey, we can abstract that Ugrešić's essays are, at their core, examinations of what V.N. Vološinov calls the "verbal responses and resonances [that] form around each and every ideological sign."[29] For my purposes, the ideological sign is understood as an item that acquires "a meaning that goes beyond its particularity" (i.e., its utility, its function) and is central to the "medium of communication [between organized individuals]."[30] The linguistic clusters that are associated with ideological signs give a view of language as an "index of social changes, and what is more, of changes still in the process of growth, still without definitive shape."[31] Linguistic units are the litmus test of the shifting tide, of the moment when glossy words on economic, judicial, and political phenomena of transition take on the role of inscribing a new reality, values, and shifting power dynamics.

The cumulative effect of this endless linguistic and visual relay in *Culture of Lies* is the production of a phantasmagoric form of social norms. Writing on the origins of phantasmagorias as "exhibition[s] of optical illusions" in the nineteenth century, Susan Buck Morss gives a concise summary of their effects: they "are experienced collectively rather than individually. Everyone sees the same altered world, experiences the same total environment. As a result ... the phantasmagoria assumes the position of objective fact ... The intoxication of phantasmagoria itself becomes the social norm."[32] This kind of "phantasmagoric nightmare" is exactly what took hold in Croatia in the 1990s – or, at the very least, it is how Ugrešić experiences the new, post-Yugoslav, post-independence years of war (69). In *Culture of Lies*, Croatia is under the pathological grip of what Ugrešić calls a "national mythomania" that fictionalizes, misrepresents, retouches, and fetishizes its own narratives and standards (104). One such norm, promulgated during the early years of Croatia's independence, emphasized that the country's departure from the "'unnatural' federal entity of Yugoslavia," from "the repressive boot of communism," was in fact a return to a seemingly incontrovertible and inherent state within which the new national identity was lauded as an "authentic replacement for an 'inauthentic,' 'schizophrenic' Yugoslav one" (250, 90, 318). Yet the claim to "authenticity" is itself the work of ideological processes, imperceptible to those subjects who have been effectively brought into those identities and into affiliation with the state building project. Ugrešić wastes no opportunities in revealing the choice irony in any appeal to a "'longstanding' tradition of Croatian statehood" because "Croatia was only ever an independent country as the Nazi puppet state NDH"[33] (320). Ultimately, the precise moment of idealizing the country's identity is a validation of it through the darkest historical hour of that same nation.

The phantasmagoric form in *Culture of Lies* is represented as a nationalist communication that signals the "collective experience" and promotes a uniform view of Croatia as valiant, victimized, suffering (the war triptych) but also as democratic, European, worldly (96). By contrast, Ugrešić experiences the new political and social reality as a scrim of language that covers stagnating social conditions. On the whole, her essays are a description of the world of spectacle that is coterminous with the development of modern capitalism and old-fashioned state control. In this milieu, with its insuperable dominance of projections and mediations in nationalist and political discourse, *image* not only becomes "the most frequent word in Croatian public, cultural and political life" but is also mass-produced and reproduced en masse. Tuđman's image is the most ubiquitous of all:

> When I go outside, I am followed by the gaze of my president from enormous posters from every which way. His eyes are shielded by glasses, but his gaze penetrates through the glass and – darts right into mine. Wherever I go, wherever I turn, his eyes bore into mine. HE knows everything, there's no way he wouldn't know, that is how omnipresent my master is, my mister President. (140)

At times, the nationalist propaganda, even if initiated by some central government organ, is commensurate with current corporate processes: the "image" of Croatia is nothing but its brand, an evocation of the contemporary world of marketing specialists and brand strategists, at times used obstructively for the memorialization of war and its signifiers. The phrase "Vukovar – *Croatian Hiroshima*" is a case in point (318).[34] Rhetorically speaking, this is an antonomasia: a figure of speech that substitutes an epithet for a proper name. Here it functions as a comparison between two proper names, Vukovar and Hiroshima, to suggest that the former is globally and historically as resonant as the latter. Hiroshima, the proper name, is in this instance also an archetypal name used to express a site of large-scale destruction. The key message behind the syntagm "Croatian Hiroshima" is to put forward a specific association: namely, to compare the offensive staged by the Yugoslav National Army (JNA) and Serbian paramilitary forces with the American nuclear bombing of Hiroshima at the end of the Second World War. The rhetorical figure enables an enlargement of consequence (from number of victims to the strength of military aggression) and gives a "global" identity to a local event.

The overall suggestion from *Culture of Lies* is that these rhetorical figures are actually given an afterlife and public circulation because they are buttressed by modern mass communications that facilitate televised streams and other media strategies. The Croatian media networks throughout the 1990s were state owned (with only a few exceptions), which meant that the press and television were mouthpieces for

Tuđman's party. State television became, in the vision of its director, "the cathedral of the Croatian spirit"[35] (97). This clash of registers – a medium of popular culture imagined as a sacred site – draws attention to the heretical gestures of how political power is exercised. The spectacle of television, as the mechanism of illusion of state building, becomes the platform of the sacred.[36]

My point is that Ugrešić's focus on symbolism and spectacle is a means to address what Judith Butler calls "the orchestrative power of the state to ratify what will be called reality: the extent of what is perceived to exist."[37] The capacity of the state to formalize and uphold what is perceived to exist is, for Ugrešić, clearly located in ideological representations of the ethnonational agenda. As such, certain semantic codes, visual responses, and iconographic images are to be understood as the manifestation of aestheticized politics that provide an affective form for particular values, beliefs, and assumptions. These forms of affect engender, in turn, sentiment and a deeper affinity with the ideals behind them: "New national states and their leaders demand a new national culture, which will be representative of the national being. They demand a new art that will, they say, have 'a spiritually renewing function'" (61). This "new art" is commensurate with what Terry Eagleton describes as "an imaginary model of the whole, suitably schematized and fictionalized for [the] purposes [of … individuals and their social functions]," adding that "[s]ince this model is symbolic and affective rather than austerely cognitive, it can furnish motivations for action as some mere theoretical comprehension might not."[38] The "imaginary model" in *Culture of Lies* is exemplified through strategies of an artistic or aesthetic provenance (such as myths, souvenirs, or turbo folk music).[39]

Out of nationalist kitsch and triviality – elements which, in Nabokov's words, "yawn so universally at times of revolution or war"[40] – emerges a serious, critical essay genre. However, one scholar in particular did not respond to this stylistic reshaping quite so generously. *Literatur und Kritik*, an Austrian literary journal, published an essay by Ugrešić titled "The Culture of the Gingerbread Heart" in early 1993 that tackles the aesthetic and affective properties of kitsch of the post-independence republics and views their pageantries of nationalism as directly descended from the spectacles and kitsch of socialist Yugoslavia. In the subsequent issue, the editorial team of *Literatur und Kritik* published a series of letters that included a strong rebuttal from Viktor Žmegač, a renowned literary scholar in Croatia. Though Žmegač finds a number of details disagreeable in her account, I will focus on his objections to Ugrešić's "aesthetic outrage," which he perceives as characteristic of her style.[41] In his account, the "aesthetic outrage" refers to Ugrešić's preoccupation with kitsch, which he finds offensive on the grounds that it presents a preoccupation with formalism, symbols, tropes, and leitmotifs of events that, according to him, should be about piety, suffering, and tragedy. His criticism, he writes, is not

> about the political convictions of Dubravka Ugrešić. It is rather about her constant talk of "kitsch." Whoever judges in this manner creates aesthetic norms. Her view is almost unbearable when the author mentions funerals ("the fallen wrapped in national flags"). It is known that sometimes, at the request of the parents, the dead – often mutilated bodies of Croatian soldiers – are buried in bunting. Whatever one might think of this, a reasonably sensitive person cannot call this kitsch. Given the infinite suffering of these people, judgments like "bad taste" or "good taste" fail.[42]

Žmegač chastises Ugrešić for forming an aesthetic judgment that subsequently governs her ethical perspective. In his sole example, he takes Ugrešić to task for trivializing soldiers' funerals by typifying (as she writes in the essay) the "bodies that lie covered in national flags" as a "common theatralization of death" (72). The problem here, from his point of view, is that when Ugrešić should respond on a moral plane – insofar as she is discussing the loss of human lives – she responds aesthetically, a mode that obscures the tragedy of the circumstances. Worse, this makes her own writing about kitsch in bad taste: a production of "meta-kitsch," concludes Žmegač.[43] The trouble with this interpretation of Ugrešić's essayistic method is that, as critic Boris Mikulić identifies, Žmegač responds to this funeral scene as if it were a natural event rather than a performance orchestrated by state actors that manipulates emotions and responses.[44] Thus, while Žmegač is convinced that he is defending universal morals from the perversion of aesthetics in the experience of tragedy, the morality he puts forward is actually deeply ideologized.[45]

Defending Ugrešić's critical discourse, Mikulić aptly notes that "her [indignation] reaches deeper than the nature of suffering: it reveals the layer of what is an already executed, falsely naturalized aestheticization of death through the symbolic means of the state."[46] What Žmegač does get right, however, is that aesthetics play a role, though he errs when it comes to recognizing where precisely that happens. Indeed, I posit that Ugrešić's actual object of critique is the aestheticization of politics itself that leads us to the destination of her "reading"/critique of nationalist kitsch.

The "aestheticization of politics" is a term that, for the purposes of this chapter, describes the process by which aesthetics is employed in the projection of sentiment, passion, and illusion in the political arena (on the grounds of nationalist values). I take aesthetics to refer not just to elements of beauty – though this dimension is present – or artistic processes, but also to a sensorial experience. I also explore what Ugrešić perceives to be the consequences of the aesthetic representation of ideological convictions of the national spirit. What are the implications of using an aesthetic frame to justify a political message – not just for public discourse and values but also for literary discourse itself?

Ugrešić's writing reveals a long-standing interest in kitsch. Her literary debt to popular culture, the mass commodity, and the lowbrow cultural product is inescapable. She has, since her very first publications, aestheticized – and thereby metamorphosed into the privileged terrain of serious writing – kitsch, pulp literature, and media slogans. Her writing from the 1980s, including *Štefica Cvek u raljama života* (*Steffie Cvek in the Jaws of Life*) and the short stories collected in *Život je bajka* (*Life Is a Fairy Tale*), is brazenly open to contamination by the popular (mass culture). Scholars who have written on these earlier works have sidelined the role of kitsch, focusing on Ugrešić's linguistic and stylistic patterns, which Nebojša Jovanović calls "a tailor's vernacular."[47] However, Jovanović suggests that her work is better approached through the "figures of waste and rubbish" and through the "abject, not the fashionable."[48] This is a call to engage with tropes of kitsch as a manifestation of cultural trash *and* actual detritus that bears a trace of its former economic, social, and historical coordinates. Kitsch is thus envisioned as a currency – a word that I use both for its figurative and actual meanings – at work in a range of historical periods (post–Second World War commodity culture, socialist realism, post-communist nationalism), all accommodated within the arc of Ugrešić's career. There is, however, no need to distinguish, as Jovanović does, between the abject and the fashionable. Kitsch is both and is susceptible to metamorphosis over time. Between the fashionable and the cast-off lies the implication that change comes, as Aleida Assmann argues, "with the loss of commodity value": we reject that which is no longer current, that which is obsolescent, and that which no longer circulates within society or the economy on the basis of exchange value.[49]

In the subsequent section, I provide an overview of Ugrešić's principles of kitsch – almost exclusively tied to representations of consumer culture – that mark her early writing. I argue that kitsch, as a product of modern mass culture, is used in an ironic key by Ugrešić to make possible a gendered critique. This results in fiction that refashions the role of women in the production and consumption of artistic creations by playing with superficial cultural representations of women. By contrast, *Culture of Lies* articulates the volatility of the sign of mass culture under the conditions of instability (war, dissolution of the republic, and economic transition). I want to stress that the circulation and application of the term "kitsch" in *Culture of Lies* is extensive: it is used to identify objects (commodities) and to conceptualize cultural phenomena as bad taste, as banal. In the latter instance, to label something as kitsch is to employ the word as a critical category without, necessarily, a material referent.

To connect these transformations in Ugrešić's imagining of kitsch and banality (from her early writing to the essays of the 1990s), I first introduce Ugrešić's mediations on popular and mass culture as refracted through her early work.

III.

Kitsch is bad taste – but very specifically, it is predominantly the bad taste of the twentieth century. It is widely accepted that the technological developments of the past hundred-odd years and the accelerated growth of capitalism contributed indelibly to its meteoric rise. Călinescu writes:

> Once kitsch is technically possible and economically profitable, the proliferation of cheap or not-so-cheap imitations of everything – from primitive or folk art to the latest avant-garde – is limited only by the market. Value is measured directly by the demand for spurious replicas or reproductions of objects whose original aesthetic meaning consisted, or should have consisted, in being unique and therefore inimitable.[50]

Expendable objects of novelty suffocate our nostalgia for an auratic (inaccessible, elusive) encounter with art. Desire is fulfilled by what the economy can offer, and it offers it in great quantity. Yet it is not so much the nature of these objects that detains us, but rather the status of kitsch as "a sign of modernization," in Călinescu's words, that emphasizes the ideological relations between mass culture and economic (capitalist), technological, political, and social spheres.[51] While mass culture is not homogeneously one of tawdry sentimentalism, for a long time it was perceived as "psychologically regressive and mind-destroying,"[52] to quote Andreas Huyssen. This is connected to the degraded aesthetic value of kitsch whose intrinsic features create an effect that is ready-made, so that, as Umberto Eco writes (paraphrasing Walther Killy), kitsch is "capable of producing an effect the moment the consumer demands it instead of venturing into the much more difficult and exclusive production of a much more complex and responsible aesthetic pleasure."[53] It is this belittled status of bad taste that is most frequently emphasized, discussed, and ironically appropriated by artists and writers.

Kitsch, in Ugrešić's early work, dovetails with mass culture more broadly: it is initially embodied in trivial genres (romance, crime), the popular press, self-help books, and advertising – all of which are imaginatively employed to challenge the parameters and intersections of high and low art.[54] The world of her fiction (particularly the "romance" novella *Steffie Cvek in the Jaws of Life*) has its historical counterpart in the world of Yugoslav aspirationalism and the pursuit of material well-being. "From the mid-1950s on the political climate in Yugoslavia permitted, and later even encouraged," writes historian Patrick Hyder Patterson, "the growth of a deep and complicated relationship with shopping, spending, acquiring, and enjoying."[55] Throughout the decades, this popular culture became more entrenched with the arrival of international fashion and culture:

> The country's "lowbrow" mass media had indeed become astonishingly attentive to European and American movie stars and rock idols, just as they closely followed the latest twists in Western lifestyles and the ups and downs of Western celebrities and their hemlines. The coverage, moreover, was rarely all that politicized or critical. Exposure to the international culture of celebrity, entertainment, and diversionary escape spawned, in turn, a host of Yugoslav variations, elaborations, and imitations, yielding a motley assortment of mass-media offerings that ran the gamut from pop stars to sitcoms to sex symbols.[56]

While popular culture was not politicized, Ugrešić's literary mediation of its codes and genres provides commentary on the intersection of gender and literary roles. Her early work tracks the processes and gestures of consumption as the promised terrain of satisfying desire that almost always remains a deferred satisfaction. The short story "Život je bajka" ("Life Is a Fairy Tale," first published in 1983) opens with "an ample young lady in a state of constant hunger" trying to satisfy her "incomplete personality," the result of an unhappy love affair, by eating an endless stream of confectionery.[57] The text reverberates with numerous "lacks," most notably exemplified by the young woman's day job on the filling assembly line at a biscuit factory, and, later in the story, by the "piteous little member" of her male guest.[58] Gratification of a kind arrives in a type of cake named "Fountain": the enmeshing of erotic (most often phallic) symbolism with consumerism is not accidental, since objects of desire are partly fulfilled through their commodity image.

Ugrešić's interest in the idea that mass culture itself consists of the production of desire is subject to a feminist critique in the 1981 novella *Steffie Cvek in the Jaws of Life*. This novel explores how mass culture can be read as an ironic rehearsal of the perception of women as "responsible for the debasement of taste and the sentimentalization of culture," a pejorative view that emerged in the nineteenth century.[59] Ugrešić overtly signals her historical awareness of this position when her protagonist, Steffie Cvek, reads (and quotes from) Flaubert's *Madame Bovary*. Steffie copies passages at length about Emma's "cold life," her expectant wait-ing for an "event, a wind that will force a sail to her," and her desire for love, which is "like a carp's desire for water when it is on the table."[60] While a number of critics have analysed this reference to Flaubert in terms of intertextuality and dialogism,[61] it is equally an affirmation of the gendered pattern of mass culture: Emma Bovary is a great reader of sentimental romances, which are quintessential examples of trivial lit-erature. Thus, women are coded as consumers of popular culture, of cultural trash, that pacifies their emotional needs, their hysteria, their insecurity, and their lack – even in Ugrešić's Yugoslavia of the 1980s. This observation can be taken further to emphasize the implications of this association between mass culture and gender. As Andreas Huyssen notes, "woman (Emma Bovary) is positioned as reader of inferior literature – subjective, emotional, and passive – while man (Flaubert) emerges as writer of genuine, authentic literature – objective, ironic and in control of his aesthetic means."[62] Within this dynamic, Huyssen adds, "authentic culture remains the prerogative of men."[63] Authenticity ostensibly offers autonomy from mass culture that, by extension, presumes autonomy from the trivial preoccupations of everyday life, as in literature.[64]

This prerogative is usurped in Ugrešić's fiction, and this is evident in the aforementioned "Life Is a Fairy Tale," a saccharine story in the grip of constant consumption, where the idea of production is treated with ambivalence. Production here specifically refers to the question of what kind of work writing actually *is*. The author character in "Life Is a Fairy Tale" is "not only incomplete but superfluous," useless with his interjec-tions: when he "boldly interrupts" the dialogue between the characters, to contribute a "brief lyrical passage," this is a kitsch gesture delivered in a nostalgic tone.[65] The action of the story incorporates elements of fantasy, folk tale, and magic, and it is predictable and scripted, with victorious and positively rewarding ends. Ugrešić is hinting here at the possibility for a literary poetics where an author, such as herself, finds originality not in an unspecified, organic talent but in rewriting, recycling, and reinserting. Ugrešić's own vocabulary can thus be imagined as a double spiral: the interactions between low and high art are amplified by a concurrent critique of male and female social and literary roles.

The female author, to put it simply, cannot occupy the same subjective position as the male author. Ugrešić's approach to writing undermines the normative association of artists and writers with originality and other sacred, immaterial notions of creativity. The problem is the nature of subjectivity in the first place. Ugrešić's novella *Steffie Cvek* is an exemplary piece of this conception of authorship in its use of sewing strategies that turn into their literary aesthetic counterpart – namely, narrative techniques. Sewing terminology begins with a key of icons: a pair of scissors indicates cutting and various punctuation combinations signify gathering, smocking, or taking in. The opening chapter, "Designing the Garment," is about "technique" – what kind of novel to write? with what kind of material to use? – and foregrounds the slippage between literary and dressmaking processes. Yet the novel never loses sight of the fact that sewing is women's domain and technology: a technology of stitching and cutting that calls to mind strategies of citation and intertexuality. Still, an important point lies behind such a construction of authorship and voice: her stories from this period are "a literary realization of some consistent literary-theoretical idea."[66] This statement foregrounds Ugrešić's recycling and reworking as serious work because of their intellectual demands. The theoretical propositions she exercises are broadly postmodern in their orientation; in fact, her "sewing" of discourse can be read as an intellectual exercise that augurs the domestication of (postmodern) literary theory. Basically, this points to the possibility of reading Ugrešić's parody as an invitation to seriously theorize about the concepts she raises.

Despite the effervescent tone and style that popular culture codes bring to her writing, a certain ambiguity about the author's relationship to triviality and kitsch is nonetheless palpable. One can detect both an attraction and repulsion towards trashy material, both a rapprochement and steely intellectual distance. As Ugrešić herself pointed out in an interview, the author-narrator of *Steffie Cvek* "tries to deconstruct the kitsch but she is at the same time fascinated by its magnetism."[67]

When the young narrator attempts to articulate the precise nature of her suspicion about the excess of kitsch, she is not able to do it, as it is implied that the clichés and banal details atrophy her thinking:

> In my fist I held a meaningless piece of paper with a recipe for stew. My thoughts resembled the recipe in style. I was thinking something to the effect that everything was a cliché, including life itself, and that I would have to think about that some more, when the storm passes; then, that the microbes of kitsch are the most vigorous organisms of emotion; then about the melodramatic imagination and how indestructible it is; ... then something ecological about our permanent exposure to unsafe levels of kitsch.[68]

The exact problem with kitsch is not pinpointed, but kitsch itself is transfigured into an ecological hazard; the subject becomes transformed into a metaphor of environmental consciousness. This prospect of pollution delineates culture as an area for conservation, threatened not just by the intellectual vacuum of kitsch but also by a key quality of its being: virulence. Kitsch, as Ugrešić's own work attests, is constantly renewing itself and occasionally thrives on its artistic re-articulations of, say, avant-garde discourses.

Reinforcing this idea is the explicit presence and influence in Ugrešić's essays of Serbian-Jewish writer Danilo Kiš and his work on nationalist kitsch.[69] Her assessment chimes with Kiš's prognosis that the banality of kitsch "gives birth to (or more correctly, multiplies) uniformity, destroys healthy human energy, multiplies the rubbish of common places ... it is, in one word, an ecological problem."[70] Or, in sloganeering terms, "*Banality is indestructible like a plastic bottle!*"[71] The implication of these metaphors is that kitsch presents an assault on the integrity of art, integrity that can only be defined and constructed in the first placed by reference to other fields of power that designate and consecrate the values of culture. This begs the question of whether Ugrešić and Kiš simply repeat the standard argument that attributes the erosion of high culture to the growth and multiplication of kitsch and whether they simply perpetuate what Sam Binkley calls the "thinly disguised prejudices of a cultural elitism" common to scholarship.[72]

If it is cultural elitism, especially in Kiš's case, then it is not predicated on the demands of consecrated taste and distinction. For him, the integrity of cultural life is located in the interplay between literature as a social and political agent of change in the world and literature as

Mallarmé's song of pure and ideal language. This tension has been noted by scholars:

> Having grown up in the virtually destroyed cultural space of Central Europe … Kiš was an essentially modernist writer whose poetics focused on a profound uncertainty over the status and legitimacy of literature in life. He considered it the writer's lot to have a comprehensive insight into contemporary developments, to testify to these developments before the world, and also to put this testimony into the service of a morally plausible purpose.[73]

He did not so much subordinate literature to the demands of truthfulness and testimony explicitly informed by his experience and knowledge of totalitarian regimes – that is, sacrifice literature to what he calls "Principles" – but he did believe that any book "that testifies against the state as an institution of violence, lies and lawlessness, gives meaning to the entirety of our writing."[74] Thus, for him, kitsch is the product of ideologically controlled art that gives rationale and justification to the very violence and perversion of totalitarianism: simply put, it does not promote artistic truth. When he describes the reading public as an audience that "lives off kitsch and common places,"[75] it is less a comment on the consumers of mass culture than about the world in which they live, a world of dogmatic cultural life.

Though he did not use the word himself, Kiš is pointing to the ethically dubious dissemination of kitsch that, for him, is less a material category than a symptom of ideology. In contrast to Kiš's explicit belief in artistic truth born of a "necessity of creation,"[76] Ugrešić's moulding of kitsch parts ways with his approach. Her early work consciously strives to demonstrate that the derivative and repetitive nature of kitsch has value in and of itself, and that manipulation of the plasticity of kitsch undermines authorial originality as the exclusive value or standard. This, however, does not negate the possibility of cultural elitism on her part: even when the boundary between high and low art is being deflated, it is still important to carry the imprint and knowledge of the boundary – otherwise the gesture of negotiation is meaningless. Works like *Steffie Cvek in the Jaws of Life* exhibit this unease though the unease never surfaces as a specific complaint.

This latent critical opinion in Ugrešić's early work emerges more fully in *Culture of Lies* via an exegesis on Nabokov's position on *poshlost*, the Russian word for banality and kitsch.[77] Nabokov's poetic attitude towards *poshlost* provides a form of cultural legitimacy for Ugrešić's own critical discourse, which is heavily invested in the outpouring of trivial imagery, iconography, and souvenirs in 1990s Croatia. A short anecdote from Gogol provides Nabokov with a tableau that sets him up to explore the double-sidedness of *poshlost*: Gogol describes a scene in which a young man seduces a woman (sitting on the shore) by swimming in a lake while embracing two swans. Nabokov claims that anyone with a cultivated cultural sensibility recognizes the sentimental tawdriness of this scene, thus rejecting its poor taste – its "aesthetic inadequacy," to use Călinescu's terms. At the same time, *poshlost* possesses another side, one that is (writes Ugrešić, citing Nabokov) "especially fearsome and vicious when its lie is not obvious and when its values are considered to belong, rightfully or not, to the highest echelon of art, thought, or feeling" (68). Thus, as Svetlana Boym argues, *poshlost* becomes for Nabokov "not merely a matter of taste, but an atrophy of reflective thinking; and thus an ethical ... failure."[78] She situates this resistance to *poshlost* as a cultural phenomenon within the writings of Russian and Soviet intelligentsia who had consistently battled against it, using the word only "derogatorily or at least ironically."[79] It was their way of asserting the cultural status of quality criticism.

This brings us back to the function of *poshlost* in Ugrešić's essays in *Culture of Lies*: the concept of *poshlost* circulates in high literature in order for that literature to defend itself against kitsch and banality. This echoes Boym's reading of Nabokov who, Boym argues, uses *poshlost* to defend his own writing from slipping into sentimentality in his evocations of his childhood. In order to demonstrate Boym's claim that *poshlost* is, above all, "an unobvious sham that deceives aesthetically and morally,"[80] in order to reveal the aesthetic as a conduit of the immoral stance, Ugrešić rewrites Gogol's scene:

> Let's return to the beginning: South Slavic leaders and their followers remind us, somewhat unusually, of Gogol's swimmer who has embraced two swans in order to seduce the young woman on the balcony. Let's add a few extra details to Gogol's scene: corpses, stranglers, grenades, red stars, Nazi crosses, dead children, and dead animals are all swimming in the lake ... The essence of the dance with the swans remains the same: seduction. Large, frowning heads of our swimmers peak out from the water and seduce Europe, who is knitting socks on the balcony. And they seduced their impoverished and starving people who are sitting on the shore. Our swimmers embrace the swans and swim without caring for the incongruous

scenography. As always, seduction achieves its goal. People on the shore, each one on their own side, clap with delight, and accept the performance as "an emanation of their own national being," as something beautiful, great, and true. (72–3)

An illustration of the leader that seduces – an embodiment of the man with the swan – appears in a different essay in *Culture of Lies*. The head of the Bosnian Serbs, Radovan Karadžić, is captured on a documentary film while "monotonously playing the *gusle*" (the single-stringed instrument used in the recitation of Serbian heroic epics) "and later pensively reciting his own poetry over the half-destroyed Sarajevo":

In a close up, the fat fingers of another killer, General Ratko Mladić, are drumming the table in the rhythm of Karadžić's stuttering folkloric rhetoric (*Secret suffer* [*sic*] *symbolizes Serbian faith* … – says Karadžić poetically to the camera). (180, original emphasis)

There is a visual concordance here between the swans and the *gusle*: they echo each other as the instrument of seduction of the audience on the shore (or on the other side of the screen). Yet the politicized use of the cultural-folkloric matrix by national leaders is semantically complex. The *gusle* represents a cultural artery that connects the medieval past and the Serbian present with a narrative that "transform[s] the murderer into a hero" (181). Also important is the venerable legacy of oral song: its age transforms its symbolic value into "pure" and epic value. This means that suffering and heroism of the past, if universal and ageless (as the oral epic is interpreted), compresses the distance between the contemporary war and past "suffering" of Serbs (which includes, invariably, the defeat in Kosovo in 1389). Ugrešić's essays codify the manipulation of the epics as *poshlost* since they are mobilized by reactionary forces for political and at times military ends.

Approached metanarratively, the creation of a serious genre out of a critique of banality (a shorthand description of *Culture of Lies*) as a defence against that banality is a modernist gesture since it seeks to protect the integrity of high art. Here, however, it comes from a self-reflexive ironizing postmodern author. I read Ugrešić's modernist impulses as a defence against the phantasm of ethnonational aestheticized politics that are ethically problematic for her. Her defence of high culture as a critical discourse does not betray an anxiety about art being swallowed up and made equivalent with the mass commodity form. Rather, she is nervous about the capacity of politicized mass spectacles to degrade cultural frames in the act of waging war – what Slovenian philosopher and psychoanalyst Slavoj Žižek calls "poetry by other means."[81] Žižek uses the expression "poetry by other means" to elaborate on what he refers to as Yugoslavia's "military-poetic complex" personified, in his view, by the figure of Radovan Karadžić, who also happens to be a psychiatrist and poet by profession. Though Karadžić is hardly a writer of great repute, Žižek asserts that a close reading of his verse provides the aesthetic construal of Slobodan Milošević's breed of politics, which can be abbreviated in the dyad of no prohibition and excessive exuberance. Žižek adds:

> War has been defined as 'a continuation of politics by other means', but the fact that Karadžić is a poet enables us to see that ethnic cleansing in Bosnia was the continuation of (a kind of) poetry by other means. True, Milošević 'manipulated' nationalist passions - but it was the poets who gave him the means to do this. They - the sincere poets, not the corrupted politicians - were at the origin of it all, when, back in the 1970s and early 1980s, they started to sow the seeds of aggressive nationalism, not only in Serbia, but also in the other ex-Yugoslav republics.[82]

Inverting the elements of Carl von Clausewitz's dictum, Žižek suggests that poetry (but also, one might add, other forms of literature) invigorates the war effort by pinning its narrative – most frequently – on mythical or medieval romantic structures.[83] The repercussions of this exposure, the purpose of locating the phantasm, argues Žižek, is "to render visible the phantasmatic support which structures the *jouissance* in the national Thing."[84] Or more colloquially, to isolate "dirty water" that stands in for symptoms and fantasies of national identity.[85] This is an equally crucial insight for Ugrešić, whose numerous examples demonstrate the culpability of the cultural arena in enabling political mechanisms: culture is the framework that crystallizes the ideological demands since it is the inverted face of national and political characteristics. This creates an environment where culture, in Ugrešić's view, is degraded in its social function by, ironically, being called into being by political demands for particular collective goals. Nonetheless, this debasement becomes precisely the justification for her defence of art's autonomy – for that modernist gesture where lines between quality, both aesthetic and ethic, are drawn against more corrupt manifestations and forms of culture.[86]

The following section tackles Ugrešić's "demystification" of commodity forms as they intersect with political, nationalist messages. The problem of *poshlost* here is narrowed down from the cultural frame to land on the trifling object – the souvenirs, the collector's items.

IV.

Politicized forms of kitsch are often understood as rooted in the symbols, rituals, and signs of totalitarian ideologies. Perhaps the most famous novelistic version of the critique of kitsch is found in Milan Kundera's *The Unbearable Lightness of Being* with the acclaimed academic counterpart being Saul Friedlander's text *Reflections of Nazism: An Essay on Kitsch and Death*. Indeed, critiques of political kitsch are numerous in scholarship, and it is not hard to perceive the presence of Cold War politics in this fact, with the imperative to dismantle totalitarian propaganda. Fascism, Nazism, and Stalinism undeniably receive the most attention when it comes to exploring the links between politics, violence, and aesthetic images.[87] But this is further facilitated by the organized and planned nature of these ideologies: in analyses of Nazi "national-aestheticism," Philippe Lacoue-Labarthe argues, one cannot avoid the overwhelming evidence that the aestheticization of politics was "in its essence, the programme of National Socialism. Or its project."[88] In other words, there is general approval for dismantling communist ideology (as in Kundera's novel) because its messages are coeval with the transgressions and oppressions of failed totalitarian projects.

In *Culture of Lies*, Ugrešić offers a critique of commodity kitsch in the context of an ethnonational project – that is to say, politicized kitsch that uses patterns of consumption to convey its principles and values. I argue that the interconnectedness of aesthetics and politics needs to be reconsidered as a far more normalized phenomenon within the horizon of the everyday, in keeping with Rey Chow's suggestion that even "the sincere altruistic rhetoric we hear in US presidential campaigns" is an example of this aesthetic.[89] This notion was earlier put forward by Susan Sontag, who argues that the broader aesthetic themes evoked by Nazi ideology – including "the ideal of life as art, the cult of beauty ... the dissolution of alienation in ecstatic feelings of community" – have been reworked into "ideals that are persistent today under ... other banners."[90] *Culture of Lies* identifies a discomfiting fit between market forces and nationalist ideology that underscores the proximity between political and commercial kitsch. This is explicit in Ugrešić's reflections on the nationalist souvenir industry.

It seems that the polarization of aestheticized (meaning self-reflexive, playful) and commodified forms of kitsch collapses not just in Ugrešić's essays but also in Mehmedinović's *Sarajevo blues.* In his collection, the experience of the siege brings out the genetic link between the two types of kitsch. In the collection, we find in a poem ostensibly about the surfeit of death in war, a sly, short reference to the topic at hand:

> There is so much suffering, so many cheap emotions: no one cries.
> Death is commonplace and kitsch is commonplace.
> What was Jeff Koons thinking
> glorifying the value of Kitsch?   (26)

These four lines pronounce an unequivocal relationship between two types of kitsch: a surfeit of death and postmodern art. The tongue-in-cheek reference to Koons, a self-styled provocateur known for bringing consumerism into the rarefied air of the art world, initiates a debate over the interplay between high and low art forms, and presumably the principles thought to lie behind such practices (parody, pastiche). Yet the postmodern play of Koons's artwork is, as critics have described it, "unapologetically flat" and "devoid of linguistic play, political commentary or psychological charge."[91] While his artwork pierces not just the elitism of high culture but also its high-mindedness, there is an overwhelming simplicity to his constructions: the commonplace takes the position of the sacrilegious, so the art gallery becomes a temple of mass culture. The symmetry is complete when we take Koons's own professional background into consideration: a former Wall Street trader, his artistry is perhaps most in evidence through his financial handling of the art market than in any craft immanent to the product itself.

The reference to Koons, however, is actually about Mehmedinović, for whom the antics of this artist suddenly become deeply reactionary when placed against a background of kitsch – represented by the surfeit of death – all his own. The cryptic "death is commonplace" can be understood through the actual fact of the endless obliteration of human life, but also as a reference to the excess of the media's reiterations of bodily horror. Importantly, the aversion levelled at Koons in just one sentence is an attempt to ward off the denigration of life that this kitschification implies. For Mehmedinović, the postmodern authorization and validation of kitschiness is a vacuum, as hollow as the subject matter that Koons exhibits (shiny giant rabbits, inflatable hearts, the latter being actually hollow). To put it bluntly, kitsch needs to be indicted as a political and moral corruption, and not simply a debasement of the principles of high art.

This sentiment, while marginal to Mehmedinović's other themes, is more fully articulated in *Culture of Lies*. In February 1994, the daily Croatian newspaper *Vjesnik* ran an article on an advertisement designed by the international clothes brand United Colors of Benetton. The billboard shows "a photograph of a T-shirt with a bullet hole near the heart along with army fatigues, followed by a text in Croatian: I, Gojko Gagro, father of the deceased Marinko Gagro, born 1963, in Blatnica, municipality Čitluk, agree to share the details of my deceased son in this advertisement for peace in the battle against war" (244).[92] The image is undersigned by the slogan "United Colors of Benetton." Ugrešić interprets this image as "a deeply ironic summary of the war story" (244): the exploitation of humanitarian discourses by a commercial enterprise as a fashionable commodity. Interestingly, the advertisement inverts the images that proliferate in other media by displacing the body and leaving the clothes as the fetish of the corpse. In this interpretation, a discord between textual and visual messages is palpable insofar as the clothes become an index for collective identity, but also fantasy, all of which are absent from the father's rather personal register. The T-shirt and the army fatigues are fetishistic substitutions, in Freud's sense of the word, for both the uniformed soldier and the missing body.[93] While there is no explicit connotation of sexual fantasy in Ugrešić's critical look at the advertisement, the signifiers lend themselves to the meaning. Equally, one can interpret the ambiguity of the image, with its spectre of the displaced corpse, as that of the missing bodies of war that will never be recovered.

We see this idea of the overt eroticization of the military body given expression by Mehmedinović. In a vignette entitled "Women," he describes how the cult of the hero has made soldiers, the city's defenders, into media stars, akin to football players or pop singers.[94] The register of mass culture, safe and sanitized, transforms these soldiers into "militaristic advertisements" and "striptease artists" for women who are, Mehmedinović continues, "most likely titillated further by the thought that they are going to bed with a potential future corpse."[95] This "future corpse" is not an empty sign: at the moment of death; instead, it becomes the repository of glory, valiance, courage, bravery, and martyrdom. This might also appear as an inverse sexual economy of war, in which women are empowered by profiting from the sacrifice made by men. This is a highly unfamiliar confluence and uncomfortable statement in a conflict with frequent gender-based violence against women. Yet Mehmedinović's point concerns the displacement of identities between those of wartime and those of mass culture celebrities: the discourses that construct the soldier and the movie star are different in their ideological aims, but they nonetheless project the same characteristics of unbridled sexual appeal, vicarious pleasure, and so on. This kitschy transformation ultimately functions to make the destruction of bodies into acceptable and enjoyable values. In turn, the ease with which this discourse is promulgated to further enact destruction underscores the indestructible nature of kitsch itself.

The dominant feature of Ugrešić's examples of political and national kitsch is their metonymic structure : the objects, like the shirt, are stand-ins for ideas that have no embodiment, what she calls "the field of war" (245). One of the more remarkable items she "collects" in her essays is a perfume named "Serb" that is packaged in the shape of a hand grenade (*kašikara*). She refers to this luxury good alongside another consumer item – the humble tie – that was transformed into a national object. The tie becomes a means by which one can "recognize Croatian identity" or, more specifically, Croatia becomes "the homeland of the first tie" (244).[96] The perfume is the more ostentatious and provocative item, seeing as it explicitly addresses (or literalizes) Serbia's vilified and aggressive image as warmongering and militaristic (Serb = bomb) for profit. Jovan Nježić, the creator and designer of the perfume, defends the provocative packaging, which is provided to the reader in a footnote in Ugrešić's essay:

'The whole world is ... aggressive, starting with movies and art and including wars across the whole planet. A bomb is the symbol of that negative energy. [The perfume] is stylized through the body of a beautiful woman who embraces the bomb and does not let it explode; we transformed that energy into [something] positive. *Our "bomb" is the symbol of "peace."*' (245, original emphasis)

The product's designer offers lines of reading that can be perceived as ironic in a postmodern sense – "critique"/subversion through the commodity form – but that ultimately remain ambiguous, both contesting and confirming dominant representations. As already mentioned, the semotics of the grenade-perfume alludes directly to the negative associations often attached to Serbian nationalism. Yet the bomb-as-perfume can be interpreted as a national self-fashioning that embraces precisely the vilifications of Serbian violent warmongering. It plays with pejorative connotations to introduce the possibility of positive identification between national identity and militarism, a link entirely plausible given some of the mainstream nationalist discourse in Serbia during the 1990s.[97] The woman's body could be read not as diffusing the grenade but as another fetishized, objectified accessory to the action of war.

However, this product placement in Ugrešić's essay suggests that it perpetuates rather than subverts certain values or characteristics. Primarily, the postmodern irony of its design cannot transcend the fetishism of the commodity: irony is here a form of capital and therefore cannot subvert the premise of "negative energy." Given the broader landscape of the essays, one conclusion seems inescapable: what she perceives in this example is the more extensive failure of postmodern irony (and play) to step out of the loop of commodification. At the same time, the commodity mechanism can take on other values (e.g., nationalist) to propagate.

This intersection of politicized kitsch with commodity kitsch works in tandem to produce what Susan Stewart calls the "privatization of a public symbol."[98] In what would become her most inflammatory essay of the 1990s, "Clean Croatian Air," Ugrešić wrote a parody in pseudo-academic language about an aluminum can (filled with air) being sold as part of Croatia's kitsch souvenir industry not long after the announcement of the country's internationally recognized sovereignty. Imprinted with the Croatian coat of arms (the *šahovnica*), the cans "resembled the cans of Coca-Cola": in other words, they themselves represented the postmodern phenomenon of popular culture, complete with image appropriation. The format of her argument, as well as her intent, is consciously styled after Kiš's famous essay about the gingerbread heart of nationalism (mentioned at the beginning of this chapter). Kiš's evocative descriptions of the gingerbread's coloured surface, adorned with ribbons, edible rosettes, and sugar lace, further underscore the quantity of bad taste.

The "can of Clean Croatian air" is nothing but a meaningless object when viewed independently of its discursive and symbolic context; the souvenir, writes Stewart, "will not function without the supplementary discourse that both attaches it to its origins and creates a myth with regard to those origins."[99] The object is incomplete as a kitsch souvenir in the hands of the one who buys it, but the story completes it by answering the demands, argues Stewart, for a "wholesome, comprehensive body."[100] The experience that the object speaks of cannot ever be possessed, but the souvenir can be an index of the event – the unobtainable event. As such, the object makes possible the experience of enjoyment of a fantasy, which it sustains. Stewart argues that in this dynamic the story authenticates the object, but the stress in Ugrešić's essays is not so much on the authenticity as it is on the idea that enjoyment and desire are always satiated through a fantasy construction. Ugrešić's parsing of the souvenir of Croatian air shows the grim consequences of one such fantasy.

This kitsch souvenir, which could be found on the streets of Zagreb in the post-independence period, coincided, Ugrešić writes, with an advertising campaign for a brand of sweets with the tagline: "It is easier to breathe" (80). These two messages Ugrešić semantically intertwines to form the slogan, "It is easier to breathe with clean Croatian air!" (80). The author's intention in combining this kitschy souvenir with advertising is to metaphorize the linguistic properties of the slogan: in six pages, she shows how "clean" becomes cleansed, or cleansing, and in turn brings forth numerous associations of expulsion, purging, purifying, sanitizing, and sterilizing – of Croatia's public sphere and its institutions and its non-Croatian populated areas. Here are some some sample extracts from the "dossier of political cleansing":

> In addition to external enemies (i.e. the Serbs, who are waging, and because of whom we are waging, this dirty war), the spirit from the bottle – like the diligent Mr. Clean or Meister Proper – has in recent months been cleansing all manner of things in Croatia …

The magic spray-formula *clean Croatian air* cleans Croatian territory not only of "Byzantines," who are of a different blood type, but of all internal enemies who are different from the ruling majority.

> Words *clean* and *air* have entered into the vocabulary of the most famous Croatian minds. V.G., a well-known Croatian intellectual, in one of his television appearances answered a stupid question from the journalist – what kind of women he loves – by saying equally stupidly: *clean women!* Some months after, the same intellectual appealed to *clean* Croatian women to give the lives of their sons for the *defense of freedom,* and some months later, he announced … that we are not allowed to defile our freedom and that *even our death must be clean.* (85, 81–2, 83–4, italics in the original)

What she is doing here is producing the supplemental narrative that the souvenir needs for its symbolic efficacy: the can of clean air asserts the singularity and exceptionalism of the national Croatian legacy against the dirt and pollution of others (ethnic others) (71). Of course, her narrative is a blow to the collective perception of the souvenir as a genuine representation of tradition and "national authenticity," but it is formally important to understand the effectiveness of disparagement. First, Ugrešić inflates the currency of the object by hosting it in her work, but deflates its symbolism by relegating the idea of nationalism to the realm of the trivial. Suddenly, the exceptional quality of ethnic or national unity becomes prosaic and banal. Second, when we look at Ugrešić's choice of propaganda, all of these images and objects are self-affirming in the opinion of the public – regardless of the ridiculous nature of kitsch, the can of clean air is, in its context, a positive image of Croatia. It is a positive image of cleanliness, of purity. So what Ugrešić discredits – and this is the kernel of her provocation – is material that forms the good face of the collective identity, of the group and its consciousness. She does not criticize violence or brutality; rather, she shows that, as Rey Chow argues in relation to fascism, "what sustains the aesthetics of monstrosity is something eminently positive and decent."[101] *Culture of Lies* was offensive and inflammatory to the Croatian public because it points to seemingly upstanding and respectable values, mediated through aestheticized politics, as the very core of moral and social corruption.

V.

The overwhelming claim of Ugrešić's essays is that the aestheticized attributes of political discourse are detrimental to the processes of civic society, where aestheticization leads to mystification. Taken holistically, *Culture of Lies* makes the case that in giving shape to the national sensibility through heterogeneous aesthetic means, the latter degrades the former. For Ugrešić, the semiotic frames, the myths, and the symbols are the distortion chambers that generate the false claims engineered by the state to legitimate its power. This view is commensurate with the dominant perspective in European intellectual thought that theorizes the interaction between aesthetics and politics – two fields typically seen as autonomous from each other, with distinct competencies and aims – as a detrimental relationship that delegitimizes political processes. In his synthesis of the ideology of aestheticized politics, Martin Jay avers that the most common cluster of the two words identifies the aesthetic "with irrationality, illusion, fantasy, myth, sensual seduction, the imposition of will, and inhumane indifference to ethical, religious, or cognitive considerations."[102] Logic follows that when this type of "aesthetic" is brought into (encounter with) the political domain, it produces a discourse that silences ethical consciousness and implications that should otherwise be taken seriously. Because the aesthetic is caught up only in principles that pertain to its own field, in its autonomy from social concerns, particularly in its more insular manifestations (including art for art's sake), it is most likely unconscious of its political entanglements and contexts.[103] In some cases, such as the avant-garde modernism of the Futurists, neutralizing the political through the aesthetic "is damned as pernicious," adds Jay, since it has led to gross excesses.[104]

Yet the idea that political ethno-myths appear, as Čolović writes, in the "form of political rituals, such as various inaugurations and funerals, political forums and meetings, or various artistic and musical symbols; [but also] tombstones, flags, emblems, hymns"[105] is part of common wisdom and is common to all political cultures, even democracies. This does not necessarily mean, Čolović posits, that one should attempt to eliminate all non-rational practices from society and the means by which society enacts politics. Furthermore, it is also impossible, he adds, to live by the simple maxim "from shadow and images into truth": no intellectual who seeks to demystify political narratives is "a distant and independent critic."[106] In other words, each individual who seeks to dismantle codes of persuasion or seduction (to use the language of *poshlost*) is beholden to their own mythologies.

This discussion is relevant for Ugrešić because one could easily claim that *Culture of Lies* is the product of an author irked by a form of "aestheticized politics" because its politics of ethnonationalism ran counter to her own conviction. In this reading, all Ugrešić then succeeds in doing is calling out the other (the majority group) for their subscription to a formulaic, falsely homogeneous view of the world. This is a gesture that marks her positively as an enlightened subject in charge of her own faculties and resistant to "ideology." In this reading, "ideology" becomes the problem of the other, the masses, thus leaving unexamined Ugrešić's own implicit and explicit allegiances that form her own schema of norms. It would, in any case, create a view in which the ideology of the other is pejorative while her own is desirable.

Her ideology, or world view, as put forward by *Culture of Lies* stands for ethnic heterogeneity, multiculturalism, linguistic plurality, and cultural cosmopolitanism – all of which are summarized in the collection's most confrontational piece called "Trash," from which I have sampled the following sentences:

> My homeland was called Yugoslavia ... Among the Slovenians, Croats, Bosnians, Serbs, Croatians, Albanians and Macedonians, I felt (and so signed in identity

papers) as a Yugoslav: a citizen of Yugoslavia, *mixed, bastard, anational, unde-fined/undetermined, nationally indifferent* ... Nationalism is the ideology of the blunt ... Language is the weapon of understanding. I don't "buy" the thesis of language as a "national substance." (320–32, original emphasis)

What this extract describes, namely, is the original, utopian vision of Yugoslavia, a myth summarized in its most famous slogan of "brother-hood and unity." Here, the political mythology of post– Second World War Yugoslavia is positively perceived since it stands for idealism and inclusiveness. If her ideology is anything, it is the evocation of a commu-nal politics of socialism. Interestingly, Ugrešić is quick to acknowledge that this ideology is fundamentally communicated through an entire vocabulary and a decades-long repertoire of kitschy phenomena:

Even though contemporary kitsch, like a duplicated photograph, breaks over its past [socialist] forms, they're different after all. Socialist kitsch proclaimed its ideology: brotherhood and unity, internationalism, social equality, pro-gress and so on. Nationalist kitsch proclaims its foundational ideas: national sovereignty and privileging of a population based on "the appropriate blood group." Socialist kitsch had a future-oriented projection and, alongside it, a strong utopian projection. Nationalist kitsch draws on a passionate sinking into a "national being" for its contents so it is oriented towards the past, stripped of a utopian dimension. The key symbols of socialist kitsch were connected to work, progress, equality (that is why soc-iconography was full of ironworks, streets, and factories with smoke, and those sculptures of happily embracing peasants and workers). (71)

In its defence of socialist kitsch, on the basis of its principles of advance-ment and equality, this extract is ultimately a manifesto of the political core of a poetics of post-communist nostalgia.

Typically perceived as a unreflexive cultural discourse, Yugonostalgia is denigrated because it is often mediated through the lens of a com-modity culture, typically taking on kitschy properties of the commodity form. However, there is distinct strain in Ugrešić's writing (evident in *Culture of Lies* and *Museum of Unconditional Surrender*) where the currency of post-socialist kitsch lies in its appearance as "a political sabotage" lev-elled against oppressive systems of rule.[107] The possibility of political mobilization of Yugonostalgia has been treated most extensively by Alek-sandar Bošković in his article *"Lexicon of Yu Mythology,"* a compendium of collectively authored entries that ironically and nostalgically describes the material and non-material Yugoslav culture.[108] Published in 2004, the lexicon can be convincingly read as political opposition to contemporary ways of governance since, in its depiction of a bygone era, it codifies the belief in the future that governed and propelled those years. Bošković writes that projects such as the *Lexicon* cannot be reduced to "a regressive idealization of Yugoslav socialist past" but offer instead "a critical intervention in both the contemporary postsocialist politics of memory and the politics of emancipation."[109] What is important about the lexicon is its "implicit critique of contemporary maladies and those who restlessly encourage present-day social ills to grow and spread."[110] That remains, in a way, the social project for Yugonostalgia, made urgent by the threats of commodification and commercialization of its aesthetics and poetics: as Ugrešić notes, "even if worthless, nostalgia can be an expensive good."[111] While nostalgia is legitimated in art and culture (e.g., Ugrešić's writing), it is also legitimated by the marketplace. Yet by being imbued with an economic value, the marketplace becomes the place of disappearance for post-socialist nostalgia since this is where the political and social agency of that kitsch is suffocated. One could argue, on a note of positivity, however, that this political project of redeeming the Yugoslav experience not as some type of passive idolization, but with a constructive role in mind for *now*, has been attempted by the new left who have sought to learn from labour and social relations of the Yugoslav era in order to redeem life in neoliberal post-Yugoslav spaces.[112]

VI.

In this chapter, I examined how aestheticized politics, a predominantly kitschy and trivial format of 1990s Croatian public discourse, is stylistically linked with Ugrešić's own poetics, which have consistently been based on pastiche and citation (the hallmark attributes of literary postmodernism). I argue that *Culture of Lies* examines what happens when aesthetic discourses are co-opted for political instrumentalization – an interest that stems from Ugrešić's own investment in strategies of decontextualization and transposition. In a way, *Culture of Lies* describes how she watches the construction of the state as a spectacle, as an image of values, history, and nationalism – a construction that mimics the very methods of her own literary practice. Yet the stakes are different in the political arena, she argues, because implicit in the construction of the spectacle is a transgression of democratic principles, a suppression of political alternatives, and minority rights (among others). The essays bring together the political variant of kitsch with its commodified version and lay to rest the possibility of the continuation of a playful or ironic commodity culture. It is not so much that these modes themselves have been eradicated from forms of representation (in both popular and high culture) but they can no longer, after Ugrešić's encounter with aestheticized politics, possess the confrontational power she believed in and practised in her early work.

4 The Search for a Language of the Historical Present

David Albahari's novels and essays of the 1990s can be described as explorations of a growing awareness of a collective historical moment that threatens to overwhelm the sovereignty of the self. This newfound consciousness of large-scale destructive social forces imbricates itself within a structure of everyday ordinariness which modulates rather than entirely destroys that ordinary life. In Albahari's book of essays *Rewriting the World*, the conflict is but one of the chronologies that compete for the author's attention in the construction of his contemporaneity. There are timelines of mortality (aging, a friend's cancer), work (deadlines), ritual (Jewish holidays); and travel, all concurrent with the metastasizing conflict. This type of synchronicity is not possible in Mehmedinović's *Sarajevo blues*, where war pervades the very marrow of what it means to be alive and so displaces other constituent elements of social organization. Albahari's physical distance from the war front permits him to conceptualize the shift as the historical present.

This schism is articulated in his fiction as a change in the temporal order. In this chapter, I consider the transformation from Albahari's assertion of the exceptionalism of the present – "other than the present, nothing else exists"[1] – into a sense of living "as a prehistoric man."[2] I analyse how the switch in the understanding of time forces Albahari to question anew the function of literary discourse while contending with the "sticky arms of history" and the "odour"[3] of both the recent and the distant past. I examine how his established techniques and metatextual experiments become tied to ethical questions, and how these interpretations shift when the historical present opens up to a more extensive historical horizon. By focusing on the skeletal, on the armature of his prose, I examine how his texts change while staying the same, while staying in place. He remains, in effect, "a habitual and loyal postmodernist."[4]

I pursue an inter-narrative approach that encompasses two novels, *Snow Man* (1995) and *Götz and Meyer* (1998), both of which address systemic historical upheaval. Where the novels diverge is in perspective and degrees of proximity (whether they be temporal, spatial, familial) to seismic social change. My exploration centralizes the means of transmission of history and crisis: the abstraction of *Snow Man* gives way to the bureaucratic archive in *Götz and Meyer*. For Albahari, the terror lies in the force of history or memory itself as much as in the content. How to tame the terror of the past in the fiction, to contain it without losing integrity and structure, all the while attempting to recover or maintain the humanity of those who have suffered and are suffering?

To begin with, I will examine how extraliterary conditions begin to characterize and inform his world view. Starting with *Kratka knjiga* (*Short Book*) in 1993, Albahari's novels become populated by nameless, unanchored men who live "in [a] history that no longer existed, a time which – it was claimed – did not happen."[5] The changes alluded to here can be conceived as the loss of Albahari's "mixed Jewish-Serbian-Yugoslav culture," a loss that invalidated his own experience of the federation's multiculturalism.[6] In an intimate filial scene in one of his essays, Albahari, standing over the sleeping figure of his son, describes his own body as an empty ruin, "devastated and buried in a time that no long means anything to anyone."[7] The image is striking because the generational gap that will no doubt mark the father-son relationship will be doubled by the political and social abyss brought on by Yugoslavia's disintegration. What forms the father's identity will be lost or irrelevant to the son. This husk, the father's husk, has been emptied of the future, and of the possibility of living in anticipation of that future.

Contemporaneous with this loss of the recent past, Albahari notes, was the arrival of stories of national greatness predicated on past glories and glorified tragedies. It was the displacement of one tradition by another as, towards socialism's official end, old histories cohabited comfortably with romantic concepts of ethnos and nation-building, cresting on a wave of religious conservatism. In this new world,, the past hurtles into the present, reflects the narrator of Albahari's novel *Mamac* (*Bait*, 1996), to justify new wars and energize the collective:

the past, life in the past, is being offered as a replacement for the life of the present ... [a demand that] life become a permanent tapping in place, a continuous performance of the past which becomes a goal in itself. If I switched on the television set or the radio, or if I opened up the newspaper or flipped through the weeklies, I could always see or hear how somebody was trying to convince me that events of the past were more important than any of the forms of reality with which I could come face to face.[8]

The end of socialism and the impending wars across Yugoslavia force a collapse of the distinct experiences of the present, the past, and the future. This is not just about the experience of duration: Albahari's prose is an aesthetic exhibit of Harry Harootunian's idea that the fall of the Berlin Wall and subsequent decline of communism magnified "the assault on the temporal order."[9] Harootunian adds that

the simultaneous manifestation of multiple fundamentalisms in the aftermath has put into immediate question the status of our received forms of temporalization by upsetting the relationship between history and the tripartite division of past, present, and future. The seemingly sudden collapse of the Berlin Wall and the appearance of movements fueled by a potent mixture of modernity and archaisms have inaugurated the removal of a conception of the future, or at least its indefinite deferral, that had once been summoned to shape the experience of the present and the expectations toward which it ceaselessly moved.[10]

For Harootunian, the events of 1989 signify the demise of a historical paradigm that had immanently accounted for the future. The experience, as this passage suggests, has now become one of "mixed temporalities." In part, this phenomenon is manifested in the presence of national and historic registers that produce strategies for justifying the historical present: a world of "noncontemporaneous contemporaneity."[11]

The translation of this "noncontemporaneous contemporaneity" into a narrative presence in Albahari's prose of the 1990s is clearly seen in the challenge to the mode of presentism so dominant in the author's poetic vision. With the reorganization of the social and temporal order, Albahari's essays and fiction become, as Frederic Jameson writes in the context of the figure of the modern reader, a "testimony as to his resistance to his own political unconscious and to his denial ... of the reading and the writing of the text of history within himself."[12] That is to say, Albahari's postmodern subject becomes aware that in any rejection of historical presence lies the imprint of historical order, knowledge, and organization. Writing in and of itself involves the inscription of history, even if that writing (like his, with its postmodern tendencies) eliminates all signs of situatedness and impact of historical time.

The very shaping by external circumstance, by decrees and standards of socialism, becomes palpable in his work at socialism's very end. In the first few decades of his writing career, Albahari had propagated and practised postmodernism on the grounds that it was a path to "a world of unthinkable freedoms" where one would live, finally, outside of history."[13] The foundational poetic attributes of his early work transformed "literature into a game, [into] consciousness about the existence of the body of literature, consciousness about the boundaries of language, and consciousness about the impossibility of precise communication. Literature is form."[14] Postmodern poetics was a means to a defence "from excessive ideology of a political system" for Albahari and his generation of artists committed to "anti-ideological growing up."[15] Thus his aesthetic position was a strike against a stifling literary milieu that bred writing "obsessed with morals, lessons, instructions."[16] Writer Vladimir Tasić echoes this position, arguing that, in addition to formal innovations, postmodernism brought with it "theories of the death of the author and the end of grand narratives, which were in one period a weapon for the depoliticization of literature."[17] A paradox in Albahari's logic of resistance surfaced on the cusp of war as he came to resist the demise of the cosmopolitan cultural sphere of Yugoslavia. The ensuing distance from Serbia (he moved to Canada in 1994) "made it possible to understand how much I owe to the mixed Yugoslav culture in which I grew up, particularly the interplay between Serbian and Jewish culture. Considering that that culture no longer exists – and considering that I refuse to give it up – it is not a surprise that I feel like a castaway whose shore no longer seems safe."[18] It is clear that he benefited from a common culture and became invested in its valences of multiculturalism. In another essay, he describes the "loss of what we call Yugoslav literature"[19] – a category that he refuses to discredit and disavow, even as he solemnly accepts the inevitable political loss of the Yugoslav project. Thus, a discrepancy emerges between the crude forms of cultural policy and the everyday that gave rise to shared forms of art. By rejecting state ideology, Albahari indirectly forged links of a supranational character; perhaps more of an embodiment of Yugoslavism than any state-sponsored activity could achieve.[20]

My concern in this chapter is to examine how this thinking about history, and his thinking historically, in the novels *Snow Man* and *Götz and Meyer* (with reference to *Svetski putnik* (*World Traveller*, 2001) intersects with Albahari's long-standing loyalty to linguistic defeat. In other words, what structural, stylistic, and conceptual strategies are destabilized or complicated by the intersecting demands of the historical dynamic and linguistic instability? I argue that the poetic and formal undertakings by Albahari during the Yugoslav wars of secession do not essentially shift in a new direction from his previous writing even as the levees break on his prose and social coordinates flood in to fill the void of dehistoricized, austere postmodern work. As Vladislava Ribnikar has remarked, the upheaval in Yugoslavia simply gave Albahari's poetics "[a] sharpened form and, until then, a non-existent tension and urgency."[21] His hallmark features – uncertainty, linguistic meaninglessness – remain constant. Rather, what changes within his poetics is the nature of the aporias themselves. The motifs of death and silence (to highlight just two) are transformed from the esoteric disenchantment of language into crises of witnessing to history. Similar disappointment, alternative uses. What used to be, as he once wrote, "the powerlessness of language to ... find the sufficient precision for expression [of narrative]"[22] is now transposed onto a field – the field of war and crisis – that demands articulate expression in order to make sense of its chaos and its overwhelming power. Yet as a conduit for this experience, and the resulting erasure of self and structure, language is underwhelmingly equipped, as seen in Albahari's introspective novel *Snow Man*:

> Everything was so sudden, I thought, the departure and the arrival, especially the arrival, I hadn't had time to gather myself, and I still existed as a series of scenes, inexpertly linked by the hand of an inexperienced montagist, as if my life was falling apart together with the history of my country, my *former* country, I have to add, and as if I was no longer one man, one being, but more people and more beings, so that I could perceive each thing simultaneously from several angles, in endless multiplied moments, just as every thought immediately existed as many thoughts, same but different, different enough to prevent me from accepting any one of them, which, at the end, left me empty, careworn, like a shell, like wreckage, namely, like shells, like wreckages into which each one of those beings and each one of those thoughts also transformed.[23]

This sentence that so desperately wants to convey the experience of a diffusive, uncertain state takes on the properties of the state itself. But there is, on second glance, a tight economy of rhetoric here. The splintering of a single being (or thought) into its multiples is duplicated in the syntax of the sentence as each possible clause, each possible meaning of a discrete phrase, is spliced into twins, each of which undergoes a subsequent splicing. Such an example is at once a demonstration of how imprecise meaning can be achieved through the precision of syntax. It also shows the consequence of external tectonic movement on a self that tries to bind himself through language (and fails).

Thus testifying to and critiquing social circumstances is for Albahari a formal and linguistic problem (rather than one of political meaning) through which he seeks a narrative form for systemic rupture of the multinational Yugoslav union. It is actually logical that Albahari's linguistic concerns should remain the same: if language was insufficient for the broad horizon of a safe, boring life – and the breadth and complexity of human experience that comes with it – then how will language withstand the demands of historical turbulence? Albahari answers this question by first taking the reader further away from the socio-historic upheaval, starting with the narrators' geographical displacement, and by letting the prose take on the qualities of rupture without naming the profound conditions that contributed to the distress. Every distancing, be it spatial, temporal, or linguistic, disguises the commentary that the narrative wishes to make of political formations, the conditions of power, and the mess of the war. Any direct attempt to diagnose and anatomize the situation and its historical reverberations is transformed into an absurd, but not meaningless, language game.

Despite diverging aesthetic visions, Albahari's prose can be perceived as a counter text to Dubravka Ugrešić's essays. Albahari and Ugrešić both acknowledge the tawdriness of politicized language as an instrument of warfare, typified by impoverished sound bites of thinkers and intellectuals who have, in Albahari's words, "surrender[ed] to the power of the media," along with the "new baroque," overblown style of writers who manipulate literature into a site of ideologically and nationally inflated claims.[24] Historians, too, are part of this cluster, and their own mythmaking is particularly frightening as their discourses open up "the possibility for the uninhibited growth of the most extreme forms of ideology, religion and politics."[25] In Albahari's view, they contribute to the progressive depravation of language: their production is in constant service to others, for other aims. This is not too dissimilar from Ugrešić's experience with aestheticized forms of sloganeering, advertising, and ideologically oriented literatures. Nonetheless, they implicate their literary projects in this state of affairs rather differently. The cacophony of *Culture of Lies* with "words reacting on words,"[26] to borrow a term from Vološinov, is startling in contrast with the starkness of Albahari's *Snow Man*. This slim novel reverberates with multiple absences that chime lyrically with the symbolism of the northern landscape of the novel's setting: "the protagonist arrives into the wild, the whiteness of the snow, the emptiness, the north of his being, the endless polar night."[27] In *Snow Man* the withdrawal of naming (of geographical locations, ideologies, people) allows ambiguity and alienation to fill the vacuum. I consider in this chapter how these strategies contribute to Albahari's attempt to shape the historical problem where shaping, rather than resolving or responding to the crisis, takes aesthetic priority.

The comparison of Albahari's two novels, *Snow Man* and *Götz and Meyer*, might seem like an untenable exercise, given the multiple polarizations – including the thematic – that separate them. The former novel is thoroughly abstract and experimental in its consideration of the historical context, while the latter is a reconstruction of a historical episode of the Holocaust in Serbia. *Snow Man* depicts a self-aware protagonist who struggles with self-understanding in the present after an almost surgical break with his past and a namelessness that comports with a blankness of his new environment. Conversely, *Götz and Meyer* combines two temporal orders: that of the archive that details the murder of Jewish women and children in 1942, and the narrator's present of the early 1990s. The novel, in its contact with the archive, proliferates with names, dates, and processes. There is even an overproduction of facts. Moreover, in *Götz and Meyer*, the task of literature is complicated by the high stakes of tackling the limit-experience of Holocaust. Representation of the Holocaust in literary discourse demands a sensitivity to a whole range of ethical considerations and historical veracity that can be complicated by the aestheticizing features and fictionalizing tendencies of novels or short stories.

These are not superficial differences, by any means, yet they cloud the structural affinities between the two novels: both texts are sites of exploration for theoretical questions about the nature of literature itself, and therefore set out to test the ground of fiction and language. The experience of the two novels is close to what the narrator of *Bait* describes as stories that "constantly fall apart under the stress and blows caused by the insertions of parallel histories."[28] Even in the absence of a corresponding historical current, Albahari's stories fail to congeal around themselves. There is no guarantee that, as one moves further into the book, meaning and significance will fall into place, either on the micro-sentence level or the more panoptic view of the whole text. Though *Götz and Meyer* buries the reader in a surfeit of empirical data, the text complicates this choice: "Knowing will never catch up to the power of not knowing."[29] In *Snow Man*, the sentences do not embroider meaning into patterns but rather undo the stitches of meaning that have been made or, as the narrator puts it, "as if the sentences were fake floors, which slip under the feet of the main protagonists."[30] Also, the yawning abyss between the worlds of the two novels allows us to focus on how the elements of his poetics are given expression under distinct demands: what happens in the switch from namelessness to naming? What happens when abstraction and concern with linguistic inadequacy open up to the presence of the archival discourse?

Current scholarship offers psychoanalytic and trauma theory readings of this period of Albahari's oeuvre. Ribnikar posits that the discourse of trauma is an organizing principle for the narrator's own wound as rupture that corresponds to his parents' – particularly the mother's – Second World War tragedies.[31] Zoran Milutinović reads *Bait* – he characterizes it as a book of remembering written "to liberate [the narrator] from compulsive repetitions" – through the Freudian *fort/da* game, where the approaching and distancing from mother, homeland, and the past determine both the thematic and formal axis.[32] Finally, with reference to the post-Lacanian psychoanalytic critic Julia Kristeva, Tatjana Aleksić argues that writing the mother's life in *Bait* should be perceived as a (figurative) murder of the mother by the son-narrator in his attempt to constitute an identity in exile.[33] These scholarly responses do credit to what is an intensely introspective reckoning with the historical caesurae: Albahari's novels resist the tide of national sovereignties and, in turn, resist being shored up against collective passions.

In addition to the internal poetic structures that inspire such readings, other (though not unrelated) factors contribute to Albahari's social distance and his abstruse position as a public figure – a theme that receives treatment in the author's essay that reveals a fascinating archive, one that conveys the complexities of Albahari's relationship to his own authorial voice, his public voice(s), and his private persona. Published in various forms of media (from daily newspapers such as *Politika* to literary journals, including *Polja* [Fields]), Albahari's essays, demand a familiarity not just with his own corpus, but with particular literary forms, literary jargon, and local as well as international debates on contemporary culture.

A theme that is given some consideration in these essays concerns his baseline position – his identity – as ambiguous and uncertain because it is integrative. Primarily, this evokes the issue of his family's mixed Jewish

(Sephardic) and Serbian heritage. In his fiction, it is a vexed and perplexing theme that is articulated through Jewish motifs and mythology. Yet the richness of this cultural and written heritage was not matched by a deep spiritual belief. By all accounts, he was raised in a secular, assimilated household (one that was not without its Jewish rituals) and he manifested belonging to the Jewish people in a way that did not presume religious tendencies.[34] His social contributions to communal Jewish life reached an apogee in the years leading up to the war as he took on the position of volunteer director at the Federation of the Jewish Communities of Yugoslavia. Being a minority in Yugoslavia in the early 1990s, outside the centre of ideological battles for sovereignty and outside the main narratives of ethnic belonging, did not mean that the political currents did not directly affect Albahari's life. The status of belonging to an ethnic minority was not one of privilege. Instead, faced with a disintegrating union, Albahari's contemplations on the idea of being a minority are informed by the twentieth-century history of European Jewry: "to be Jewish in Yugoslavia today means knowing the expertise of walking on a rope, because only that degree of balance will save us from falling into the abyss."[35] His sense of marginality reveals a deep precariousness and insecurity. So, rather than being invisible because one belongs to a group outside the dominant narratives of religious, national, and historical origin, the minority may find itself the scapegoat, framed as a threat to the integrity of the mainstream body. On this note, it is telling that the theme of anti-Semitism haunts Albahari's essays and writing from the late 1990s.

The structure of this chapter is as follows. First, I consider the fundamental tenets of Albahari's poetics in order to foreground how stylistic and prosaic patterns contribute to a conception of time that is predicated on the mundane diurnal stretch. This routine, boring and repetitive, still proves inscrutable and perplexing to Albahari the grammarian. I then advance the idea that this tight unity between the ongoing present and language experiments comes undone with the break-up of Yugoslavia. My case study for this is *Snow Man*, where I demonstrate how Albahari's form is transposed onto new spatial and temporal coordinates. I discuss two concerns emerging from this literary experiment: the lack of naming and the disappointment of postmodern theory. The chapter concludes with an analysis of *Götz and Meyer*'s linguistic strategies for writing about the bleakness and tragedy of the Holocaust. The linguistic dimension and features of this novel, I argue, are still inherently Albaharian in their compulsion to discover the effects of naming.

II.

Albahari's life and writing have always been somewhat homogeneously characterized by their high degree of autonomy from social and political conditions. It is widely accepted that throughout his career he has occupied "an unambiguously ignorant stance towards political questions"[36] since his true interests are far more conceptual, pinned together by the notion of writing as an investigation into the viability of language and its non-referential status: "I like things, I like objects on their own as they are. I know something exists behind them, and I know that I have not succeeded yet in approaching that something. Words get in my way," writes Albahari in an early story.[37] One strand of Albahari's literary apprenticeship consisted of his own translations of American postmodernists (including John Barth, Donald Barthelme, Robert Coover, and Kurt Vonnegut) whose ideas were "blasphemous" to him because they dethroned the author as an all-knowing, godlike figure, and also actively sought the participation of the reader in constructing meaning.[38] These sources instructed Albahari in matters of metatextuality, through which he developed a style of writing that doubled as autocritique, as its own commentary: "No matter how much I try, and how much effort I put in, I have never found a way to give things new meanings, to make a defined movement mysteriously new. The key in the lock is the key in the lock."[39] The narrator of these experimental short stories starts from defeat, from living in the exhaustion of narrative expression. In thrall to post-war masters of America and continental Europe, Albahari's prose unites a philosophical, contemplative strain with a certain irreverence towards genre, a lack of concern with literary conventions, and (unsurprisingly) a suspicion of metanarratives. His prose constantly returns to ideas of the imprecision of language and the futility of writing when faced with the resistance of language to representation, and so he attempts a departure from these "poetic problems" through an elaborate scheme of fragmentation.[40] This splintering once risked total self-erasure – a literal, ontological, and philosophical silence – as Albahari's short form inched towards Wittgenstinian minimalism. In "The Story of the Koan," the single question "If I raise my hand, says he, where will my hand go?" is the threshold that keeps the author away from the emptiness of the blank page.[41] This overt formal and stylistic parallelism with Wittgenstein's *Philosophical Investigations* is accented by a common concern with ordinary language that is also centralized in the work of Samuel Beckett and the mid-twentieth-century Austrian novelist Thomas Bernhard.

A figurative way to consider these experiments is to posit that Albahari, in wrestling with what language can express, is not showing off the skills of the craftsman but is exploring the material possibilities of language itself. The literary discourse this leaves behind is the sculpture hewn from this material. Language can thus be conceived as an organic entity with fallible properties, some of which do not stand up to the demands of moulding, squeezing, and stretching; the surface of language is worn thin by repetition and cliché. But it is also susceptible and weak when faced with the demands of expressing meaning, verisimilitude, and cognitive and physical experience:

> If the boundaries of our language truly determine the boundaries of our world, as it was once said, then we are condemned to a slow, long-lasting distancing from the correct understanding of reality. For the endless multiplicity of constantly different happenings, we possess only a limited and always the same number of words. The lover, the storyteller, the scientist, the shaman, and the child know well the powerlessness of language. Each one of them, in their own way, attempts the impossible: to honourably express the reality of their experience. And each one, after the incomplete task, withdraws into silence.[42]

The opening sentence – yet another allusion to a Wittgensteinian maxim – underscores what is at stake in the hewing of language. Language is necessary for the constitution of the speaking subject and for that subject's existence and movement through the world.

If this presentation of Albahari's poetics suggests an alienating, impersonal, and impenetrable prose, then this impression has been mitigated by the domestication of Albahari's writing, and of the author himself. I use domestication to signify a number of things. First of all, the compulsion to query the status of language, author, and text has become a conventional strategy in postmodernist fiction, and one to which contemporary readers have become accustomed. Prose of Albahari's quality, with its high degree of self-reflexivity, has become domesticated in the landscape of literary fiction. Second, Albahari's stature as a writer of elite literary authority has grown, reflected in the number of prestigious literary awards he has won, and this status has been accompanied by popular and critical acclaim (particularly in the 1990s). Finally, since his poetics has been conscientiously analysed by literary critics, their work has unveiled the structure of meaning behind the author's ambiguous writing. In a way, they have provided the key to reading his work. They have, in other words, tamed the novelty of his prose.

In many of these discussions, very little is made of the domestic in Albahari's own works, though I use the world "domestic" loosely to refer to the familial and the everyday [*svakodnevnica*]. The more appropriate word, in fact, would be prosaic: that which is in the realm of the ordinary, including the commonplace habits and actions that constitute life. (Prosaic also means dull, mundane, and lacking poetic beauty – the negative connotations to which I turn later.) *Porodično vreme* (*Family Time*), the title of Albahari's first collection of short stories (1973), is a signal of the prosaic, and of the temporal and spatial coordinates that organize his fiction. The ritualistic elements of quotidian life (seasons of the year, season of childhood and adolescence, seasons of midlife and death) produce in the first collection an effect of "changing scenes without the use of a curtain," a phrase that the narrator uses to describe his first experience of opera that reveals to him "the lies of theatre" in which he sees an analogy with fiction.[43]

Albahari's prosaic style refrains from the precise, material observation and description that some domestic chronicles indulge in; that is, a world of observation and record where "things" become constituent of life but also conduits of character, plot, and foreshadowing. (Exemplary of this writing is Danilo Kiš's *Bašta, pepeo* [*Garden, Ashes*]). Nor is Albahari's a world of torturous intergenerational relationships: the family's discussion of their Jewishness is not a source of filial conflict, but a shared exploration that touches upon the limits of the family's religious belief and their identity as "half-Jews ... (given mother's conversion in 1936 from the Christian Orthodox to the Jewish faith)."[44] There are no gnawing authority issues even if the narratives do not entirely disband the hierarchy of the family. Family time is, however, ritualistic and gives a good sense of what Albahari rejects: social and historical frameworks, ideological agendas – namely, salvific narratives. What is absent is a sense of a shared past, a continuity of tradition, an organized life beyond the family – all of which would signify the presence of historical organization.

The domestic should in some senses hinder poetic evolution: repetition, limited world view, no possibility of heterogeneity through its immobilization of characters and dearth of locations. Nine years after the first collection of family stories appeared, Albahari expresses concern about rehearsing this type of narrative form: "I am just retelling the same old story again, bringing myself into danger that the reader will give up only after reading a few lines." He worries that narrative, if delineated by filial and paternal dynamics, will simply bore.[45] But, in one fell swoop, he recovers his sense of narrative justification:

> But if prose gravitates toward the everyday, if Hegel's prophecy is already reality, then am I not on the right, the best of all possible roads? … If everyday life is as I show it – monotonous repetition, endless walks on strictly fixed paths, regular hourly wages, always the same answers, never "yes" instead of "no," the roaring laughter of my mother at four in the afternoon – if it is all like that, then where is my error?[46]

Albahari is of course referring to Hegel's notion of "the prose of the world," the phrase that, according to Lorri Nandrea and Michal Ginsburg, "indicts all the external factors that limit an individual's freedom and independence," be they social obligations, collective institutions, the insistence of others, or simply accidents.[47] According to Hegel, the prose of the world – "as it appears to the consciousness both of the individual himself and of others: – a world of finitude and mutability, of entanglement in the relative, of the pressure of necessity from which the individual is in no position to withdraw" – impedes the "higher aims of the spirit."[48] However, does Albahari's fiction hold up the idea that prose is inimical to "inner essence"?[49] Does the regularity and monotony of life undermine aesthetic or spiritual animation?

Albahari might not be much interested in spiritual development of the self, but his short stories foreground the enigmatic gesture of the everyday. This daily routine might be banal, but it is no less mystifying for it. However, he also uses prose in a way that Hegel does not: prose as a means of expression, defined as direct, unadorned form that is not restricted by metre, measure, or rhyme (features attributed to verse).[50] The prosaic forms of life and prose as a way of inscribing everyday life are made interdependent in Albahari's short stories and novels, and this taps into a broader conceptual concern of his: the observation of gestures, ones that can be infinitely repeated and observed as the perfect crucible for linguistic experiments, for language games. Yet literary theorists of prose posit that one of the fundamental characteristics of prose is the notion of forwardness. It is: "pro-vorsa; forward looking or front facing."[51] Albahari demonstrates in numerous ways that he has grasped this point, starting one of his novels with the phrase "after the first sentence there's no return."[52] Then, there are more embedded structures, including the device of taking a walk by the river (in the family stories) – a movement that suggests syntactical forwardness even when the thoughts and conversations do not march along in a progressive manner but interrupt and disrupt each other. Yet Nandrea and Ginsburg posit that if prose is irreversible, if it does possess this singular orientation and direction, then it surely cannot have "an internal principle of ending."[53] They arrive at this position after examining the relationship between the terms "prosaic" and "prose," a discussion initiated by Hegel's formulation of "the prose of the world."[54] The pair highlight the essentially positive connotations of the term "prose" (accessible, honest, direct) and the pejorative adjuncts of the "prosaic," which is defined by a lack – whether of beauty, imagination, or feeling. The idea of prose as never-ending comes from its attachment to the prosaic, the pejorative furthering of which – the authors argue – Hegel supports. How is prose to find closure if the material of which it speaks, the stuff of life, is unceasing? Is this not another way to think about Albahari's statement: "the story, when left to itself, gives itself up to the wind"?[55]

Albahari's writing leaves the reader with the sense that a reduction, or a stripping away, of mimetic mechanisms does not in fact inhibit prose; it does not shorten it. This is demonstrated by his elision of conventional mechanisms that would determine and hasten the end of narration, such as plotting. Albahari has consistently mocked literary constructions such as "the right Moment" that forces the narrator "to stop and explain, to breathe," and offer psychological motivations for the characters' actions, making the literary text suffer from "excessive digressions and laments of the main protagonists."[56] There is no "ballast," such as long descriptions or extensive dialogue, that weigh down the writing.[57] There are no structures of anagnorisis and peripeteia that function to reveal the moment of recognition of truth. Yet – and perhaps somewhat counter-intuitively – the result is that Albahari's prose need not stop even as it undoes itself (as its meaning unravels). The following quotation exemplifies not just this dynamic but also the captivating rhythm of forward motion. I quote from a story from Albahari's most experimental collection at a point when the narrator withdraws into an internal monologue in order to answer a question he has been posed:

> I knew I wouldn't tell the truth but at the same moment I asked myself how I knew that it was not the truth, maybe I use the wrong words, maybe I call things by names that do not belong to them, but if that is the case, how are we to understand each other, if we understand each other, do we understand each other, we don't understand each other, though there were moments when we clearly spoke of the same things using the same words, but how do I know that it was not simply an accident, a coincidence resulting from some

cosmic probability, a result of endless division and multiplication, the product of her ability to adapt, or my ability to adapt, because I remember many more situations when, using the same words, we spoke past each other, evidently imagining different worlds, or better yet: each imagining their own thing, even though the words were, in appearance, were the same, if it is possible to say that words have an appearance that can be compared.[58]

The hypnotic sentence, which continues for two pages, is indicative of the self-questioning and self-investigation typical of Albahari's metafiction. This passage is organized around a series of antitheses and contradictions. Despite the primary conclusion that one cannot ever answer because one has not understood and will subsequently not be understood (identified right at the beginning), the narrator cannot stop. He is incapable of stopping because, it seems, it is important to understand what underlies the misunderstanding, to probe its nature rather than accept it passively. Another issue with such a passage is its overwhelming abundance of clauses and subclauses, making it hard to distinguish the important detail. Nandrea and Ginsburg argue that this type of prose leaves the impression that though the semantic content (the characters, the accidents that befall them, and the time and place in which they are located) is propelled by syntax, "the syntax is in some sense 'indifferent' to it, that it would have been the same if the characters and events were totally different."[59] This type of interaction between syntax and semantic planes is just another example of Albahari's relegation of the authorial platform of creation: "A writer who starts with the form of the work does not have an active role. He is used by language, he is used by literature."[60] The problem of hierarchy (of meaning) in Albahari's fiction is compounded by a once marginal device that has become central to the aesthetic project of Albahari's 1990 novels: the sentences flow in a continuous, thick style with no paragraph or chapter breaks.[61] Such prose continuously pushes the reader forward (underscoring the notion that reading unites cognitive and experiential abilities) and is closely related to a literary form with predecessors including Beckett and Bernhard. Of his own motivations for the use of such a prose form, Albahari has said: "It is a text which flows … The text cannot have a rupture through which the reader can escape. Instead, once he's in, he's got to go on till the end."[62] Such a prose style sacrifices hierarchies and order: the details of the sentences themselves (whether they include information, dates, names, thoughts, or actions) are all piled on at once, thereby making it nearly impossible for the reader to stop, reflect, and deduce the order of meaning.

As much as the tight uniform style suggests unity, the story does not build up itself. For Albahari, syntax relinquishes (or approaches a precarious point of relinquishing) its relationship with the semantic dimension, thereby relinquishing rootedness, grounding, breaks, and pauses. This comports with what Jameson identifies as a rejection of the hermeneutic or "depth model" in postmodernism.[63] One relationship that has been rescinded in the post-hermeneutic state is "a breakdown in the signifying chain, that is, the interlocking syntagmatic series of signifiers which constitutes an utterance or a meaning," conceptualized through Lacan's model of schizophrenia.[64] The implications of this breakdown are intimately tied up with the inability of the schizophrenic to unite and coherently organize their biography, their self, into a temporal order. The literary – or aesthetic – results of such an experience points to "something closer to a sentence in free-standing isolation."[65] In Albahari's prose, the signifying chain has been broken – the syntax is not in servitude to meaning because it is not in servitude to time – but its results, while reminiscent of Beckett, develop in a different direction. What the two writers share is the "primacy of the present sentence," to borrow Jameson's words, which "ruthlessly disintegrates the narrative fabric that attempts to reform around it."[66] However, Albahari's formal intervention is to veil the break of the signifying chain through visual unity, to disguise it through the endless piling on of sentences – "a syntax which gushes out," as he puts it[67] – which graphically suggests anything but dissipation, loss of meaning, or lack of internal coherence.

In turning towards Albahari's novels from the 1990s, the significant narrative shift the reader experiences lies in the recalibration of family time into collective time that is imbued with the weight of historically monumental events. How does the social turmoil of the 1990s enter into this dehistoricized fiction? How does historical consciousness find expression? Is the enigma of everyday life wholly supplanted by the sense of a historical crisis? Despite the acknowledgment of the limitations on his narrators' sovereignty, the novel *Snow Man* still recognizes the need for autonomy and the idea that by looking askew at one's circumstances might reveal them in fuller light.

III.

A short, experimental novel, *Snow Man* transports an unnamed writer to a distant, unnamed country in the north for a stint as a writer-in-residence at a university. The plot is minimal: it concerns the circumscribed everyday routine of the protagonist-narrator, whose complex insecurity deepens throughout the course of the novel. Troubled by the conflict raging in the country he left behind, his displacement and its repercussions on his identity and subjectivity form the core of narrative development. Despite the prevailing diffuseness of the narrator's mind, the novel is itself characterized by a tightly structured repetitive loop of daily activity that takes him past the same urban features (a church, a bus stop, a highway). Repetitions are also embedded as echoes of recurring phrases ("I will grow old here"); conveyed as images (drinking a glass of orange juice, sweeping hair from his forehead); and expressed through the narrator's understanding of time itself, such as "If this day differs in any regard from other days, I thought, it is only because it won't ever end."[68] The passage of time is disproportionate: his own activities at home – standing up, sitting down, exiting, entering, falling – are minutely reconstructed (and take up the bulk of the narrative) while conversations and interactions with others are broadly sketched. Given the dominance of the present – the novel is sealed off from the past, from intrusions of memory ("I couldn't remember a single memory")[69] – and the narrow window of happenings within that present, how does the novel manifest the urgency of the historical crisis?

The answer to this question is complicated by the novel's insistence on a reading that must involve the figure of the narrator, a self in displacement, dissociated from "the place I really belonged."[70] The origin of the narrator's instability remains linguistically vague and unspecified, making the figurative representation of his psychic turmoil a primary focus; a reading of the social and collective coordinates necessitates reading through him. A man stifled by circumstances and numerous inertias, he is a writer who cannot write, a man afraid of disappearing, a man "who is not sure that [he] can talk."[71] The struggle with language is a struggle of presumed belonging: "I hesitated a bit until I could shape the word 'home' but I shaped it in the end"[72] is a moment that testifies to his struggle with signifiers of attachment, rootedness, affiliation. The house he inhabits so precariously, suspicious if not outright frightened of its recesses, appears to him as a burial ground: "I thought, it could collapse into itself, like a bucket into the well, like an echo into the ravine."[73] Finally, in the last pages of the novel, in a sequence equally realistic and metaphysical, he merges with the snow. While he thought he would perish in the rooms of the house – "each one ... a hole, an opening, a trap that lured me" – it is the snowfall that dissolves him: "I opened my mouth, and the snow rushed in to the emptiness, it coated the tongue and the palate, filled the cheeks, slid down the throat, erased every lasting difference."[74] The novel's overarching threat of disappearance is the figurative threat to the ego, to the coherence of the subject, its existence as an autonomous being. Crucial to the self's organization and knowledge of himself is the possibility of speech, but the final tableau eliminates all such likelihood, by tampering with the instrument of speech, the location of verbal construction.

I explore two strands of commentary regarding the Yugoslav conflicts that are distinguished in the novel. First, I discuss how the novel does *not* discuss the wars, nor the political upheaval, nor the sense of historical instability, through the strategy of not naming. This is fundamentally a reflection on discourse, about trying to name a personal experience that needs to be iterable and understandable to others but that is not contaminated by other forms of discourse with their unexamined claims. Then I turn to the problem of postmodernism that is emphasized in the tension between the end of history (as theory) and lived history.

The signification of the conflict in Yugoslavia and its context take shape through a limited vocabulary and ambiguous references to historical circumstances in *Snow Man*: his "country is falling apart," it is "in war."[75] Even these are a generous indication of what historical upheaval underlies the narrator's turmoil. More frequently, the references are outright enigmatic: "I left, I thought, because space had begun to get smaller, the walls had begun to suffocate me, because I no longer recognized myself while I walked on the street, while I read the papers, bought bread, threw pebbles into the river."[76] These explanations resist being assimilated to markers of regulated and unregulated violence, from the political to the military, to specific historical transformations that would appear in the novel as plotted affairs. The narrator favours, rather, the explicitness of despair. Yet it is not clear whether the lack of signifiers in *Snow Man* are a sign of the unnamable or the unutterable. Ribnikar leans towards the latter: the narrator is possessed by what cannot be said after the traumatic event that inflicted his wound, so that not naming can thus be read either as a rejection or an impossibility of utterance.[77] Yet *not naming* is pervasive in the novel to the degree that it exceeds the trauma mechanism evoked by Ribnikar. It concerns, for instance, the narrator's as yet unknown present, here exemplified through the topographical: "I still could not call the road I lived on my own, in fact, I did not know what it was called, I walked like someone who is leaving rather than someone who is arriving, least of all did I walk like someone who lives there."[78] Having the privilege to call a thing by name or to call a thing one's own is a symptom of stability and dependence, neither of which is available to the unformed subject caught between symbolic departure and arrival. Arriving "into the world," a recurring shorthand for his journey to the north, the narrator hopes that language will return to its prelapsarian state where "every thing will have a name" and therefore "belong."[79] The implication here is that re-establishing the signifying chain is commensurate with his own integration or affiliation. For this to work, language has to be conceived not as an interiority, as something that testifies to the self's most secret avenues and uniqueness, but, argues Eagleton, as an "'interior' [that] is constituted as a ceaseless opening to an "exterior," a constant self-surpassing or surge towards objects."[80] Even if he never succeeds in expressing his turbulence to others, the express hope that the links in the signifying chain can be reconstructed is to acknowledge language as a medium that exists outside of him, first and foremost.

It is also clear in *Snow Man* that historical and political matters are unnamed rather than unspoken or forbidden from speech. Even the superficiality of the debates and interpretations offered to the narrator by professors and students at the host university are nonetheless an avenue where the subject of the disintegrating Yugoslav reality surfaces residually. The members of academia, ostensibly neutral observers surveying the embers of the former Yugoslavia, speak of the country as "an unsuccessful experiment."[81] They are messengers of empty phrases, including the standard "it could all have been avoided," whose words anatomize the conflict as if it were an animal for dissection and not the narrator's present – a narrator who "experiences it all [the war] on his skin."[82] Their appearance in *Snow Man* is crucial precisely because their speech fails to signify anything (of value) to the narrator: "I missed the meaning of [the professor's] comparisons, metaphors in which the nation was a human body, then a royal palace, then a heavenly kingdom. He spoke about sovereignty as if it were a meal, a spread for sandwiches, exotic fruit."[83] Eschewing proper naming, these speakers name in other ways: they diagnose, prescribe, and pinpoint. Their discourse is a translation of perturbing events (the external, unspecified reality) into the most sanitized and insufficient language of rigid clichés.

While journalists and the media are most often guilty of such inscriptions, *Snow Man* goes after the well-intentioned institutionalized scholar who spins a diagnostic discourse about the unravelling state of affairs in Yugoslavia. In the following scene, the narrator of *Snow Man* is in conversation with a professor of political science at a university somewhere in North America, where, as a writer, he has taken a fellowship. In their

encounter, the professor takes the opportunity to indulgently and author-
itatively hold forth on the nature of historical interpretation. The professor speaks first, putting forward a somewhat postmodernist position:

> Every historical subject seeks a different point of observation, he claimed,
> because history is not a unique totality, he claimed, history is the sum of
> individual histories, something resembling a church organ, where every
> pipe stands for itself but not a single one, on its own, means anything, and
> their sense is only complete in unison. "I never loved the organ," I said.
> "History doesn't care for love," said he after wiping his lips.[84]

The narrator's response is a resistance to the metaphor and by extension a resistance to the analysis: his statement "I never loved the organ"
literalizes the comparison that the professor made and thereby displaces
the attempt to govern or master the understanding of the world. The
witty response (witty in its effect, but not intent) returns the reader to
the professor's words and the self-confidence inherent in them. The
phrase "I never loved the organ" rejects the authority of his interlocutor's
discourse without having to mean anything itself, or to offer a counterpo-
sition. The point is to call into question the unthinking ease with which
one dives into language as a medium, and this doubt is inserted precisely into a discourse where the thinking is presumed to have happened
(intellectuals, scholars). More broadly, this conversation is characteristic
of Albahari's resistance to transparency.

A key strategy of the novel is to arrest the authoritative judgments of
these pronouncements – "the architectonic shells, the skeletons of language."[85] This does not happen through a denial or a counter-discourse.
Instead, the narrator usurps the communication by challenging the fundamental linguistic proposition of his interlocutor's speech. This happens even in the most ordinary exchanges, where, in fact, it is the most
important: "The professor of political science wanted to know if I had
watched the news last night. I hadn't. Did I know, he asked, that an ulti-
matum was placed on my country, just as he had predicted during our
lunch. I wasn't sure which country he meant."[86] A similar response from
the narrator – "What country are we talking about?" – is repeated later.[87]
"Country," from the narrator's perspective, is a multivalent signifier, splintered into multiple signifieds – of the delegitimized socialist Yugoslavia; of
the new political and national narratives underpinning Serbia's claim to
sovereignty; of a contested war zone. But even without this supplemental
logic, the narrator's response is a rejection of the transparency or clarity

implicit in the professor's words without purporting to offer alternative definitions or his own coherence, a choice duplicated in his own form of enunciation in answering to the professor: "Staring at my bare feet, I mumbled my answers, mainly negative ones, shorter than the nails on my toes."[88] The lack of naming, then, is not so much about focusing attention on the most irreducible, most essential characteristics of the situation as it is about focusing the reader's attention on the units of vocabulary, or, as the narrator puts it, "the presence of the fragment."[89]

There are two functions of the fragment in *Snow Man*: one that pertains to the conception of time, the other to linguistic experiments. In the first place, as Albahari's essayist self declares, "[f]ragments ... speak of the despair of a world that's falling apart"[90] Suddenly, and in contrast to its previous manifestations in Albahari's prose, the fragment stands for the dissociated figure, not one that is rejected from the system but the one produced by the suspension of the whole itself. The fragment – that is, the subject – can no longer "depend on the passage of time, on spatial and spiritual co-ordinates, on the connection of the past with the future," a subject position available to one of the students the narrator encounters in *Snow Man*.[91] Disappointingly for him, the spatial distance that separates him from his homeland does not intervene in the temporal order of the "whirlpool" imposed by the war: "I came ... because I believed that life could be existence again, and not just a chain of discontinuous sequences, always new beginnings, never ends, and I found myself in a web of new beginnings, in constant repetition."[92] The disruption of time as a result of the historical crisis has an interdependent connection not with the geographic location one occupies but with one's own body. Interestingly, this points to one of the conditions that makes the novel so introspective and self-focused: the experience of systemic crisis is thoroughly proprioceptive. It manifests itself in bodily stresses and adjustments. In the following scene, the connection between the two is demonstrated:

> "I'm going home," I said, this time out loud, and I started moving, leg after leg, just the way people walk when they know exactly where they are. I even started to sing, at first silently, it wasn't different from muttering, and then later, when I found myself on the flyover, above the highway, I began to sing in full voice. It was a real song, it didn't have the real words, I was interweaving, in fact, words from several languages ... all until I realized that, in following my steps, I had slowed down to the rhythms of a solemn march, that I was singing the anthem of my former country.[93]

Despite the overt symbolism – the body still marches to the internalized rhythm of the state – it is the formal relationship here that is reiterated throughout the novel: the physical gestures and contortions are influenced by the background pressures and developments of his "former country." This behaviour, and symptoms of certain affective states, infuses the entire novel as his body responds through fatigue, extreme thirst, and nausea. One of the disappointments of *Snow Man* is that a new ordinary horizon is not established by the end of the novel, that the body does not adjust to a new temporal order.

Second, the fragment in *Snow Man* – whether a syntagm or, as in the example, a word such as "country" – dislodges the sure-footedness of language and decelerates reading. The fragment acts as a force of dispersion rather than a synthesis for the text that surrounds it (or the interpretation being imposed). The story dissolves around such particles instead of accumulating meaning. Its manifestations are numerous, sometimes distinguished through a graphic mark, as "'in my country,' I thought in speech marks."[94] Often, the fragment is perceptible because it disobeys the realist mode that dominates the narration, evident in the scenes that involve the narrator's domestic meanderings and musings:

> I closed my eyes. When I opened them, the hot water bottle, as happens with these things, slipped from my embrace and fell on the floor next to my bed. I got up. In the bathroom, on a cardboard box with tissues, it said 'I will grow old here' in printed letters, in the Latin alphabet, with an exclamation mark at the end that somebody had crossed out. In the kitchen already warm from the sun, I opened a new bottle of orange juice.[95]

The sequencing of this extract does not account for the semantic counter-realism of the middle section: the slogan on the box of tissues cannot be accounted for by logic and instead has to be read as part of a psychic projection of the narrator's mind. Yet the extract is written as if all events were responses to stimuli external to the narrator, to his body. These subtle slips between planes are the core of the linguistic precariousness in a novel that attempts to relate a precarious situation yet is faced, at every turn, with linguistic genres and contexts that describe this extraordinary situation in rather ordinary terms. The ease of this communication flattens distinct spheres of experience so that "the number of artillery, and war fronts, are dictated as if a recipe for a fruit cake."[96] A similar critique is voiced in *Bait*: "By that point the war had become a monotonous daily occurrence, news was read in the daily papers with the same care devoted to the continuation of a comic strip [or] sports results."[97] These communications are offered as a disambiguation, while Albahari's *Snow Man* demands a perturbed language that will reroute and recircuit the consequences of historical commotion. Each word needs to draw attention to itself and then shatter that attention into a multiplicity of meanings in order to undercut the security of presumed significance.

This is part of the novel's demand: inverting the expectation of common sense, avoiding a discourse where, as the narrator claims of the professors and students, "language was continuously being expended, constantly being thinned out in its repetition ... in the never-changing phrases and exclamations."[98] The task, as Albahari sees it, is not to design a program for meaningful language, but to use literature as the interruption of that common flow of language. He must un-write ready-made sentences by expanding the "space between words ... silence between sounds ... whiteness between pictures" in order to focus attention on what is lacking.[99] In a sense, this produces a novel that wards off and defers the core of its neuroses: it displaces names and forms of real life. It focalizes the problem of their representation while looking away from them.

Inasmuch as the narrator is dismayed at the linguistic presentation by the professor and the sphere of academic discourse, there is another interpretation to be extracted from this dynamic that pertains to the vicissitudes of the postmodern. The cascade of events in 1989 catalysed anew the debates about history that did not leave Albahari indifferent. Yet in *Snow Man*, various figures who step forward to espouse historical views appear to be in the grip of arguments about the "end of history" that culminated with the publication of Francis Fukuyama's refuted 1989 article on this subject.[100] Coming at the tail end of communism in Europe, Fukuyama's thesis prognosticated that history would no longer be a battleground in the coming decades given that the struggle between liberalism and communism had ceased to exist. There was to be no further ideological embattlement as communism gave way to forms of liberalism, free-market economics, and civic societies. The end of history was to be a post-ideological condition. In Albahari's novel, the spectral beings who broadly ventriloquize this postmodern view on history and historical thinking are blunt about the state of affairs. "History is dead," says a woman to the narrator, "and what is happening in your country ... is, in fact, taking place in the past, in a movie from the cinema, in a play that nobody wants to watch anymore."[101] Once the past is displaced onto a film, it becomes another text, another representation, another simulacrum, without referent. Furthermore, the trope of the dead is later echoed by the professor who exclaims to the narrator, "I think sometimes that you [people] over there are already dead."[102] On another occasion, the narrator comes to represent a specimen from a fast disappearing era when another professor calls on him with the following statement: "this is an ideal chance for us to find out something about the world that is disappearing." The pre-1989 order is collapsing and with it the idea of history itself.

These statements cannot be divorced from the context within which they are uttered – in that regard, the university campus is not a neutral locale in the novel. The university campus, particularly in North America, writes Tasić, is a "haven of postmodern theories and aesthetics ..., the place from which the world can look out in a postmodern manner, if it so desires, because of its extensive choices."[103] This multiplicity, the freedom of choice, is represented in the novel through identity politics. It is implied that the ideology of political correctness has substituted the historical paradigm:

> I listened to two students exchange pretentious phrases about the end of history. Behind their backs, a poster printed in pink invited us to a discussion about political correctness of feminism. Another poster, next to the elevator buttons, warned about inequalities in women's employment, employment of minority groups and native Indians. In fact, the whole of the campus was plastered with placards and leaflets and as I passed through the corridors, they flapped from notice boards, carried by the air current and the hurried passage of bodies. The campus was deserted.[104]

As another professor puts it, "this is the new world" and the university, therefore, a duplication of the dominant values of liberalism.[105] The ideas behind these statements are unpacked in Albahari's 2001 novel *World Traveller*, which mirrors the structure of *Snow Man* (with variations, including a full roster of names): a Serbian writer, Danijel Atijas, is on a writing fellowship in a art centre in the Banff area. During his stay, he engages in theoretical-conceptual discussions with a Canadian painter of landscapes, who is the novel's narrator. The "new world" is defined in this novel by the visiting writer who shares Albahari's initials as a place of economic development "where standards and fortune enable the easy belief that history is finished, unnecessary, unimportant, superfluous and excessive, and used up like, let's say, sandpaper."[106] Here, the connection between late capitalist societies and lifestyles and postmodern variations on history is made explicit. The postmodern investment in the end of history has an ideological provenance. Resulting from the fissuring of totality (an unnamed grand narrative), Danijel Atijas postulates, are identity politics – those alluded to in *Snow Man* – that are the new (relativized) micro-histories of the victim. The problem is that the emergence of these attachments – those on "the social, sexual or religious margins" – are discontinuous with each other.[107] Their aims and objectives cannot be grouped under one system of historical objectives.

The narrator in *Snow Man* rejects these abstractions of the new world formed as they are by figures "scrunched down in an armchair ... sharing lectures, preaching and sermonizing, even though in reality everything was different."[108] The narrator's antagonism could function as a surrogate for the conflict between theory and reality, with him as representative of the latter. It would be more accurate to state that *Snow Man* is about the transaction between the two in which the status of reality and its temporal order have shifted but where the theoretical components have remained inert. The (theoretical) stasis stems from the relatively easy horizon of late capitalist society. Even so, as I demonstrated in the preceding section, reality does not take over in terms of the mimetic framework: it is the object that barely makes it into peripheral vision. This can be attributed to Albahari's linguistic philosophy, where the smallest of distances that has to be covered, such as movement through a room or a gaze aimed through a window, introduces the greatest challenge in terms of expression and meaningful articulation: "Every time, even if they look the same, words say entirely different things."[109] Signifiers are interminably unbounded, but can bind themselves to signifieds that spoil communication (at least according to social rules): "A branch would tremble outside, a cry would ring out, and I was thinking 'trap,' 'betrayal,' and 'loss.' Quickly, everything I looked at became one of these words, without resistance, without effort, as if language did not need any more words."[110] In sum, reality announces its dominance (post-socialism, war, post-Yugoslavia), but its representation remains elusive.

By embracing these explorations of language and meaning, *Snow Man* puts itself in a bind when it has to address history from a postmodern aesthetic plane that includes extensive fragmentation. Glancing back over his career, Albahari has remarked that the novella *Cink* (*Tsing*, 1988), which charts the death of a father (based on Albahari's own), belongs to a "time which has ended with no chance of return" given that "it stands at the end of a period during which it was believed possible to live without history."[111] The sense of living in history is there, but interpretation is a problem. The theoretical paradigm that might have once facilitated an explanation to this quandary has been undermined. This theoretical blindspot is another disappointment in a novel that already has a surfeit of them.

On a final accounting, *Snow Man* reverberates with the emptiness of lost beliefs, of recalibrated perspectives even though this mood is rerouted through the critique of the professors. Plus the point is muted somewhat by the postmodern key in which *Snow Man* itself is written. The narrator is not sure what model of historical knowledge or experience should fill the post-socialist ideological vacuum nor accommodate for the reality of a military conflict. The notion of history as a totality of sorts is alluded to through a set of metaphors that have nothing to do with history:

> I was explaining water, but maybe I was really thinking about oil, or some other liquid, or a substance whose molecules were more tightly connected. History is elusive, a constant fight of internal forces, like mercury, I thought, a permanent gap between the piece and the whole, so that there is always a piece that, crazy from cohesion, attempts to move away from the rest a bit, not knowing, I thought, that he is repeating models that others have left behind them, that he is climbing where others have slid down, that he is falling to the bottom from which others have already climbed."[112]

The imagery and allusion leave no ambiguity about the inescapability of historical forces – the impossibility of overcoming or extracting oneself from whatever social, political, or economic conditions are arrayed against the individual. The choice of a molecular structure is crucial here because it is a system of signs and forces that have nothing to do with language (even if they are represented here through words, these systems can be given scientific formulas or can be diagrammed). Therefore, it is a representational system that has no perspectival biases, inequalities, or prejudices of speech. There is no Othering to which the narrator himself is subjected to by those he encounters in the new world. Finally, even if the narrator cannot settle with a full understanding of what it is that constitutes history (whether it is a totality or a teleology), he is more than certain about what should be surrendered.

IV.

The status of the theoretical and the real is rewritten in *Götz and Meyer* as a bind between the imaginative tendencies of literature and the force of historical fact. This novel dispenses with a lot of the preliminary anxieties of *Snow Man* and concedes immediately to history. *Götz and Meyer* is an unusual book to consider in this study since it does not deal with its primary topic, namely, the wars of the 1990s. Yet the novel's indirect but significant relation to this theme is evident in Albahari's rising interest in emerging anti-Semitism in the Balkans during a decade of intense nationalist chauvinism across the region.[113] Furthermore, the thematic base of *Götz and Meyer* – the experience of the Holocaust in Serbia – opens up an interesting discussion of the problem of Holocaust representation during the reign of postmodern poetics. On the one hand, the "real" of the represented world in *Götz and Meyer* is negligible because the book starts off from the basis that even historical fact is now discourse. (There are no surviving witnesses; all living links to that time and to that experience have been severed.) On the other, the imperative to witness is no less demanding decades after the event as the threat of oblivion yawns large and menacing. The "real" is ultimately reinstated through language – a position complicated by the relationship of language to fiction that can at times lie about or cover up experiences.

Götz and Meyer is an archive-based meditation on the tragic events that took place in Belgrade's Old Fairground Camp (also known as Judenlager Semlin), where some seven thousand Jewish women, children, and elderly people were gassed in a Saurer truck throughout the spring of 1942.[114] The middle-aged narrator, a bachelor teacher, is compelled to discover the fate of his family – most of whom perished at the camp – and so begins to "search, tour dusty archives, visit museums, haul new books from libraries, peer into group photographs, compare different reports, collated lists."[115] In the absence of direct testimony – within the world of the novel, there are no survivors who can witness – the narrator relies on official records, ranging from Wehrmacht correspondence and paperwork, to the holdings of the Jewish Museum in Belgrade, and historical scholarship on the Old Fairground Camp (acknowledged in an author's note at the end of the book).[116] In its commitment to its documentary strand, the novel offers an objective treatment of events for the purposes of minimizing the distortion of the historical subject: it offers a breadth of logistical, technical, and bureaucratic detail regarding the daily life of Jewish prisoners. This is information, the novel makes clear, that has been neglected in public memorial discourse: after the last truck of Jewish prisoners departed, in May 1942, "a fluffy cloud of silence descended on the camp."[117] Nor was the cloud to lift even five decades later, according to the observations of the narrator: while Belgrade "was not the same city as the one towards which the camp prisoners had stared at in hunger, it kept silent in the same way."[118] In seeking to be a witness to this history, the novel addresses what Sarah Horowitz calls "the moral weight of Shoah writing" that contributes "to a reluctance to read Holocaust narratives as 'mere' art – that is, as imaginatively generated and artfully structured rather than historically determined, transparent texts."[119]

Yet the documentarian thrust is impeded by a concurrent strand in the novel that belongs to the speculative and imaginative terrain. Chancing upon the names of the two SS non-commissioned officers who were tasked with driving the gas van on its daily routes – Götz and Meyer, the duo of the book's title – Albahari's narrator begins to imagine and construct the two drivers out of limited information, confined to their names and the anecdote that one of them "according to witnesses, went inside the camp, played with the children, took them in his arms and even gave them chocolates."[120] This anecdote opens the novel and sets the narration in motion: "So little is necessary to imagine a different world, isn't it?"[121] The gesture of giving children the chocolates is an acute moment of contradiction for the narrator because it intimates a degree of human kindness and care in a man who was about to, very shortly, drive these same children to their death. The hint of decency is almost grotesque in the SS officer whose job is basically murderous. Yet the narrator progressively sutures Götz and Meyer into his own present, his embellishment of their lives expressed through archetypes of decent, working-class men. Götz and Meyer have wives, sick children, aspirations to become pilots, landscape preferences, and, like most workers of the world, experience boredom in their jobs. They are ordinary people who, as projections of the narrator, have commonplace conversations: "Götz, or Meyer, whichever one is married, is somewhat concerned about his daughter Hilda's constant sore throat. That will go away by the time we return, says Götz, or Meyer, the one who is certainly not married, but it is true, he adds, health must be looked after and cared for from a young age."[122] Already, from this quotation, it is apparent that something unusual is happening here through the interchangeability of their names – a feature which I will focus on shortly.

Both the documentary and fictive strands are connected by perpetrator history in the novel, a narrative gesture which is open-ended to our interpretation. The narrator of *Götz and Meyer* is at pains to demonstrate the public oblivion towards events that had happened at the camp, a silence that is paralleled by the real-life systemic neglect of the Old Fairground Camp as a site of suffering.[123] With this in mind, a novel that focuses on representations of perpetrators is enigmatic since it must somehow poetically employ the radical otherness of the perpetrators to help recover, dignify, and commemorate the victims. I first consider the implications of naming for the ethical and formal plane of the novel. To name by fictionalizing or by lying in *Götz and Meyer* becomes a question of moral acts. This argument is extended in a final section on irony.

"One can understand the reluctance of serious fiction writers," writes Susan Suleiman, "to portray a Nazi perpetrator's inner life" because "even if the character is loathsome, he or she must at least be recognized as human, hence sharing some characteristics with the rest of us."[124] To this, we could add other risks of this narrative strategy. It forecloses the voice of the victims, a silence that duplicates the silence of their death: the victims were denied humane treatment at the hands of their murderers and so to grant the act of speech to their perpetrators seems morally wrong. Also, it can lead to the possibility of identification or recognition between reader and transgressor. Albahari sidesteps these issues, to a degree, by eschewing the first-person narration and thereby avoiding the mire of their psychological introspection:

> To truly understand real people – that is, my cousins, I first had to understand unreal people – that is, Götz and Meyer. Not to understand them: to create them. Therefore I simply had to be Götz and Meyer sometimes to learn what Götz, or Meyer, rather, what I, actually think about what Meyer, or Götz, also me, wanted to ask him. Götz who was not Götz spoke to Meyer who was not Meyer.[125]

The description of his method here is one of ventriloquism: there is no disguising that their voices originate with him. For all intents and purposes, he uproots Götz and Meyer from their historical plane of existence – one that involves witness documents and archival dossiers – into his own present. This transforms the novel, writes Ribnikar, into one which collapses the distinction between its ontological planes, namely, the real and the fictional, so that the experience of the textual world is "disruptive and troubling."[126] She adds that this slippage makes the present an insecure territory, calling to mind the forces of destruction that are silently and invisibly gathering pace in the background of the novel, set in early 1990s Yugoslavia.[127]

In addition to blurring the fictive with the historical, the novel is also ambiguous about Götz and Meyer. Or, rather, the narrator is explicit about the fact that they are undifferentiated, often signified by the preposition "or" ("Götz, or Meyer, is full of praise for the organizational capabilities of *Untersturmführer* Andorfer").[128] At other times, it is not just a syntactical gesture: "Anyone could be Götz. Anyone could be Meyer. But then again, only Götz and Meyer were Götz and Meyer, no one else could be that. It doesn't surprise me that I constantly felt like I was slipping even when I walked on flat ground."[129] I argue that this dynamic of interchangeability is resonant across the novel in an ethical, linguistic, and generic sense. The interchangeability of their names – it functions as a sign for their perpetrator identity – is meant to evoke the possibility of switching subject position. As such, it casts light on the role of the narrator, who engages in victimizing behaviour, a role he himself foregrounds. On a number of occasions, he bribes a senile diabetic cousin with chocolates in order to extract from him, through this bribe, the names of his family who died in the camp so that he could complete the family tree. He does this in the full knowledge that the chocolates are hazardous, if not lethal, to his cousin's health: "While I was wiping the pieces of chocolate and bubbles of spit from his face, I decided to stop with that masquerade because, if I continue, I thought, for certain I will accelerate his end, which would make me equal with Götz, or Meyer."[130] The narrator, in evoking the figure of Götz and Meyer, uses them as an archetype of a transhistoric model of perpetration: their form of violence sheds light on other modes of oppression and victimization that exist beyond the concentration camp.[131]

This question about the nature of the human condition is placed within another constellation at the end of the novel. The denouement involves a scene of what Marija Mitrović calls "situational education":[132] the narrator, a schoolteacher by profession, takes his students on a field trip to the Old Fairground Camp where, collectively, they re-enact the displacement of the Jewish children from their home, their time in the camp, and their final journey to death, under his instruction. The narrator becomes a storyteller whose words have a spellbinding effect on his young charges. As they sit in the bus hired for the occasion, the pupils lose their breath, their faces become "twisted, contorted in nausea or pain."[133] The narrator's verbal skills are a form of hypnosis (to which he alludes) that has a stupefying, crushing effect on the children.[134] The lesson of history has exceeded its aim and, instead of instructing them and "spilling the seeds of memory," it paralyses them.[135] The mistreatment in this scene is stressed by a linguistic homology: earlier in the novel, the narrator speculates, Götz and Meyer must have considered their task to kill seven thousand Jews in the Old Fairground Camp "as some sort of excursion."[136] A cautionary scene, scholars agree, that highlights the victimizing potential of identification and the questionable morality of this endeavour.[137] This reconstruction is also a metanarrative gesture since it calls into question the role of the medium itself (in this case, literature) as the means of transmission. *Götz and Meyer* perhaps warns against the strength of the imagination, arguably a feature inherent to the act of artistic creation. But equally the novel could be pinpointing fictionalization as the broader problem, given the degree to which fictional strategies were employed within the ideological language of the Third Reich to justify their actions or to use the language to divorce the act from its immorality.

In addressing this matter, it is crucial to focus on the hypnosis analogy within which the scene is framed by the narrator. The release from the "spell" comes not from the narrator but from the driver with the question "So ... we're going towards the school now?"[138] The driver is outside the time of the tale, outside the captive audience. He is the observer (or a type of reader) who breaks the magnetism of the narrator's words. This leads the students out of their debilitating identification with the victims and ends the illusion that had held them in sway. The novel thus comments on what it sees as a role of the reader to end the illusion it has itself spun; to release the narrator, too, from his own story, if the capacity of the text is to be perceptible. The power of a text is multiplied when its illusion is revealed or destroyed because its impact upon the world beyond its borders becomes evident. To summarize, then, what began as discussion of the narrator's potential to victimize – even if that potential stems from a dignified, humane task to commemorate – culminates in a pointed commentary about the task of literature. In particular, it is a comment about the necessity of literature to declare its borders: the fictional must expose its narrative tricks in order to make its ethical intervention perceptible.

Beyond this thematic-moral or thematic-metanarrative axis, the notion of interchangeability is present in the formal dimension of *Götz and Meyer*. The dynamic of the *and/or* that is linguistically bound up with the exchangeable personalities of the two drivers is most obviously in the type of splitting and switching that lies between history and literature embodied in the documentary and imaginative paradigms I outlined at the beginning of this section. On the whole, *Götz and Meyer* does not choose one or the other but animates the dynamic: it cannot rest on the historical sequence (and, and, and) nor on the literary potential for alternative (or, or, or). The literary dimension, typified by the alternative sign ("or"), is given direct expression in the novel. When the narrator takes the children to the camp for the educational re-enactment, he constructs the fictional Adam – he is a fantasy – and through him, articulates the realization "that parallel worlds exist, and that these worlds are created through language, and that it was enough to change the meaning of some words in order to change an existing world or to create a new one."[139] The teacher's imagining of what Adam might think reads both as a description of the literary method (literature creates alternative worlds), but it is also an echo of the fundamental structure of the Golem myth. In the legend of the Kabbalistic figure, the Golem's creator brings the creature to life by changing one letter – from the Hebrew "emet," to "met."[140] This linguistic detail of the Golem myth can be read as making the case for the creative potential of the word to create. Thinking in terms of Albahari's novel, I argue that *Götz and Meyer*'s investment in the imaginative realm of literature, which only exists as a sequence of words, is the "or" that reroutes meaning, that can bring to life what is perceived to be dead or disappeared.

How does this reverberate with the conclusion of the novel? For Ribnikar, *Götz and Meyer* is defeatist towards the prospects of literature in its encounter with historical outcomes or historical truth. She quotes the narrator's line that "in history no one chooses" to demonstrate how the attempt to "correct [history's] flow" through fictional experimentation fails (the case for this disappointment lies in the fantasy figure of Adam). "You still think of reality as a work of art," the narrator tells his pupils, "in which you have the possibility of choice, but in reality there's no choice, you have to participate in it, you cannot step out of it and into something else."[141] This statement potentially diminishes the capacity of literature's alternative (the "or"), particularly in the face of the sheer insurmountable tragedy of the Holocaust experience.

My interpretation of *Götz and Meyer* stresses a more nuanced mediation of the polarization signified by *and/or*, by the history-literature tandem. The novel upholds a more diffusive structure to which even the narrator calls the reader's attention: "the worlds are easy to create, but difficult to maintain, and collision, interweaving, and equivalence between their co-ordinates can happen with ease."[142] When we consider how this is manifest in the novel, it becomes clear that the alterity of literature is not just about the ethical hope that the pain and trap of history can for a moment be suspended or evaded (the hope most clearly intoned in the narrator's creation of Adam). Rather, literature, as Albahari's novel shows, also possesses the capacity to house the volatile and the murky claims (the claims of the perpetrators) by modifying the world of the archive, which is the pervasive and most dominant discourse in the novel. Not only is this exemplified through Götz and Meyer, who are referred to as "lighthouses" that "illuminate the mud and nothing else"[143] (the darkness of this historical abyss), but also through the linguistic inclusion of the archival material and the narrator's manipulation of the very same.

Götz and Meyer is a novel of meticulous historical research where archival data is often not adapted in tone to suit a more lyrical or aesthetic mode. The discourse remains, for the most part, unadulterated and unadjusted from its bureaucratic and military sources. Information and details are transferred directly from sources and recontextualized within the logic of the novel.

> Later, in a book, I came across some German correspondence from June 1942 which ... lays out the problem of the stability of the gas trucks. The opinion of the manufacturer is mentioned ... if the body of the truck was reduced, the entire balance of the vehicle would be disturbed, and the front axle would have to withstand an incomparably larger pressure. In practice, however, the signatories claimed, the cargo rushes towards the doors that are closing and it is right there that they are found in largest numbers, which means that the pressure of the cargo is aimed towards the last axle.[144]

One could simply overlook this feature of *Götz and Meyer* and suggest that the transposition of impersonal language limits and flattens the tone of the novel, making the entire endeavour stylistically uninteresting. However, the visibility of the archival discourse – it is perceptible insofar as the words are not absorbed within the narrator's linguistic identity – is not a neutral rendition of historical facts, particularly in the case of euphemistic terminology. In the extract above, the word "cargo" – referring to the Jewish prisoners who are on their way to their death – is one such example: it transforms them into an inanimate bulk for transport, a thoroughly dehumanized label. What happens when the idiom of the bureaucratic and military language with its "simulated innocence," in the words of Shaul Esh, is reinscribed in the novel?[145] How do the codes, conventions, and substitutions in language, all of them veiling the violence and murder, accord with the novelistic universe of *Götz and Meyer*? Are they refuted, exposed – and if so, how?

Overall, the labour of the narrator-researcher produces a narrative that details what he calls "the economic and efficient workings on which the functioning of the Reich was based."[146] Viewed comprehensively, Albahari's novelistic accounting of this historical episode favours the functionalist approach to the Holocaust combined with the modernity paradigm. The former focuses on the technocratic and bureaucratic aspects of the institutions of the Third Reich, while the latter invokes the Holocaust as an outcome, rather than a failure, of modernity.[147] Most strongly associated with Zygmunt Bauman's work *Modernity and the Holocaust*, this interpretation posits that "[t]he Holocaust was not an irrational outflow of the not-yet-fully-eradicated residues of pre-modern barbarity."[148] Rather, Bauman adds, it was "a paradigm of modern bureaucratic rationality," a bureaucracy whose organization approached the standards of "a textbook of scientific management."[149] The narrator of Albahari's novel perceives the Holocaust as sourced in the "enormous structure" of the Third Reich within which even comparatively small tasks, such as driving the Saurer truck, contribute to the functioning of the whole, "the security of the entire foundation depends on their competency."[150]

If there is a single trope that displays the intersection of these two currents in *Götz and Meyer*, it is the Saurer truck, a technological feat that is the historical precursor to the gas chambers:

> This truck, it must be said, had a forerunner in a hermetically sealed vehicle used as part of the "Euthanasia" program for mental health patients, in which victims were killed with pure carbon dioxide. An ingenious concept that enabled the actualization of Himmler's idea that was, after all, necessary for further development of the technology of mass killing, and that consists not of pure carbon dioxide in steel bottles but that uses the gas from the exhaust pipe, all of which didn't just make the whole procedure cheaper but had the effect of making the interior of the truck seem completely innocent: like a *real* interior of a *real* truck, which would no doubt have a beneficial effect on the victims.[151]

Viewed in a broader perspective, the truck is a figure of the "concentrationary universe" that is to come with the death camps in Poland.[152] From the historical perspective of the reader of *Götz and Meyer*, who knows the outcome of the Holocaust and the Second World War, the death by gassing in the truck cannot but call to mind the subsequent terror of the stationary gas camps. Yet the novel's presentation of the truck, informed as it is by the archival material, transforms the Saurer truck into an object that is fetishized for its engineering efficiency; it is emblematic of the apogee of logistics, industrial design, and rational thinking. This vehicle (entirely neutral in and of itself as an object) proves, the narrator tells us, that "the spirit of modernity prevailed" since it demonstrates the Nazi regime's "support for further development of more humane and less painful murder."[153] Moreover, the narrator continues, "when all the costs were laid out on paper, it was most economical to send one gas truck to Belgrade as was advocated by those who believed in the development of scientific thought."[154] This claim is substantiated by precise mathematical calculations, provided in Albahari's novel, that demonstrate the optimal conditions for an ostensibly painless death by suffocation: "Only a hundredth of one percent of carbon monoxide in the air can cause symptoms of poisoning – headaches, nausea, and tiredness – and a fifth of that same percentage brings about death in less than half an hour."[155]

There is a vertiginous quality about these quotations and the stratification of discourses within them: the logic of scientific design is co-opted by the rhetoric of social engineering. The detached language of observation and experiment, both scientific and industrial, is interwoven with clichés about a more humane death. It becomes hard to distinguish between the idiom of Nazi German scientific discourse and phrases like "spirit of modernity": in Albahari's novel they seep and support each other, they substantiate each other's claims. They spin a web of deception and defer the articulation of reality that services both the German soldiers and their victims. Götz and Meyer, the narrator tells us, make use of such stock phrases: they "did not use that word [death], instead they spoke of 'relocation' or 'treatment'."[156] The ultimate deception befalls the victims, played out in the extract above as a game of the signifier/signified: they see a truck so it must be a truck – a vehicle that will transport them, not kill them. They are outside the idiom, the language system, that would enable them to read this sign, to decipher its monstrosity.

Since the archive is exposed in *Götz and Meyer* as a site of explanation and rationalization, we have to consider what happens to the disseminated justification of the perpetrator when it is aped and mimicked by the narrator. On the one hand, the novel approaches a point of unthinking fascination: after presenting the case for murder by gassing in the truck, the narrator adds: "I had to admit that you rarely encounter such a crystal clear and iron logic."[157] There is a dangerous subtext in this sentence. While it is an expression of praise for the structure, and not the content, of the logic, it is not entirely clear that the two categories should be divorced in discussions of this particular ideology, in the context of the Holocaust. On the other hand, the book neatly shows what happens when the narrator takes the plunge towards "identification" and "complicity" with the perpetrators instead of tiptoeing around its threshold.

The narrator escalates his own participation in the recounting of the events: dispersed throughout the novel are numerous instances where the narrator's own interventions extend the rationalization of the bureaucracy, where his own narrative voice supplements the logic of what he had read in the archive. The following extract begins with a routine description of the camp:

> In the fourth pavilion, they later opened a kitchen; in the beginning, food was brought by truck from Belgrade. The Jewish men, those who had been spared executions, lived in the fifth pavilion. The second pavilion was set aside for the Gypsies; some time later, those quarters were converted into numerous camp workshops: locksmith, cobbler, and carpenter. The camp had its own hospital and pharmacy ... A true small town, no doubt about it. It's a shame that prisoners, when they had to go to the toilet, had to go outside. Had that situation been better resolved, the Old Fairground could have become a model Nazi camp.[158]

The detached, somewhat routine description of the organized life in the camp is undercut by the final sentence. The list is neutral in tone, the narrator's voice dissolved in the facts. This is modified by the phrase "It's a shame," which, on a surface reading, reveals some identification between the narrator and the perpetrators. To rephrase: it's a shame that the desired efficiency could not be achieved so that the regime's demands could be better facilitated. ("It's touching, their concern for the welfare of the prisoners" is another recurring phrase.)[159] Yet the sentence is simultaneously a sabotage of that reading: "shame" is an excessive utterance and signals the ironic tone. The profound degradation of the prisoners is brought to the foreground by the narrator's mimicry and extension of the rhetoric of this modern bureaucracy. In order to reroute the sterile descriptions towards their opposite meaning, he has to perpetuate the euphemistic terminology of the archival material. The narrator replicates more than just the language code of the "officialese" (*Amtssprache*): he also matches the tenor of what was considered immoral to the Nazis. That is: it's a shame that the facilities could not have been made more *humane*. The language here is mimicking the moral travesty of unnecessary hardship, rather than expressing disgust at the murder itself.[160]

This interplay between complicity and irony is the dominant dynamic of the novel. Irony, as the supplement produced by Albahari's narrator, deepens the guilt of the perpetrators by exposing the camouflage of the language and the passivity of the bureaucratic process. To rationalize an idea is not to justify it or to endorse it, particularly within a literary text by a writer whose basic premise is that language can be easily destabilized. The ironic tone does two things for the novel as a whole. First, toying with the language of the archive does not manipulate the historical retelling. The armature of empirical details necessary for the knowledge of the event is preserved. Second, irony offers an alternative way of knowing the systematic murder that took place at the Old Fairground Camp in the spring of 1942. Importantly, it is an alternative to the knowledge accrued through the transmission of trauma that defines the narrator's relationship with the victims. By focusing on the fiction of language codes of bureaucratic rhetoric, Albahari demonstrates how language produced a violence that was frightening because of the passivity it engendered. Moulding and twisting the language does not dispel the horror but brings it into focus (through detail and perspective). This language dimension is profoundly connected to Albahari's own interest in calling a thing by another name. In *Götz and Meyer*, the narrator is assembling the archival remnants of a time when murder was not called murder and facing the horrendous outcomes of "a dictionary in which nothing expressed the thing that language usually expresses."[161]

In these reflections on the dangerous fiction created by the language of the Third Reich and Albahari's ironic take on that same language, *Götz and Meyer* becomes a novel that does not incorporate the real but demarcates the boundary between aesthetics and the physical, existing world. The novel's language is used to call to attention to what lies beyond the text as the only possible ethical gesture of narration when the historical event is not recoverable by other means.

V.

In this chapter, I demonstrated how Albahari's reckoning with the historical present and the agony of the past is staged in two novels. I began by arguing that the explicit anti-ideological stance towards the monolith of socialist administration that defined Albahari's poetics was not sustained to the last. While he objected to literature that was duty- and task-bound, the dissolution of Yugoslavia's pluralist cultural sphere and the stability of the union left a disorienting mark on his prose. In *Snow Man* the lacuna of this historical shift is revealed through the hollowness of theoretical positions but also the staleness of the unaware, unreflecting academic idiom. The novel has a bifurcated identity, then, when it comes to the postmodern: the narrator, in actual physical displacement, also seeks to reposition his thinking on history (theoretically), but the novel remains attached to cultural attributes of postmodernism. The novel cannot step outside its own skin, to borrow from the narrator's lexicon, outside of its aesthetic paradigm. It can, however, attempt to re-evaluate material that exists beyond the border of the text; a world that is just coming into view for Albahari's narrators and subjects that populate his fiction.

This idea of the border plays a central role in *Götz and Meyer*, a novel that crosses or obliterates numerous thresholds: imaginary/real, historical past/recent present, victim/ victimizer. Principally, the real is already complicated by receding into history and into textual representation: the narrator is seeking some trace of the victims of the gassings at the Old Fairground Camp, to recover their lives and their deaths, and comes across the archive. Within the documents, he stumbles across a world made entirely of false language that excised all capacity for the expression of morality or, for that matter, immorality. In my reading of the novel, the literary text engages with this idiom in order to reinstitute the horror and extremity of these events. The novel also emphasizes the distinction between the fictionalizing tendencies of Götz and Meyer – the language codes of administration and bureaucracy – and the strategies of literature. In literature, I conclude, calling to attention the illusory premise of a story or novel is what makes the lesson acute and visible in the border beyond the text.

5 The Quickened Moral Pulse

I

The Bosnian conflict of the early 1990s became famous through the combined power of modern technologies of mass communication. The story of the wars' prominence and distinction – and also their infamy – takes shape against a background of enmeshed discourses, including geopolitical negotiations, advocacy, compassion, human rights, intellectual engagement, and activism. Abetted by highly visible humanitarian interventions, the region and its populations were cloaked in a symbolic function – that of a suffering and endangered species, the fate of which continuously elicited the moral and rather naive responses of celebrities and intellectuals.

The media apparatus, in bringing news of the war, "quickened the moral pulse of intellectual Europe," writes Dubravka Ugrešić, revitalizing "forgotten phrases about political engagement" in complacent, consumerist Western cultures, and "about the role and responsibility of the intellectual in historical events."[1] Quite predictably, the three writers in this study do not take kindly, or passively, to the imposition of the international gaze and rhetoric – and sometimes, like David Albahari's narrator in *Snow Man*, they indulge in humorous scenes of violent fantasy towards those whose bombastic phrases and appeals are seen as merely condescending chatter.[2] The virtue of intervention is both self-serving and a perpetuation of tropes about areas in crisis. The individual who rallies behind the cause of the dispossessed, writes Ugrešić, is "superfluous" in the "clinch" between the subjugated and the empowered: neither "the aggressor nor the victim needs the intellectual."[3]

This chapter is concerned with two problems. First, I examine intellectual engagement under the sign of the media. If in the age of postmodernity the television is unavoidable as a channel of communication for political activism, how does this modify or transform the types of ethics proposed by various intellectuals? This is particularly pertinent when we take into account that most foreign intervention comes from the "centre" – Western countries – and interferes with marginal or peripheral spaces. In addition, the media, as Michael Rothberg puts it, is also "disruptive of the face-to-face encounter that has traditionally grounded the ethical."[4] Thus, any interaction or dialogue between the two parties runs the risk of objectifying the survivor or witness. I focus on intellectuals because they are distinguished by their disinterestedness, or impartiality. Susan Sontag's definition of that freedom is emblematic of this position: "By intellectual I mean the 'free' intellectual, someone who, beyond his or her professional or technical or artistic expertise, is committed to exercising (and thereby, implicitly, defending) the life of the mind as such."[5] Here, Sontag exercises a definition not too far from Pierre Bourdieu's own construction of the cultural field in which consecrated authors are propelled beyond their specialized arena (say, scholarship) to a position from which they can access a general audience and critique political, fiscal, and state affairs, but without recourse to the tools of those particular domains. Yet Bourdieu clearly asserts in the final chapter in *Rules of Art* that the autonomy of intellectuals is threatened by "new forms of stranglehold and dependence," represented by "the major cultural bureaucracies (newspapers, radio, television)."[6] It is important to understand what role the frame of the media plays in underwriting these sincere claims of intervention, particularly when we consider that these individuals do not profit in the same way as actors and singers, who more obviously embody "the money form" through their acts of celebrity diplomacy.[7]

The second part of this chapter considers the image and performance of the authorial persona – specifically, the three writers considered in my study – in light of intellectual responsibility. The claims of engagement are supported by the construction of an authorial self, an "I" that speaks. When it comes to writers, that "I" is valued because of the sign of their authorship. For the writer or philosopher who attracts media attention, their status is based on a life devoted to thinking, a life whose production is ostensibly in opposition to economic and political profit in "the field of power."[8] That is, in opposition to the field that projects them into the glare of public life. It is their authorship that imbues their public persona with intellectual distinction. "The matrix of associations supporting [authors'] reputations," writes Aaron Jaffe in his illuminating study on the modernists, "is not intrinsically image-based but predicated instead on a distinctive textual mark of authorship, a sanction for distinguishing a high literary product from the inflating signs of consumption."[9] The "textual mark of authorship" follows the authorial persona on the screen or the radio. Yet the notion of authorship is complicated in the context of postmodern practices.

Postmodern authorship is strongly influenced by the theoretical and literary models that desacralized and demystified the author figure as so many signs and practices conditioned by social, economic, and ideological forces. That Ugrešić absorbed this lesson is manifest in her humorous short story "Posudi mi tvog lika" ("Lend Me Your Character"), first published in *Life Is a Fairy Tale*, that with its epigraph "Is the pen a metaphorical penis?" alludes to the opening line of the classical piece of feminist scholarship *Madwoman in the Attic* by Sandra Gilbert and Susan Gubar.[10] Much like the two scholars, who seek to demystify the tradition of literary paternity that sees male sexuality as "not just analogically but actually the essence of literary power,"[11] Ugrešić's stories tackle the conditioning of social roles (subservience of women, for instance) in order to explore how they reveal entrenched prejudices in the literary creation and authority of voice. With Albahari, as I discussed in chapter 3, his poetic voice was invested in writing as a matter of enunciation in the manner described by Roland Barthes in "The Death of the Author":

> Linguistically, the author is never more than the instance writing, just as *I* is nothing more than the instance saying *I*: language knows a "subject," not a "person," and this subject, empty outside of the very enunciation which defines I, suffices to make language "hold together," suffices, that is to say, to exhaust it.[12]

The premise here is that the "I" is characterless and identity-less and should not consequently be typified by vocabulary that appeals to creation and origins. This chimes with Albahari's frequent statements that language – and the form that is carved out of it – escapes from the author, that the utterance possesses an internal self-renewing principle of creation.[13] It is easy to understand how this argument would have been an oblique rejection of the functionalized figure of an author in a socialist environment.

It is this particular theoretical conceit of authorship that is problematized by the events of the 1990s, which, by provoking individual commentary on social affairs, demand a more disambiguated relationship between subject of enunciation and the text. It less acceptable, within the text's circulation in the media or other arenas of public discourse, to foreground the principles of disavowal and abnegation of authorial voice. If we accept Sean Burke's view that postmodernism celebrates the very premise of a "textuality defenceless before its clients, unable to answer for itself, only capable of returning the same form of words in the face of numerous conflicting interpretations, powerless to predict or programme its own audience and reception,"[14] the conflict in Yugoslavia presents an opportunity to reconfigure that position vis-à-vis literary and critical discourse. I examine how the values of an author's individual aesthetic pursuits get rejected or embodied in their own projection of an authorial persona.

II.

For the purposes of this chapter, I distinguish between two forms of international humanitarianism. The first category involves multinational organizations (such as the UN) that were instrumental in providing peacekeepers during and after the conflict, relief agencies, and global NGOs (Human Rights Watch, among others) that arrived to aid the state-building process. The aid here was both military and diplomatic. The second category is that of non-institutional humanitarianism, comprising a disparate cohort of individuals, writers, actors, thinkers, and musicians whose symbolic gestures of solidarity with victims of the war resulted from the common assertion that something should be done. When I speak here of engagement, it is with an eye on the latter category: the troop of celebrities – headed by Susan Sontag – whose impact, while culturally significant and emblematic of particular networks of power and Western myopia, has hardly been commented on at all. My reason for foregrounding their presence is that they captured the attention of writers in the region, an attentiveness that can be partly justified by the fact that they could enter into dialogue with the personal claims of another writer in a way that was harder to achieve with representatives of Western political power.

Straddling the frontier between the two categories were the numerous journalists whose careers were made in the wars – including Ed Vulliamy of the *Guardian*, who famously reported on the prison camps in northwest Bosnia held by Bosnian Serbs, and who went on to testify as an eyewitness at the International Criminal Tribunal for the Former Yugoslavia. Faced with the inhumane treatment of civilians, many perceived a duality in their journalistic assignments: while reportage was the main goal of their work, many used their medium to mobilize geopolitical opinion in favour of

Western military intervention.[15] Objectivity was considered a prerogative, but neutrality was not. This, it must be stressed, was not a point of view shared by all journalists. Nonetheless, the media has set the agenda for humanitarian interventions (strongly in evidence in the last twenty years or so) and has created a forum for debate on humanitarianism and the ethical and moral obligations of the developed world. It has done so through the construction and evocations of compassion, where compassion translates into financial aid, food relief, and other modes of charity.[16] One consequence of committing to such a task is that by the late 1990s, the noun phrase "compassion fatigue" had "entered modern dictionaries such as *Chambers* and had become an example of late-twentieth century language innovation":[17] it describes the state engendered by overexposure to images of death, war, and famine – images that can no longer stimulate.[18] Wars are tragic, but not always tragic or aesthetic enough, and some journalists have been candid about their own efforts to return the aesthetic frisson or tension to a tableau of war in order to re-engage the audience.[19]

If the standard trope of the other in the media reports was their difference – as impoverished, silenced, and dead – then for the intellectuals who came or spoke of Bosnian citizens' plight, identification was the primary quality. Part of the responsibility of their engagement revolved around an imagined solidarity with the city of Sarajevo and its population, who so unflinchingly and with dignity bore the indignity of war. This sense of fraternity was a false identification and recognition, seeking as it did to collapse the image of the other into the image of the self.[20] Jean Baudrillard criticized this relationship:

> They [the Sarajevans] were not in need of compassion, they were in fact the ones to take pity on our dejected condition. "I spit on Europe," one of them was heard saying. No one indeed can be more free, more sovereign in a rightful contempt, directed not so much at the enemy than at those whose good conscience balks in the sun of so-called solidarity. And God knows that they have seen lines of those people pass by.[21]

Baudrillard's broader critique, in addition to attacking a global society that universalizes victims, makes the victims virtuous, and subsequently makes them into exemplary human beings, focuses on the political and democratic orders of Western Europe that, according to him, deny their own countries' inter-ethnic problems, but slowly institutionalize the type of ethnic violence evident in Bosnia.

Other writers, including Bernard-Henri Lévy, Juan Goytisolo, Peter Handke, and Alain Finkielkraut, demonstrated a particularly shrewd knowledge of the potential for mass media to expose or highlight their agenda. Most of the time, this meant their agenda at *home*. The social breakdown of Yugoslavia and the humanitarian crisis that came in its wake actually threw into relief domestic or national tensions elsewhere. The rush to support the cause of Bosnia in particular, Phil Hammond notes, "was animated by the desire to define what the West stood for."[22] Importantly, the disintegration of the Yugoslav union – as a historical juncture – was abstracted to illuminate the ethical core and standards of other historical junctures. This was the case with three German and Austrian writers characterized as "left-liberal, former '68ers,'" argues Karoline Von Oppen, who "were ultimately first and foremost concerned with the reactions of their own generation to this war and its significance to its most cherished ideals."[23] The escalating crisis was imagined both as a cipher for another country's domestic issues (multiculturalism, inter-ethnic relations) and a blank canvas of silent, mediated suffering to which any message could be ascribed.

The intellectuals themselves were undeniably visible, televised in action, propagating the further engagement of the media (as a mechanism for distributing the spectacle) and the political elites. In a poem by Bosnian writer Ferida Duraković, we read about Bernard-Henri Lévy:

> There came
> instead a Professor, Parisian in manner: *Mes enfants,*
> he began, and his fingers repeated: *Mes enfants, mes enfants, mes enfants,* in
> the middle of the Academy of Sciences grey heads thought
> only of his shirt, conspicuously white,
> *Mes enfants, Europe is dying here.* Then he arranged
> everything in a film, in picture, in large words, such as
> *histoire, Europe,* such as *responsabilité* and, of course,
> *les Bosniacs.*[24]

Duraković's depiction of Lévy – who is *only portrayed* as having uttered those words – stereotypes his figure (the shirt, "Parisian in manner") to the same degree he objectifies the Bosnian people. The political message is this: Lévy's "patronising" compassion is here ironically juxtaposed with what Damir Arsenijević calls "the continuation of normalcy in the state of exception," demonstrated by the "desire of the other ... for a clean, white shirt"[25] – the other that is consistently characterized by a mute victimhood of extremity. The poet's contrast of saviour/victims is also marked by the infantilizing appellation "*mes enfants*," a rhetorical embellishment (or affectation) that this fictional Lévy might have perceived as a closure of distance: he extends the possibility of a filial relationship between him and *les Bosniacs*. "*Mes enfants*," however, achieves none of that, as it is frankly insulting and ultimately distancing. The decision not to translate "Lévy's" words into Bosnian in the original poem underscores how Duraković's see the position of such foreign visitors: the intrusion of a foreign language echoes the broader cultural or political interpretation of "*les Bosniacs*" by European political and intellectual elites for their own purposes, and hypotheses, on history and multiculturalism. The ideological issues behind this and similar acts of engagement can be read as the work of liberal-capitalist societies that are attempting to argue for the collective struggle for human rights.

Susan Sontag's time in Sarajevo also offers an opportunity to consider what kind of victim can be identified with and what implications that has for the ethical foundations of intellectual engagement. Sontag staged Beckett's *Waiting for Godot* during the siege, working with local, emaciated actors in dire conditions. Defending the project as, in Sontag's terms, an "expression of human dignity," she argued that culture had become the only acceptable redress to tragedy because it refuses to speak the language of destruction. While expressly rejecting all media appearances (aside from one press conference) during her staging of *Waiting for Godot* in Sarajevo, Sontag wrote about the project in an essay that was published by the *New York Review of Books* that same year. Sontag's travels to Bosnia earned her a certain credibility in America – accolades that made academics shake with fear at their own "intellectual mediocrity," "idiocy," and unworldliness.[26] So Sontag's intervention becomes, intentionally or not, an opportunity to position herself within a moral corner of the American intellectual field. She justifies her involvement through the medium of theatre on the premise that Sarajevans were admirers of "serious culture" of which the siege had deprived them.[27] Her commentary following the performance betrays this (Eurocentric) elitism:

> What my production of *Godot* signifies to them ... is that this is a great European play and that they are members of European culture. For all their attachment to American popular culture, as intense here as anywhere else, it is the high culture of Europe that represents for them their ideal, their passport to a European identity.[28]

Requirements of civility and sophistication as criteria of humanity are coded into this expression of solidarity. The citizens of Sarajevo are saved because they are visible, and they are visible because they are civilized and posses all the qualities that diminish the distance between them and the nebulous West. Here Sontag's justification becomes indicative of a wider "urban bias" that was in evidence among other self-appointed humanitarian ambassadors.[29]

Celebrity activism underscores how the margin is colonized anew by the centre, even as the margin moves into a postmodern space of mediation as one of its many narratives and discourses. The marginal is appropriated with the consequence of consolidating the centre. The margins are reified as the space that cannot be anything other than the initial victim status that was attributed to it. Sontag and Lévy recognize that Sarajevans are the same as Europeans – connoisseurs and producers of culture – but then freeze the image of them as helpless victims of their own circumstances. Their gesture, like that of many others, cannot overcome the very thing they purport to break down. This type of rhetorical transformation eclipses the flourishing heterogeneous cultural life in Sarajevo that included the establishment of the popular Sarajevo Film Festival, magazines like *The Phantom of Liberty*, publication of poetry collections, journalism – and local theatre.[30]

The act of intellectual engagement, because of its visibility, tends to distract with its image and performance – over and above the content itself. I now turn to Semezdin Mehmedinović, who considers the implications of intellectual engagement within the writer's field of specialty, within the field that consecrated them, rather than with the act of commitment itself.

III.

In *Sarajevo blues*, Mehmedinović writes about an episode of literary notoriety involving the Russian writer Eduard Limonov: a moment that undermined an author's celebrity status as an outcome of their political action, resulting not in the loss of fame but the further fetishization of their personality – what Bourdieu calls "a negative sanction."[31] In 1992, Eduard Limonov, a Russian writer famous for his provocative anti-establishment commitments, made a visit to Sarajevo and was filmed, in the company of Radovan Karadžić, shooting at the city from the hill of Lapišnica, where a contingent of the Bosnian Serb army was stationed. The video footage was part of a documentary film titled *Serbian Epic* that has since been used as evidence in the trial against Karadžić at The Hague.[32] Limonov's actions estranged him from Western European literary circles and jeopardized his publishing contracts on the Continent.[33] In his micro-essay on Limonov, Mehmedinović pointedly does not interpret this moment through the symbolism of Orthodox fraternity and a glimpse into the Russian-Serbian political alliance. He sees it instead as a demonstration of Limonov's "literary consistency": this Russian author, celebrated for his explorations of underground, furtive life in autobiographical fiction, "aggrandizes the position of the outsider who possesses enviable physical strength and ... who is ready at every moment to prove it" and offers his support to the international scapegoat *du jour*, Serbia itself.[34] Clearly, Mehmedinović is ready to accept a straightforward interface between (authorial) action and text, and between political action and aesthetics, suggesting that literary value resides in external validation, predicated on social and political forces. The prominent Austrian writer Peter Handke found himself in a similar situation: perceived as a pro-Serbian sympathizer in the 1990s, his literary reputation suffered as a result of his association with the perpetrators of violence. The point here is not the question of political allegiances and loyalties, or whether someone is pro-Serb or pro-Croat, but rather the loss of authorial and literary distinction. Alongside the moral judgment that is passed on the authors' actions and ideological sympathies, moments like this bring into sharp focus the inability to socially support literature when it is marked by an author's discriminatory activities (even if this involves misreading their writing, or not reading it at all).

Thus, for Mehmedinović, the matter becomes clear-cut: this is not about the virtues of intellectual engagement but about the literature itself. When a writer strays beyond their field of production (artistic, literary) and manifests political views, their work is retroactively subject to a reappraisal on the basis (and popularity) of their actions. Whatever the literary work itself endorses is later read against current social values, political correctness, and public morality – and is then attached to the author. The relative autonomy of literature, whatever its devices, strategies, and techniques, is relatively dependent "with respect to the field of power."[35] This idea of the field of power must be understood in its multiplicity, since the reader deals with both the national and local arenas of power, but also the transnational or global. What interests me about this position, and Mehmedinović's attitude to Limonov, is that he himself asserts a claim to autonomy for his own work: in *Sarajevo blues*, as I argued in chapter 1, Mehmedinović argues for the possibility of an art divorced from moral considerations. Rather than give himself over to this current, his prose and poetry collection keeps the tension going between the social, communal sphere and the aesthetic topic. Nonetheless, he makes a political demand of others when he conceives of himself as a member of a community. In a sense, the demands of the public sphere cannot be satisfied by what satisfies the aesthetic field.

This anecdote confirms the renewed importance of authorship and its relationship to social mores. Mehmedinović does not go so far as to suggest we apply an ad hominen argument in attempting to evaluate the Limonov affair. Instead, he points to that gap between dominant theoretical constructions of authorship and the image of the author that is held in high regard by a community united by particular morals and values. That space contains, for Mehmedinović, human agency – something which the postmodern stress on intertextuality and verbal structures cut out. The agent of writing has returned as a figure of intellectual responsibility.

IV.

Political and social notoriety consolidated Ugrešić's own literary celebrity in the 1990s – or some might say that her political and social bravery against nationalist dogma thrust her into a successful and critically acclaimed career. This depends on whether she is perceived through the frame of an emerging Croatian literary culture (post-1991) or through the "international literary space" that consecrates authors on the basis of their affinity, promotion, and collusion with a select range of European intellectual values.[36] What I investigate in this section are the formal principles by which Ugrešić consolidates her writerly authority.

The sequence of events that thrust Ugrešić into public view in the early 1990s has been well documented, partly because the story involved the media itself, and partly because it has been central in the construction of Ugrešić's subsequent authorial persona and her presence in European literary circles. In an interview from 2007, she gives her own summary and impressions of the polemic events that led to her departure from Croatia:

> The publication of my first essay, titled "Clean Croatian Air," in a German newspaper, was sufficient for an attack on me to appear in a Croatian newspaper the very next day. The author of this article, a fellow writer, accused me of being insufficiently patriotic or "indifferent" to patriotism, of advocating "Yugoslavism," of an unpardonable anti-war stance, of ridiculing Croatian national symbols and Croatia's "thousand-year longing for national independence." … My colleagues at the Faculty of Art at Zagreb University, where I had been employed for 20 years, withdrew their support. Practically

overnight I became an "enemy of the people," "traitor," "suspicious character," a person of "suspicious background" – in one word, ostracized. The
speed at which I was being excommunicated was surreal.[37]

After being discredited locally, Ugrešić's writing in exile found a
positive reception from the international literary market: she became a
proponent of free speech and an authoritative commentator endorsed
by associations such as PEN. Her own literary celebrity seems to have
benefited greatly from the mechanisms of contemporary publishing,
including efficient promoters, timely endorsements, and her own public
appearances. In both the local and European context, the recent biographical events constructed a character of Ugrešić, a fictionalized persona that does not need to be accompanied by a reading of the work
itself; the hardships but also the romance of dissidence possess their own
narrative appeal. Plus, for a multicultural and secular Western Europe,
her politics were right: moulded as a feminist writer, committed to truth
seeking and challenging political and national orthodoxy comported
with general anti-ideological discourses. Her first essays, published in the
international press as early as 1991, were also in vogue across a continent
curious about life in the other Europe emerging from communism. In
sum, the reading public, both at home and abroad, took heed of this
personal dimension, of Ugrešić as a character.

Yet her essays partially solicit these readings: biography is a tempting
filter for her writing, especially encouraged by the more personal and
confessional aspects of the essay genre itself. Theorists of the essay frequently emphasize a distinction of the self as public and private that
come together in the essay to convey "a multistable impression of the
self ... in the process of thought and in the process of sharing thought
with others."[38] If one insists on the personal/public dichotomy, it brings
into the foreground other binaries that have consequences for the status and effect of the essay itself (such as subjective/objective, personal/
impersonal). The tendency towards the personal, which is the dominant
mark of Ugrešić's writing in *Culture of Lies*, is perceived as undermining
the authority of her utterances. However, on closer inspection, Ugrešić's
essayistic voice, no matter what representation of the personal she provides, actually employs rhetorical mechanisms of inscription that dep-
ersonalize her communication. That is to say, she demonstrates how
a personal discourse can enact the effects of (seemingly) impersonal
discourse by moulding its style. I argue that the narrative strategies of
Ugrešić's essays chip away at the image of her personal self, in order to

objectify their content and furthermore to undermine the claims made about her political betrayal. I posit that through this recourse to means of (essayistic) depersonalization, her essays refocus the attention on the author's use of citation, in turn revealing some quite traditional and surprising tendencies.

In particular, her mode of depersonalization draws on the generic proximity between the essay and its professional counterpart, the academic article: what Oraić Tolić calls the "scientification of poetry" but can be extended to include other types of literary creation.[39] It must be said that Ugrešić is not deeply interested in the development of an argument but in the rhetorical modes by which authority is implied, circulated, and extended. Citation is one such technique of embedding one's personal view within a community of established voices that conversely adds integrity, weight, and tradition to one's own line of argument.[40] While this is such a standard course of action in scholarship that it seems superfluous to even mention it, it is often neglected in interpretations of Ugrešić's essays. Her multiple references to esteemed Croatian writer Miroslav Krleža (1893–1981) throughout the essays in *Culture of Lies* demonstrate this efficiently.[41] Writing about her aversion to contemporary writers who employ "*spray* sentences" in public interviews to manifest their patriotism (there are no dissident writers in this country, says one prominent writer, "*because we're all in love with Croatia*"),[42] she undermines such posturing by evoking Krleža. In particular she quotes from a 1926 essay titled "O malograđanskoj ljubavi spram hrvatstva" ("On the Petty-Bourgeois Love of Croatianess"). By introducing the essay as "an unsurpassable and actual analysis of Croatian patriotism," her own critique becomes rooted in a historical current that bypasses her pro-Yugoslav politics by predating the period of the socialist republic altogether. That is, she needs not just Krleža but the idea of his context through which she can avoid the charges of her critique being a cry of nostalgia for a lost Utopia (socialist Yugoslavia): Krleža brings in a different era beset by the same problems.[43] In addition, while her evocation of Krleža is one of a writer of superior talent (his writing is "unsurpassable"), formally this type of intertextual relation is nonetheless predicated on equivalence insofar as Ugrešić's ideas (the content) converge with his: her own writing is thus to be seen as a direct inheritance of his ideas.[44] The assessment that echoes throughout the century is of Croatia's blind self-love that perceives itself as a cultured, civilized, and European country that has no relationship to the eastern provincialism of its neighbouring regions.

Of course, citation demands analysis beyond the placement of the individual quotation. The symbolism, the association (or identification) with the writer – or the distancing from the writer – are all involved when it comes to understanding the function of citation. As Ken Hyland notes, "citation plays … an important role in mediating the relationship between a writer's argument and his or her discourse community."[45] This dialogism between Ugrešić and esteemed authors and thinkers (Krleža, Nabokov, Kiš, György Konrád, and so on) doubles and then triples the extent of Ugrešić's themes, muffling her personal dynamic and amplifying the socio-historic resonance beyond *Culture of Lies.* But what is the quality amplified in this intertextuality? The map of literary affiliation drawn by Ugrešić is a map of a literary canon that is not necessarily counter-traditional or subversive. It is true that a constellation through East European sources is "a form of 'minor transnationalism'" that troubles the dominant blueprint of global literature based on "Western Eurocentric universalism."[46] Yet, followed in another direction, this gesture is not liberating or provocative. Instead, all Ugrešić can reanimate and extend is the cultural capital of already canonized male authors: precisely the qualities she sought to vitiate with her fiction in *Pose for Prose* and *Life Is a Fairy Tale,* which is why this oversight cannot go unmentioned in this instance.[47]

This returns me to a famous quotation often evoked by scholars when they want to argue for Ugrešić's unaligned, autonomous political perspective with a cosmopolitan orientation. Suspicious of collectivities and institutions, imposed values and identities of political and ideological movements (communist, feminist), Ugrešić has famously claimed literature as the single ethical refuge for her curious, itinerant mind: "I believed that a writer should have no homeland or nation or nationality, a writer must serve neither an Institution nor a Nation, neither God nor the Devil, a writer must have only one identity: his books, I thought, and only one homeland: Literature."[48] Free from external dogma, "Literature" emerges in her vision as the product of independent enquiry and reflection, even when beholden to forces of the market. What such a portrayal of "Literature" risks, especially when we read it against the intellectual sources that compose it in *Culture of Lies,* is the possibility of shading into a recognized canon. The canon here is not so much organized on national principles and borders but rather opens up to the authority of the male writer. Thus, while destroying one dominant thread of selfhood that relates a subject to the broader collective of the nation, she supports another dominant model – that of literary tradition. Crucial here is the awareness that tradition is determined through certain impersonal configurations and forces, and not Ugrešić's own immanent subjectivity, which is somehow unanchored and free from influence.

This rhetorical manoeuvring is disguised partly by the fragmented essay form she so keenly practices: the aggregation of discreet and episodic thoughts never solidifies into a progressive, considered argument. Discontinuity is at once indicative of a broader freedom from systematic constraints, but also of fragmentation from context, field of references, and background. Both strains are crucial to Ugrešić's essays. A book like *Culture of Lies*, notes Ugrešić, "does not have a proper ending."[49] She imposes "an arbitrary end" to the collection, but a similar enforced closure is at play in the essays. The essays, in addition to the thesis or central idea that causes their constitutive parts to splinter into sections, are fragments of the broader historical narrative on which they comment. They play the part of the footnote, "a writer's gesture of self-defense, [that] turns into an exhausting race in which the runner never reaches his goal ... Each footnote is turned into a layered metaphor of literary and human defeat. Everything that this author has written is but a footnote to the long lists of people who have lost their lives, their loved ones, their homes or their country."[50]

Yet while the fragment does refuse totality, Ugrešić's transgression of certain ideals and values consolidates others: she might reject national mythologizing of the Croatian literary canon, but her embrace of the more metaphoric aspects of exile – and with it a community of transnational writers – reinforces the authority of Edward Said, Joseph Brodsky, Breyten Breytenbach, and Vladimir Nabokov, among others. (On this theme, it is worth pointing out that her appropriation neutralizes their politics of exile in order to favour the more metaphysical reflections their writing puts forward. This is problematic for a figure like Edward Said, whose reflections on literature cannot be divorced from the postcolonial project.) In rejecting the perspectives of nationalist politicians-writers, she reinforces Krleža and Kiš. This transforms intertextuality into a practice that achieves precisely the opposite to some of its original claims; it is a strategy that reawakens suppositions it had sought to discard. That is to say, intertextuality is presumed to decentre the authorial subject, the site of enunciation, by pointing to other utterances from which the "I" derives its authority. Yet in this function – whereby the accumulated social capital of Krleža, or Kiš, or Edward Said is transferred onto Ugrešić's writing – the stature of the author figure is affirmed. After all, for Ugrešić's citation to make an impact on the broader field (the reader, the collective), the concept of the author must still hold an unchallenged, unreconstructed status in the cultural field, otherwise we could dismiss her dependency on the heritage of these authors. This intertextuality bestows on them attributes typically offered to consecrated, deified figures of a cultural sphere.

V.

There are very few attempts to understand the socially and culturally specific circumstances in which Albahari's authorship operates. His name brings up connotations of a non-politicized, disengaged biography, and the more institutional aspects of his professional life as a writer tend to get overlooked. However, Albahari has led a life of letters with membership in literary institutions including Serbian PEN – where he often argued against censorship measures undertaken by the Yugoslav government – and the Serbian Academy of Science and Art (SANU).[51] He participated in literary institutional life when membership of such organizations took on a politically sensitive dimension. The most illustrative case of this took place in 1993 when Albahari travelled to Santiago de Compostela as part of the Serbian PEN delegation that was attending the organization's world congress. Together with writer Vida Ognjenović, Albahari was tasked with defending the existence of Serbian PEN after demands were made by the Slovenian contingent to disband this particular branch. Serbian writers, at that time, were perceived by some PEN factions (Predrag Palavestra notes the objections of Croatian, Slovenian, Bosnian, Esperanto [*sic*], Scottish, and English delegates) as nationalist propagandists, instrumental to the government's machinations.[52] Albahari himself has not written on these activities – there are no accounts yet relating his experiences of representing Serbia as a writer who is both Jewish (an ethnoreligious minority) and Serbian. What we can glean from his presence there, and his years-long involvement with PEN, is the commitment to the public defence of literature that takes place on a national platform. It is a platform that connects him to a collective, to a literary field in which his own distinct poetic voice gets absorbed into a broader matrix.

Since the war, and despite his residence in Canada, Albahari has continued to move towards the centre of Serbian literary life, a journey that peaked with his 2006 membership in SANU. This is an institution that has had, since the 1980s, a complicated and at times problematic reputation. The leading centre of its kind in Serbia, it is infamously affiliated with a memorandum released by its members in 1986 describing eth-nonationalist ideas that numerous observers perceived instrumental in abetting the populist politics of Milošević's government.[53] SANU's legacy and standing in Serbian society is still troubling for a new generation of young critics who perceive it as an institution that embodies the contact zone between intellectual production and politics. The year that Albahari was initiated into the academy, *Beton* (*Concrete*) – a left-leaning cultural and literary magazine – wrote a satirical article congratulating the new members:

> It is important that you are orthodox, that you don't write anti-Serbian books in which you muddy the heavenly people. You are not a common, poor scribe, you are the pagan priest of goddess Nation that was born in the blood of ethnically unfit blood groups. If you listen to my well-intentioned advice, you could publish, of all things, an atlas, or a microbiology textbook, and if you put a genre marker saying *novel,* the NIN book prize will be yours.[54]

The mocking and prickly rhetoric characterizes SANU as a reactionary and conservative presence on the culture scene that propagates and further reproduces unexamined but readily acceptable values about the nation. While SANU is not the sole organ that arbitrates on cultural matters in Serbia, its role seems symptomatic of a broader problem that has beset the practice of literary criticism. Primarily, as Boško Tomašević suggests, it works on the principles of neo-Zhdanovism with its own ideo-logical code that favours a select grouping of Serbian authors (at the exclusion of others) onto whom it bestows elitist values. Albahari, with his long list of prizes, is listed among those who are favoured in such a set-up.[55] The intellectual distinction of these writers is not celebrated, adds Tomašević, but *fetishized* by the officious body.[56] However, it is not just the fetish of a work of art that should be emphasized here but also the idea of value that is produced, as Bourdieu argues, not by the artist but "the field of production as a universe of belief which produces the value of the work of art as a fetish *by producing the belief in the creative power of the artist.*"[57] This circuitous process of validation is crucial in the sub-sequent discussion of Albahari's authorship and his own ideas of how it should be practised.

I bring up this aspect of Albahari's public signature not because I wish to offer a revisionist history of his public identity; nor to pass judgment on his activities; nor to suggest some sort of latent nationalism on his part; nor (finally) to invalidate his fictional writing. Instead, I am curious about the notion that his own ideal of authorship, most strongly articulated in his essays, is at odds with the circulation of his own authorial identity in the Serbian literary milieu – a fact that has been little remarked upon. I am particularly interested in the significance of the space that arises between the concept and the practice of authorship, and, subsequently, what this dynamic communicates about Albahari's own status in Serbian letters.[58]

Rewriting the World, his first collection of essays, is interesting in this regard because it marks the appearance of a narrative voice of the living author who becomes the repository for the social, political, and ethical turmoil experienced by the man himself.[59] That author appears in various guises through references to his Yugoslav citizenship, his presidency of the Federation of Jewish Communities of Yugoslavia (at that time headquartered in Belgrade), and his practice of Jewish rituals. This figure is tasked with the burden of embodying the historical caesura of a disintegrating federal state. Albahari also appears as a father, as a friend, as a guest on a radio show, and as a reader (to name a few of his roles). At times, he circulates as a figure who offers self-commentaries, interpretations of his own literary positions, exegeses on literary form, and so on. The essays keep in play a tension between two categories of the writer as a creative self and a social self in order to privilege the former.

All manifestations and descriptions of Albahari, in these essays, are part of the author function, in Foucault's meaning of the term, that refers to "a projection, in more or less psychologizing terms, of the operations that we force texts to undergo, the connections that we make, the traits that we establish as pertinent, the continuities that we recognize, or the exclusions that we practice."[60] The figure of the author function is an apparition of a composite, made up of all the qualities associated with the proper noun "David Albahari" that accompanies his short stories, novels, interviews, public speeches, and so on. In this interplay, the essays promote a circuitry of appearances within which the living author is a construct who is eventually absorbed into the author function, but this author function is external to Albahari's text, and therefore thrust into further existence and circulation (such as in this very chapter).

What is intriguing about the *Rewriting the World* as a collection is that it presents, among other topics, the author's reasons for staying outside the clamour of intellectual engagement. The essay collection cultivates an impression of Albahari's courtship of silence as an ethical gesture in a milieu characterized by a heavily ideologized culture. His fictional work, by contrast, explores the principles of silence as a linguistic-ontological paradigm: it is marked by formal and narrative atomization leading to fewer and fewer words; death; namelessness and anonymity; speechlessness; emptiness; and the proliferation of speech to justify recourse to silence. "The true thought," writes Albahari, "lies outside [form]: in the inexpressible, inexplicable, uncommunicable."[61] Silence more often than not stems from a crisis of language and its hopelessness in offering meaning that has not been worn down by conventional use. As with all writers, there is the suspension of words between sentences, where the reading is directed by punctuation and controlled pauses. To a degree, this is a writing style predicated on "an administration of linguistic shocks,"[62] through which Albahari attempts to return power to literary language by threatening to dispense with language altogether. It is the prospect of Albahari's extreme reduction that is more disruptive than the actual silence itself.

Conversely, the essays extract silence as an immanent presence in linguistic communication and transform it into his chosen interface for the encounter with the social dynamics (and dimension) of literature. He writes: "I choose silence because I don't believe in social engagement of the artist, nor in the duty and the ability of art to give answers to social questions."[63] In line with this rigid divorce between the world of literature and social mechanisms (of his milieu), his essays project degrees of disdain for the circuit of literary institutions, establishments, and pageantry; for didactic, moralizing storytelling (storytelling as mythmaking), programmed literary writing of socialist Yugoslavia. To be sure, he rejects dissidence as an equally frustrating and pointless mode of authorship: the objections of "internal dissidents" to socialist authority were only articulated from the platform of another trap: nationalist ideology.[64] All associations with the public dissemination of an author's image are negatively portrayed, leaving behind an impression of writing as a practice that should take place beyond the pettiness and regulations of everyday life. As he states in an interview in 1992, writers are "humanists, people who understand the human heart."[65]

His attitude towards the politicization of language further underscores this. In one sense, his negative view of politicized language is comparable to Ugrešić's apprehension and disgust as expressed in *Culture of Lies*. However, unlike her rhetorical unpicking of conventional, clichéd nationalist phrases through which meaning is undone and deflated, Albahari refuses to engage with social texts in this manner or bring them into his own writing. While Ugrešić's essays demonstrate the rhetorical range of this conventionalized language, in Albahari's work it is alluded to as uniform, degraded content: "the language of politics is the language of powerlessness, language of poverty, and uniformity."[66] By contrast, artistic expression possesses "power ... abundance, and richness"[67] – all of which it risks losing in its transformation into political art.

Essentially, Albahari constructs a social distance (absent from Mehmedinović's and Ugrešić's work) between the literary, public persona of David Albahari (the author of cerebral, conceptually led fiction) and his own private life that he refers to at one point as the life of "a citizen."[68] (The essayistic writing in no way embodies that distance: the style possesses a surprising transparency and clarity; there are no twists or turns of language; no repetitions, no evasions.) When he "participates in reality" Albahari is a citizen, but when he is a citizen, he cannot (or at the very least, he *should not*) be a writer.[69] It is on the grounds of this separation that he makes his claim "I am, as a writer, totally indifferent to our reality."[70] Thus privacy and anonymity of the author, as surrogates for silence, represent ideals for a model of authorship that seeks to deflect social engagement. Thomas Pynchon is admired by Albahari on the grounds that his long-standing "disappearance from public life" signifies a veritable "death of the author."[71] The lesson of this anecdote is crucial: the seclusion ("death") of this American author and his overt resistance to the machinery of literary promotion is a withdrawal that has only increased his standing, intrigue, and value – maybe even his aura. An important element of this idea is that the "death of the author" does not deface the author but adds to his or her individual currency. There is symbolic capital in receding from the public. Albahari has grasped this lesson by using Pynchon as a foil for his own authorial signature: "[When a writer] participates in reality, which most of us do, the writer contributes – as I am doing now – to an inflation of meaning and possibilities. Language becomes declarative, authoritative."[72] The effect of the Pynchon anecdote is that Albahari's critique of the public appearance of an author becomes a platform for the valorization of his own position: even if he cannot perform a high level of anonymity, his self-consciousness contributes to that deficiency.

I take these statements from the essays as elements that constitute the paragon, in Albahari's own chosen vocabulary, of authorship. In sum, he privileges a cluster of features the principal of which is autonomy (from the state, from pressure, from dogma, from literary machinations, from institutions). Autonomy safeguards the act of creation and preserves the writer's capacities and energies for the production of "pure" and intellectually honest material. At the same time, however, the detachment from various systems and institutions can be transformed into a value to be leveraged, if need be, as a site from which disinterested critique can emanate. That is to say, (public) silence provides a model of authorship that transcends social reality both in the sense that it can rise above its conditions and that it can judge and pass comment on that social reality from a position of unaffiliated subjectivity.

What is valorized in Albahari's vision closely resembles the beliefs that proliferate in the field of cultural production about the "creative power of the artist": it is a figure validated not immanently but by external configurations that Bourdieu calls "the entire set of social mechanisms which make possible the figure of the artist as producer of that fetish which is the work of art."[73] Thus, when Albahari says, "I cannot completely renounce my authorial persona," this persona is a construct, already circulating as a reified model of values that are privileged by elite discourses.[74] By extension, Albahari's essays reproduce "the belief in the value of art – and in that power to create value which belongs to the artist."[75] I am arguing that Albahari invests in a paradigm of authorship that feeds off certain cultural myths that further compliment his own aesthetic production, that endow his fiction with the appropriate signifier of difficulty and intellectual accomplishment. If anything, he supports the literary field as it is.

For Tatjana Rosić, however, the literary field *as it is* is the actual problem in Serbia: an establishment that has nullified the radical potential of postmodernism by bestowing upon it a cachet of its own.[76] Albahari cannot help but collude with processes of authorial consecration but, as I have shown here, that goes beyond institutional membership and receiving literary prizes. More illuminating are Albahari's own attempts to justify and square his ideals vis-à-vis cultural and historical visions of authors; though interestingly, it is clear that much of what his fiction postulates has no bearing on his understanding of authorship as laid out in his essays. It seems that very few of his literary experiments are transferred onto the arena of authorial practice. If anything, the distinction he enforces onto author identity – the self who writes, and the self who exists socially as a writer – keeps the idea of the mystery of writing going.

VI.

Solipsism, ideological betrayal, complicity with the media or institutions – these are all the risks that writers run in stepping outside of the purview of literature. There seems to be an impasse between two genres of writing: what is championed in literary discourse cannot hold for writing that bleeds into the factual, socially relevant territory. This is very much the case for Mehmedinović, who self-consciously aestheticizes war but is also mindful of the implications of this type of enjoyment – a kind that might appear callous and unethical.

Yet even those who seek to distance themselves from the social arena are moving into a space of autonomy that is sanctioned by social processes since a writer can never fully deny him or herself the connection to a literary field. That is to say, even the most broadly conceived idea of a writer as humanistically minded – with appeals to the universalism of the human condition – upholds certain traditions rather than some innate, innermost quality of writers themselves. The question that then arises is whether individual writers problematize or challenge the establishment within which their authorial signature circulates. This is not so much the case with Albahari; in fact, one could claim that he fronts a particular type of postmodern poetic fetishized by the Serbian literary establishment. Ugrešić, on the other hand, seemingly destabilizes all sorts of collective categories, including national and political, but a closer look at her aesthetic practice reveals her dependence on a rather established literary tradition.[77] What is at stake in these discussions, particularly with Ugrešić, who is fashioned more and more frequently as a subaltern, transnational intellectual, is whether they write from these liberated, anti-elitist positions (from the position of subalterity, for instance), or whether they just write of them.[78]

Conclusion

This study does not follow the historical developments after 1995. Even after the Dayton Peace Agreements had been signed and after hostilities in Bosnia had ceased, the long decade of the war in Kosovo and the NATO bombing of Serbia was still in the future. The work of transitional justice was yet to come, as were the years of poverty, confusion, and repression, but also the implementation of neoliberal capitalist practices across the countries of the former Yugoslavia. Yet I pause at this particular year in order to capture the moment of living in history without the knowledge of new rules, new laws, new governances, and new narratives. The voices of the authors examined in my study are animated by the crumbling state of their environment, but they have no perspective from which to consolidate the narrative of what has come to pass. This precariousness has receded over the years as writers have, like other commentators, incorporated and responded to post-war and post-communist divisions.

A generational divide is already palpable. Younger writers – those who were on the cusp of adulthood at the beginning of the war – already form the literary establishment across the former Yugoslav territories though some are based overseas (including Miljenko Jergović, Aleksandar Hemon, Vladimir Arsenijević, Saša Ilić, Faruk Šehić, and Adisa Bašić to name a few). This shift is occasionally matched by the passage into war of ever younger and younger protagonists in their writing, from the adolescent to the child who possesses residual and spectral memories of socialist Yugoslavia.[1] That the wars will continue to mould established poetics and literary phenomena is beyond doubt: a new literary genre can been identified, for example, with the recent spate of plays, novels, poetry, and memoirs that broach the Srebrenica genocide. Interestingly, it is a genre that shares much with the testimonial literature of the Holocaust both in its formal tendencies and meta-literary questions that revolve around the moral weight of representing such a singular experience.[2] Broadly speaking, any future cultural output will be intensely informed by external values, circumstances, and conditions since it will internalize – but also challenge and demystify – whatever societal beliefs, historical interpretations, and political appropriations gain traction in the public sphere.[3]

The work examined in my study straddles a temporal border between the temporality of a federated union of republics and that of sovereign nation states that was sharply thrown into relief by the destructive waging of war. However, this time of insecurity – the parentheses of war – reveals literature as the foothold on which the crisis is endured, even if it endured in pain, in indignation, and in defeat. Multiple, simultaneous processes in the field of literary studies and artistic creation inform this period of Yugoslavia's dissolution. The decline of and suspicion towards postmodern practices took place at the same time that the literature received critical approval, when the postmodern poetic became institutionalized as part of the Serbian, or Croatian, or Bosnian sequence of literary history. Something similar happens with the writing itself. The prose and poetry of the three authors is fully self-revelatory and demystifying about postmodern poetics *and* strategies of social cohesion (various ethnonationalisms, narratives of justifying war). Plaguing this critical, questioning discourse is the consolidation of their work as part of canons that are deaf to the messages of the texts themselves: patriarchal, masculinist, or ethnonational structures become the filters for the reception and dissemination of these texts. By aligning Mehmedinović with Ugrešić and Albahari in one study, I have overcome this type of essentializing but without holding up the postmodern aesthetic practice as the correct, uncompromised thread that binds. After all, the development of postmodernist poetics can itself become an overarching narrative that suits the demands of the local literary field. Rather, by focusing on the ethical implications of their aesthetic experiments, I foregrounded the political blind spots residing within a certain type of postmodern poetics, particularly in the intersection between linguistic structures and the referent (of war, destruction, trauma). The unarticulated ideologies of postmodernism were acutely important to address on a literary level given that, as Terry Eagleton writes, "political interests ... govern cultural ones."[4] Since cultural mechanisms mitigate the political message by offering aesthetics or affect as a hook, they make the investment in political ideology possible. In this way, forms and genres compound their own erosion of autonomy.

The literary texts that I have examined are organisms that metabolize this problem – the problem of culture and its relation to forms of power – and discover, in the process, that their means of metabolizing are insufficient (as tools of critique, opposition, integrity). This manoeuvring takes us back to the quotation from Danilo Kiš at the opening of this book: literary form is a discovery of a new level of reality previously unknown but, in the production of the text, other issues arise along the way. (Issues that complicate the telling, for instance.) If the writers of this study abandon anything perceived as essential to the postmodern trope, it is the renunciation of history and a particular ironic reflexivity towards mass culture.

This book opened with a chapter that situated literary practices of the late and post-socialist Yugoslav contexts within international postmodern currents. Here I will consider briefly what other implications of the postmodern are at play in this contemporary but marginalized literature. I want to signal towards the possibilities of understanding this writing within a more global configuration. Mehmedinović, Ugrešić, and Albahari produce literary works that speak about what Debjani Ganguly calls the new "geopolitical deathworlds": this includes places as diverse as Bosnia, Kosovo, Palestine, and Rwanda, among others.[5] Specific to such literature, argues Ganguly, is "the intersection of post-1989 geographies of violence, hyperconnectivity through advances in information technology and the emergence of a new humanitarian sensibility in the context where suffering has a presence in everyday life through the immediacy of digital images."[6] Her own focus is on how the politics of pity and suffering in the anglophone novel are narratively and ethically manifest in a globalized world of terror and genocide. The nature of her literary selection, which includes popular and even some bestselling novels, pins her to an examination of the centre that commodifies local, lived experiences of war and trauma. Examining the marginal and the distant is not possible through those novels, but a discussion about the relationship between those spaces cannot be overlooked, particularly because the local experience of extremity is flouted as a universalizing trope.

The local experiences are included as part of the global circulation of "deathworlds." This movement is framed as a "trauma economy" by Terri Tomsky since "local traumas are turned into mainstream news and then circulated for consumption."[7] In the contemporary context of these global media practices, trauma must be read as "overdetermined by capitalism."[8] However, Tomsky underscores that the trauma economy can function as positive practice: she demonstrates how a graphic novel by Maltese-American journalist Joe Sacco "highlight[s] this mediation" and "explicitly challenges the politics that make invisible the maneuvers of capitalist and neo-imperial practices."[9] Despite the institutional inequality that arises in this flow of information, Tomsky posits that despite the overwhelming commodification of local experiences, self-reflexive means of representation (such as Sacco's work) give rise to "unexpected if transient solidarities across cultures."[10] The salient point here is that the trauma economy, in Tomsky's definition, is not just another road towards the expression of moral outrage. It can have a constructive role in intercultural and transnational media (as well as artistic dialogues), but only on the condition that we recognize its instrumentalities of power.

While this argument is successful in renegotiating trauma as a zone of inclusion, rather than exclusion, its application in the context of my study is limited. Given the inequalities in the circulation of literature, a text like *Sarajevo blues* cannot break through into the trauma economy even though it is a text of critical and acutely penetrating perspectives (as much as Sacco's). If a text and author receive recognition in the dominant literary market, then the type of trans-solidarity Tomsky speaks of can take place. But relations between peripheral and central literary industries have not changed, thereby disadvantaging writers who cannot enter into processes determined by capitalism. Even Ugrešić (as I discussed in the final chapter), who has notable literary authority in the European literary space, finds her writing conditioned by demands of the market, as well as other factors of prestige, status, and trends.

This type of inequality is relevant not just for the discussion of trauma but implicates this book's discussion of postmodernism. As I highlighted in the opening chapters of this study, the appearance of aesthetic postmodernism in Yugoslavia across the arts was coeval with its Western counterparts – in both high and low art forms, in art and literature. However, the cultural production of late-socialist Yugoslavia is hardly ever brought into a comparative frame with these analogues. While my study focused on the consequences that the migration of postmodern theory holds for the local environment and how this is modified by the arrival of war, the reverse research agenda should be undertaken. Namely, these writers must be read as agents of what constitutes postmodern aesthetics and not solely as postmodernism's alternative practitioners (Balkan, East European, lagging). When Mehmedinović asks in a poem about Sarajevo during the siege – "What was Jeff Koons thinking/glorifying the value of kitsch?" – there must a situation in which he is heard asking that question as an equal – and not as a vulnerable, defensive author. In much the same way, the theoretical complexity with which Ugrešić and Albahari imbue their prose, particularly when it comes to discursive strategies and self-reflexivity, should contribute towards understanding and defining the global postmodern aesthetic. This type of research would challenge the reification of the margins and contribute to the central claims of postmodernism – from decentring to decanonization.

Notes

Introduction

1 Mehmedinović, "Izbaviteljska gesta poezije," 31. All translations in this book are my own unless otherwise indicated.

2 Norris, *Writing War in the Twentieth Century*, 99. Original emphasis.

3 By ideological values of socialism, I am referring to both the positive and negative practices in Yugoslavia between 1945 and 1991. The Yugoslav system sought to provide, on the one hand, full social security (from health care and free education to apartments and pensions) as well as full employment. It was also a state that promoted brotherhood and unity: the equality of all peoples in Yugoslavia. The values were an important part of the state's founding narrative and existence even though their implementation was uneven from republic to republic. On the other hand, many were critical of the abuses of power made possible in the context of a single-party state and the repressive measures often meted out to those who held contrary sociopolitical convictions.

4 For more on how socialist experiences were framed and interpreted – as well as how they informed post-socialist societies – see Katherine Verdery, *What Was Socialism and What Comes Next?* (Princeton, NJ: Princeton University Press, 1996). On Bosnia and Herzegovina specifically, see Andrew Gilbert, "The Past in Parenthesis: (Non)post-socialism in post-war Bosnia-Herzegovina," *Anthropology Today* 22, no. 4 (August 2006): 14–18.

5 Kiš, "Ne usuđujem se da izmišljam," in *Homo poeticus*, 199.

6 Vogler, "Poetic Witness," 180, 203.

7 Rothberg, *Traumatic Realism*, 8.

8 Ibid., 104.

9 Ibid., 2.

10 Ibid., 15.

11 Peréz-Torres, "Nomads and Migrants," 163.

12 Rothberg, *Traumatic Realism*, 96.

13 Ibid., 182.

14 See Maria Todorova, *Imagining the Balkans* (Oxford: Oxford University Press, 1997).

15 Victimhood has been traditionally constructed as a space of no agency, in order that the victim might not be implicated in the violence that they experience.

16 Rothberg, *Traumatic Realism*, 13.

17 This discussion is more extensively covered in chapter 2.

18 "Populist literature," writes Mirko Đorđević, refers to a work that "is accepted as some sort of program or sum of national interests." Furthermore, such literature is easily put in the "service of goals that are not immanent to literature." Dobrica Ćosić's multi-volume *Vreme smrti* (*Time of Death*) and Danko Popović's *Knjiga o Milutinu* (*The Book of Milutin*) can be considered representative of the main elements of populist literature – namely, as fiction that fulfils political desires. See Đorđević, "Književnost populističkog talasa," 438 and 434. For a consideration of Ćosić and Popović, especially the political and historical motivations manifest in their fiction, see Nikola Bertolino, "Vreme inkubacije," 87–115.

19 The postmodern and the populist were not the only literary currents of this period but they were both domains that were gaining ground.

20 Mehmedinović, *Sarajevo blues*, 89. This edition contains material from Mehmedinović's earlier poetry collection.

21 Erjavec, "Introduction," in *Postmodernism and the Postsocialist Condition*, 26.

22 Miško Šuvaković, "Art as a Political Machine: Fragments on the Late Socialist and Postsocialist Art of Mitteleuropa and the Balkans," in Erjavec, *Postmodernism and the Postsocialist Condition*, 94.

23 For two very different readings, see Jakovljević, "Human Resources," 38–53, and Oraić Tolić, *Paradigme dvadesetog stoljeća*. For Jakovljević, the 1968 student protests represent a lost moment that, had it not been for the official government response, had the potential to reconfigure the leftist positions of Yugoslav socialism. The suppression of this fledgling revolt, he argues, would reverberate right through to the 1990s. By contrast, Oraić Tolić also sees in 1968 a significant historical moment but she ignores the student protests altogether to focus on the Prague Spring that, to her, had its analogue in the Croatia Spring a few years later (1971). The year 1968 thus represents for her the beginning of separation of national cultures from the Yugoslav union, rather than a chance to revivify the concept of revolutionary Marxism, as the student protests had sought to do.

24 Tatjana Aleksić writes, "Directed against undesirable social tendencies, the Belgrade student protests were Marxist in essence and did not envision a change of the Yugoslav political system. Quite the opposite, the New Left insisted on socialism, but on so-called socialism with a human face, without social stratifications and fractional nationalisms." Aleksić, *The Sacrificed Body*, 126.

25 Participants of Croatian spring, including Croatia's future president Franjo Tuđman, faced dire consequences for their activities related to this movement, including loss of professional positions. Others who faced equally punitive measures for expressing national interests include Bosnia's former president Alija Izetbegović, who was imprisoned in the 1980s for allegedly inciting Islamic nationalism. Izbetbegović wrote about this experience in *Moj bijeg u slobodu: Bilješke iz zatvora 1983–1988* (Sarajevo: Svjetlost, 1999).

26 Enver Kazaz, "Mehmedinovićeva mistika emocija," 218.

27 Mehmedinović, *Sarajevo blues*, 91.

28 Erjavec, "Introduction," 4. This argument is heavily influenced by Mikhail Epstein's work *After the Future: The Paradoxes of Postmodernism and Contemporary Russian Culture*. Translated by Anesa Miller-Pogacar (Amherst: University of Massachusetts Press, 1995.)

29 Ibid., 25.

30 Ahmetagić, "Fantom postmoderne," 17.

31 Bošković, *Zablude modernizma*, 146.

32 Albahari, *David Albahari*, 210.

33 McLoughlin, *Authoring War*, 112.

34 A good analogy for this idea are the numerous photographs that were taken of civilians running across Sniper Valley in Sarajevo. Photographers captured them at the moment of their flight, a flight that remains frozen on the image. This singular moment does not reveal the moment after and thus captures an evocative melancholy as their future, so precarious, remains outside the frame and beyond the viewer's knowledge.

35 Crnković's recent publication *Post Yugoslav Film and Literature* is a rare example of a transnational, post-Yugoslav study that delves into pre-war fiction. Most academic approaches focus on a single national literature. See, for instance, Strahimir Primorac, *Linija razdvajanja: Hrvatska proza o ratu i njegovim posljedicama 1990–2010* (Zagreb: Naklada Ljevak, 2012); Enver Kazaz, *Bošnjački roman XX vijeka* (Sarajevo: Naklada Zoro, 2004); David Norris, *Haunted Serbia: Representations of History and War in the Literary Imagination* (Oxford: Legenda, 2016); Silvija Novak Bajcar, *Mape vremena: Srpska postmodernistička proza pred izazovima epohe*, trans. Ljubica Rosić (Belgrade: Službeni glasnik, 2015).

36 By emphasizing this tendency towards more "isolationist" practice of literary studies, predicated on national literature, I do not want to diminish recent and welcome conversations about the meaning, possibility, and significance of comparison between South Slavic literatures. The most extensive discussion on this theme took place on the pages of the journal *Sarajevske sveske* in 2011 (in two special issues) and has, more recently been extended by Tihomir Brajović in *Komparativni identiteti*. Though too diverse to summarize adequately here, many of the articles in *Sarajevske sveske* call for a re-examination of literary culture during the existence of Yugoslavia (as well as the post-Yugoslav period) but interrogate also the means by which comparison is undertaken and what the premise for such studies might be. See *Sarajevske Sveske*, nos. 32/33, "Interkulturno-poredbeno izučavanje književnosti," June 2011. Also, Brajović, *Komparativni identiteti*. It should be noted that Zvonko Kovač, a scholar of South Slavic literature at the University of Zagreb, initiated this discussion with his book *Poredbena i/ili interkulturna povijest književnosti* published in 2001 (Zagreb: Hrvatsko filološko društvo, 2001). It is this text that helped Kazaz and Brajović develop their own work.

37 See Rem, *Slavonsko ratno pismo*.

38 Kazaz, "Prizori uhodanog užasa," 137–65.

39 Ibid., 137.

40 Ibid., 139.

41 Sokolović, "Susret sa odgođenim krajem dvadesetog vijeka," 164.

42 Ibid., 154 and 161.

43 Moranjak-Bamburać, "Signature smrti i etičnost ženskog pisma," 115.

44 Moranjak-Bamburać notes that in an influential anthology of Bosnian and Herzegovinian literature (published in 1998), only a handful of female writers are recognized as worthy of inclusion in the national literary canon. This is indicative of a broader problem where women's writing often gets analysed through the prism of "universal," namely, male, values and thereby relegated to a secondary literary position. Ibid., 115–16.

45 Moranjak-Bamburać, "Ima li rata u ratnom pismu?" 81.

46 Ugrešić, *Kultura laži*, 137.

47 Albahari, "Balkan: književnost i istorija," in *Teret:eseji*, 7.

48 I chose to focus on Albahari's *Götz and Meyer* instead of his 1996 novel *Bait* [*Mamac*], which would be the more predictable choice on the subject of history and the dissolution of Yugoslavia. The reason for this is that *Götz and Meyer*, in my reading, emerges as a novel where an aesthetic struggle over language and its relationship to history and reality is more explicitly waged than in the earlier novels of the 1990s. I explain this position in more detail in chapter 4.

1 War, Postmodernism, and Literary Immanence

1 Pavičić, "Prošlo je vrijeme Sumatra i Javi," 126.
2 Denegri, "Inside or Outside 'Socialist Modernism'?" 171. A caveat about literary history: in this book, I will not cover the formal and informal literary networks that existed during socialist Yugoslavia. Though the practice of literary criticism would reveal insightful information about various relationships and dynamics (state, academia, authors), the primary focus for this study is on war writing.
3 This chapter does not give a full account of intellectual history of this period but foregrounds the main developments that are relevant for my argument. I also rely exclusively on published material – journal articles and books – which do not always reveal the conditions and influence of the environment in which they were produced.
4 Buck Morss, *Dreamworld and Catastrophe*, 232.
5 For an overview of the theoretical discussions surrounding the term, see Perry Anderson, *The Origins of Postmodernity* (London: Verso, 1998).
6 See Callinicos, *Against Postmodernism: A Marxist Critique* (Cambridge: Polity Press, 1989).
7 Eagleton, "Capitalism, Modernism, Postmodernism," 61, 62. My preference for Eagleton and Jameson on this point is informed by the fact they were the first to attempt a theoretical and historical periodization of the term. Linda Hutcheon, in contrast, does not offer a periodization of the term's evolution.
8 Radhakrishnan, *Theory in an Uneven World*, 4 and x.
9 Erjavec, "Introduction," *Postmodernism and the Postsocialist Condition*, 24.
10 Jameson, *Postmodernism*, 9, 12.
11 Jameson, "Regarding Postmodernism," 4.
12 Visković, *Umijeće pripovijedanja*, 144.
13 Flaker, *Proza u trapericama*, 318.
14 Here I am speaking about my sample of authors and their particular generations of prose writers. This statement does not account for other artforms (conceptual or performance art, cinema, music) that were contemporaneous to this literary fiction nor to more explicitly subcultural movements, such as punk or new wave, of the 1980s. It is impossible to account for the complexity of the bourgeoning Yugoslav cultural landscape during late socialism and, as such, the statements I make pertain to a select literary grouping. They do not function in a diagnostic and generalizing manner that accounts for all strains and variants of cultural production, especially since I do not tackle the visual arts nor the youth movements

that emerged in the last decade of socialist Yugoslavia and that, in Tatjana Aleksić's words, function as the redirection of countercultural movements of the 1960s with their concern for "the total idea of the liberation of the human subject." From Aleksić, *The Sacrificed Body*, 192.

15 Silvija Novak Bajcar argues that this "formal liberalism" was also a characteristic of high modernism in Serbian literature (her case study) and that it continued through to the early years of postmodernism. See Novak Bajcar, *Mape vremena*, 38.

16 Jelčić, *Povijest hrvatske književnosti*, 356.

17 Ibid.

18 Visković, *Mlada proza*, 12.

19 Slapšak, "Šta si radio u ratu, sine?" 161.

20 Ibid., 160.

21 Novak Bajcar, *Mape vremena*, 47.

22 Kazaz, *Neprijatelj ili susjed u kući*, 113.

23 Ibid.

24 Ključanin, "Ushit ljepotom svijeta," 745.

25 Mehmedinović, "Izbaviteljska gesta poezije," 27.

26 Josip Osti, "Razotkrivanje obrnute perspektive svijeta," in Ključanin, *Bošnjačka književnost u književnoj kritici*, 749.

27 Kazaz, "Mehmedinovićeva mistika emocija," 220.

28 Enver Kazaz's collection of essays in *Neprijatelj ili susjed u kući* provides the most coherent overview of this situation. The debate about the canon is of course not new but it possesses, in the 1990s, an entirely different accent and orientation given the altered political context. For an earlier discussion of what constitutes Bosnian and Herzegovinian literature, see *Savremena književnost naroda i narodnosti BiH u književnoj kritici*, ed. Ivan Lovrenović, Vojislav Maksimović, Kasim Prohić (Sarajevo: Svjetlost, 1984/5).

29 Jerkov, *Nova tekstualnost*, 17.

30 See, for example, the book *Postmoderna: Nova epoha ili zabluda?* ed. Ivan Kuvačić i Gvozden Flego (Zagreb: Naprijed, 1988). The book is a collection of essays that were presented as part of a colloquium titled "O postmoderni" ["On the Postmodern"]) in Zagreb, 24–7 March 1986.

31 The breadth of this debate can be see in the variety of the journals themselves, which encompass both the literary, the philosophical and the cultural. For example: *Delo* 35, nos. 4–5 (1989); *Marksizam u svetu* 13, nos. 4–5 (1986); *Kulturni radnik* 38, no. 3 (1985); *Theoria* 29, nos. 3–4 (1986); *Treći program radio Beograda* 68, no. 1 (1986).

32 On the former, see Gvozden Flego, "Postmoderna – nova epoha?" in *Postmoderna: Nova epoha ili zabluda?* On the latter, see Milorad Belančić's

critique of Derrida's position, "Postmodernistička zebnja," in *Delo*, 35, nos. 4–5 (April/May 1989): 132–40.

33 See Buck Morss, *Dreamworld and Catastrophe*, 230–51.

34 This issues are thematized in an interview between Mladen Kožul, Ivailo Dičev, and Jameson for the Croatian journal *Quorum*; see "Postmoderni prostor," *Quorum* 7, no. 1 (1991): 3–18.

35 Jameson, "Postmoderni prostor," 6.

36 Ibid., 6.

37 Erjavec, "Filozofija kritičke teorije i postmodernizam," 142.

38 See, for instance, Jovan Deretić's *Kratka istorija srpske književnosti* (Belgrade: Beogradski izdavačko-grafički zavod, 1987). As an example of the latter, see Dubravka Oraić Tolić, "Citatnost u avangardi i postmoderni."

39 Ugrešić, *Život je bajka*, 129–30.

40 This evocation of postmodernism and plagiarism calls to mind the most famous literary affair of Yugoslavia in the 1970s: the trial of Danilo Kiš's *A Tomb for Boris Davidovich*. The overt narrative presented by the prosecution revolved around Kiš's lack of citation in what was a novel bursting to the edges with sourced material. The covert narrative of the trial revolved around the political critique of Kiš's book that attacked Stalin's gulags and extended parallels with Yugoslavia's own state system and repressive measures. On the more literary front, Kiš's detractors accused him of plagiarism, demonstrating, as Vladimir Zorić writes, "a somewhat anachronistic approach to authorship and originality" to which the author replied with a defence of intertextuality (in a now famous essay entitled "The Anatomy Class"). While the core of the affair is the political lesson, the proceedings underscore the literary conservatism of that time and the intersections of literature and politics. Zorić, "The Poetics of Legend," 165.

41 Aleksandar Jerkov's *Nova tekstualnost* (published in 1992) is the most extensive theoretical treatment on the subject of literary postmodernism in Serbian literature. To my knowledge, it is also the most comprehensive analysis and position of postmodernism vis-à-vis literature across the former Yugoslavia at that time. In Croatia, it was articles that made the most impact (in particular those by Dubravka Oraić Tolić and Viktor Zmegač). This changed in the mid- to late 1990s, as the period saw an increase in book-length contributions to this theme from critics including Milivoj Solar (*Laka i teška književnost*, Zagreb, 1995) and Milo Lompar (*O završetku romana*, 1995). In the Bosnian and Herzegovinian literary context, according to Kazaz, postmodern pluralism and hybridity flourished in the 1990s. See Kazaz, "Krvavi lom društva i poetički prevrati romana," in *Neprijatelj ili susjed u kući*, 111–55.

42 For example, Oraić Tolić talks about the contemporary epoch as either one
   that is facing the consequences of totalitarian regimes ... or of mass media"
   ("Citatnost u avangardi i postmoderni," 160) – a statement about which I
   will say more shortly. Jerkov, in a footnote, foregrounds the asymmetry in
   conditions between first world and socialist Yugoslavia but then adds the
   interpretation of postmodernism for the Serbian literary scene "need not
   be so embattled" (*Nova tekstualnost*, 17). The implication here seems to be
   that certain aspects can be sidelined in favour of establishing the literary
   credentials of postmodernism.
43 Dragan B. Bošković, "Politike srpskog postmodernizma," 12.
44 Ibid., 13.
45 Ahmetagić, "Fantom postmoderne," 16 and 14–15. The broader context of
   Ahmetagic's work on postmodernism, especially as laid out in *Unutrašnja
   strana postmodernizma* (Belgrade: Raška škola, 2005), is to dismantle what she
   sees as the more fatuous claims of the postmodern theoretical apparatus.
   Her ideas are put into practice in a section on Serbian writer Milorad
   Pavić, whose reputation, she argues, solely rests on the work of critics who
   institutionalized him as an archetypally postmodern writer.
46 Oraić Tolić, "Citatnost u avangardi i postmoderni," 160.
47 Ibid.
48 In the mid-1990s, after the disintegration of Yugoslavia, Oraić Tolić
   reframes her approach to postmodernism. This is discussed shortly.
49 Kazaz, "Mehmedinovićeva mistika emocija," 218. See also Žmegač, *Povijesna
   poetika romana,* and Milivoj Solar, *Retorika postmoderne.*
50 See Lydic, "'Noseological' Parody, Gender Discourse, and Yugoslav
   Feminisms."
51 I expand on this point further in chapter 2.
52 Kulenović, *Istorija bolesti,* 109.
53 Hutcheon, "The Politics of Postmodernism," 179–80.
54 Šuvaković, *KFS,* 148.
55 Aleksić, "National Definition through Postmodern Fragmentation,"
   89–90.
56 Šuvaković, *KFS,* 154.
57 Denić Grabić, "Kraj dvadesetog stoljeća," 287.
58 Eagleton, *The Ideology of the Aesthetic,* 373.
59 Brajović, "Kratka istorija preobilja," 195.
60 A more extensive discussion about the end of history vis-à-vis the work of
   David Albahari can be found in chapter 4.
61 Brajović, "Kratka istorija preobilja," 192. Brajović's article also details how
   the more conservative quarters of the critical elite in Serbia turned against

postmodernism in the 1990s, treating it as an imported, foreign poetic that should be abandoned in favour of more autochthonous forms.

62 I must acknowledge the counterpoint to the anti-war literature that I will discuss in this study and signal to the main representatives of the nationalist-realist canon in Serbia, Croatia, and Bosnia. In Serbia, Dobrica Ćosić, Rajko Nogo, and Matija Bećković were all crucial in articulating political sentiments through their literature in the 1980s. Ćosić was also president of the rump Yugoslavia (known as the Federal Republic of Yugoslavia) from June 1992 to June 1993. In Croatia, Ivan Aralica was the writer closest to Tuđman's regime and was a member of the ruling party. In Bosnia, Džemaludin Latić and Zilhad Ključanin wrote distinctly ethnonational prose and poetry.

63 Novak-Bajcar, "Zašto je postmodernizam u Srbiji (ipak) moguć," 129.

64 Hebdige, "Postmodernism and the Other Side," 184.

65 Albahari, *David Albahari*, 217.

66 Oraić Tolić, *Palindromska apokalipsa*, 35. She also advances this argument about the loss of utopia in 1968 in *Paradigme dvadesetog stoljeća*, see chapter on "Hrvatska Postmoderna," 111–38.

67 Oraić Tolić, *Paradigme dvadesetog stoljeća*, 136. This descriptor of "postmodern war" remains quite vague.

68 These ideas are give exposition through the case study of Croatia author and scholar Pavao Pavličić.

69 There is a certain ambiguity about this spirited defence because it could be read as ideologically motivated, even if Oraić Tolić's periodization is firm in its account of the loss of *grand récits*. To begin with, Oraić Tolić chooses to frame her theoretical reflections on postmodernism with her own involvement in the events leading up to Croatian Spring in 1971: she writes in support of the "Declaration on the name and position of Croatian literary language" (1968) that rejected the imposition and expansion of a uniform Serbo-Croatian and snowballed into the Croatian Spring in 1971 (*Palindromska apokalipsa*, 33–4). In turn, this political narrative – that she sees as achieving its goals in 1991 – is woven in with the entire postmodern narrative. Further, by stripping postmodernism down to the principle of "morals" in wartime, it is clear that what is being kept behind lines up with the demands of national and ethnic existence of 1990s Croatia (the book was published in 1996, a year after the Dayton Accords for peace in Bosnia and Herzegovina were signed). I am not suggesting that her own ethical or political position might be nationalist but that, in the chaos of a country at war and a nascent liberal democracy, critical thought had to dovetail with collective values.

70 This, in part, is the topic of chapter 3, where I examine how Ugrešić's undermines this so-called real: her own reading of the social and political environment as a text discloses the extent to which the "real" is an instrumentalized simulacrum in the hands of both the state and market forces.

71 Here I refer to Rosić's work in *Mit o savršenoj biografiji* (*The Myth of the Perfect Biography*). Rosić's application of gender studies to the theme of the author-function and its ideological significance for Serbia, particularly as read through the authorial personality of Danilo Kiš is multifaceted in its argument. For my purposes here, I will focus more on the repercussions of this model for postmodern writers.

72 Rosić, *Mit o savršenoj biografiji*, 182.

73 Rosić, "Slepa mrlja realnog," 150.

74 Rosić, *Mit o savršenoj biografiji*, 182.

75 Ibid., 184.

2 The Spectacle of the Siege

1 Kazaz, "Prizori uhodanog užasa," 139.

2 Kebo, "Pismo iz Sarajeva," 49.

3 These figures were first reported by the Istraživačko dokumentacioni centar Sarajevo (Research Documentation Centre of Sarajevo) and published in their 2007 *Bosanska knjiga mrtvih* (*Bosnian Book of the Dead*) that was subsequently updated in 2012. The total figure is still being disputed since a number of deaths cannot be confirmed due to a lack of reliable sources. See Tokača, *Bosanska knjiga mrtvih*, 107. For more on displaced persons, see the Internal Displacement Monitoring Centre, http://www.internal-displacement.org/.

4 Campbell, "Atrocity, Memory, Photography," 6.

5 Andreas, *Blue Helmets and Black Markets*, 4.

6 Jergović, "Sarajevski Marketing," 39.

7 Mehmedinović, *Sarajevo blues*, 57. All references to the text will henceforth appear in parentheses in the body of the text.

8 Hemon, "A Coin," in *The Question of Bruno*, 126.

9 Jay, "'The Aesthetic Ideology' as Ideology," 44.

10 Ibid.

11 Benjamin, "The Work of Art in the Age of Mechanical Reproduction," 242.

12 Buck Morss, "Aesthetics and Anaesthetics," 4.

13 Ginzburg, *Blockade Diary*, 88.

14 Dauphinee, "The Politics of the Body in Pain," 145.

15 Vogler, "Poetic Witness," 174.

16 Iordanova, *Cinema of the Flames*, 235. In his book on the Bosnian war, *Love Thy Neighbor: A Story of War*, Peter Maass insists that journalists who "found safe spots near a sniper zone and waited for someone to be shot" were at work, not voyeuristically exploiting a fatal mise-en-scène. See Maass, *Love Thy Neighbor*, 146.

17 Agamben, *Homo Sacer*, 119.

18 In his book *Forgotten Future: The Politics of Poetry in Bosnia and Herzegovina*, Damir Arsenijević also uses Agamben to highlight the context of biopolitical control. He identifies Mehmedinović's poetry as a strategy for "mounting a critique of sovereign biopolitics." In an analysis that includes Asmir Kujović, Marko Vešović, Ferida Duraković and Mehmedinović, he examines the manner in which their poetry "reappropriates and re-politicises corporeality in order to expose the violence of and intrude into the permanent, ahistorical present moment of war biopolitics which de-politicises individuals." Arsenijević, *Forgotten Future*, 146.

19 Burt, "Must Poets Write?" 34.

20 Osti, "Razotkrivanje obrnute perspektive svijeta," in *Bošnjačka književnost u književnoj kritici*, 748. Mehmedinović's two collections of poetry written before the war are *Modrac* (1984) and *Emigrant* (1990).

21 Lovrenović, "Je li kasno za Bosnu?" 2. There is an undeniable poignancy to these words: the threat of starvation and its drawn-out desperation was eclipsed by the towering knowledge of the genocide of some seven thousand Bosnian Muslim men and boys half a year later.

22 Felman, "The Return of the Voice: Claude Lanzmann's *Shoah*," in Felman and Laub, *Testimony*, 207.

23 Both of these editions are held by reference libraries across the former Yugoslavia. For the purposes of this article, I will be consulting the edition from Biblioteka Dani (2004), because it is the only widely available edition of the text.

24 *Sarajevo blues* was translated into English by Ammiel Alcalay and published by City Lights Books in San Francisco in 1998.

25 Kermode, *The Sense of An Ending*, 25.

26 Ibid., 30.

27 McLoughlin, *Authoring War*, 107, 119.

28 Indeed, in the English translation this is doubly significant because of the overlap in the verb forms "grenading" and "raining." In the original, "padaju granate" is not as close to the phrase "pada kiša" ("it's raining"), but the linguistic echo is strong enough to suggest a connection.

29 McLoughlin, *Authoring War*, 119.

30 Blanchot, *The Gaze of Orpheus and Other Essays*, 109.

31 Bernstein, *Foregone Conclusions*, 16. Italics in the original.

32 Berman, "Falling," 129–30.

33 Scarry, *Body in Pain*, 61.

34 Shaw, "New Wars of the City,'" 149.

35 András Riedlmayer, *Destruction of Cultural Heritage in Bosnia-Herzegovina 1992–1996: A Post-War Survey of Selected Municipalities*. An expert report prepared for the International Criminal Tribunal for the Former Yugoslavia (ICTY), The Hague, this document is available online as part of the Milošević Trial Public Archive, Human Rights Program, Bard College, http://hague.bard.edu/reports/BosHeritageReport-AR.pdf.

36 The destruction of the library has significant currency for this very reason, and it received much attention in the press. It was also a piece of information needed to bring the siege of Sarajevo conceptually closer to European and Western values. See, for example, Lovrenović, "The Hatred of Memory," and Fisk, "Waging War on History."

37 Benjamin, *The Origin of German Tragic Drama*, 178.

38 Moretti, *Signs Taken For Wonders*, 112.

39 "I once wrote": in *Modrac*, Mehmedinović's 1984 poetry collection, a poem titled "City" speaks of precisely this image and this sentiment: "a future song should smell/ of the soft paper with which market sellers/ wrap oranges." See Mehmedinović, *Modrac*, 34.

40 Hell and Schönle, "Introduction," in *Ruins of Modernity*, 5.

41 Simmel, "The Ruin," in *Essays on Sociology*, 261–2. It is important to stress, however, that Simmel had an interest in ruins brought about by natural decline, rather than man-made destruction.

42 A kiosk is a small hexagonal street stall, ubiquitous in Serbia, Bosnia, and Croatia, and very much part of the landscape of everyday urban life. Kiosks sell newspapers, cigarettes, transit tickets, etc.

43 Consider also the title of Rossellini's film *Germany Year Zero*. This film of ruin, as implied in the title, suggests a clock that is "reset" after which counting can begin again.

44 Hell and Schönle, "Introduction," in *Ruins of Modernity*, 7.

45 Kant, *The Critique of Judgment*, 39.

46 Ibid., 39–43.

47 White, "Figural Realism in Witness Literature," 114.

48 Hell and Schönle, "Introduction," in *Ruins of Modernity*, 6.

49 This intersection of warfare, violence and enjoyment has a frightening presence elsewhere – that is, frightening in its implications. This happens particularly in the documentary formats that have surfaced since the war. For example, the video of the Srebrenica massacre that was broadcast in June

2005 (and eventually used in the International Criminal Tribunal for the Former Yugoslavia for prosecution of war criminals) shows the shooting of a group of Muslim prisoners from Srebrenica by the paramilitary formation The Scorpions [Škorpioni] in Trnovo, a small village on the Treskavica mountain. The video was made by the executioners themselves. Art critic Dejan Sretenović writes: "The recording ... metaphorically suggests that the media image of the war in Serbia actively 'participated' in the crimes committed by organizing visible enjoyment of violence, by producing a collective 'metastasis of enjoyment' (S. Zizek), which arises as a consequence of deliberate abuse of the symbolic order through the reification of signs (the war, nation, leaders)." See Sretenović, "A Journey Through the Pictures and Phantasms of the 1990s," 192. Moreover, in this discussion of the commodification of violence, it is worth mentioning that the video itself circulated freely before it was shown at the ICTY trial against Milošević: a witness statement during the trial confirmed that the video could be borrowed from a local video club. See Kandić, ed., "Škorpioni," 297, 629, 637.

50 Structures of feeling, writes Raymond Williams in *Marxism and Literature*, "do not have to await definition, classification, or rationalization before they exert palpable pressures and set effective limits on experience and action." See Williams, *Marxism and Literature*, 132.

51 In the original, the word is "bol." It was translated by Ammiel Alcalay, the English-language translator of *Sarajevo blues*, as "sorrow." Mehmedinović's own phrase is tuned in to this ambiguity.

52 Gérard Genette defines "paratext" using two related categories: firstly, the term refers to an epitext which comprises drafts, autobiographies, diaries, letters, interviews, and other self-commentaries associated with the writing and, secondly, it refers to the material found on the periphery of the literary work, such as titles, prefaces, footnotes, epilogues. The paratext, among other functions, shortens the distance between the reader and the (main) text itself. Genette, *Seuils*, 10.

53 Ó Tuathail, *Critical Geopolitics*, 193.

54 Ibid., 189–93.

55 Jakovljević, "Theatre of Atrocities," 1816.

56 See Binder, "Anatomy of a Massacre." I am grateful to Branislav Jakovljević's article cited above for drawing my attention to Binder's work.

57 Virilio, *A Landscape of Events*, 24. The first of these was, of course, the Persian Gulf War, which, Virilio argues, "is inseparable from its cathodic framing."

58 Frye, *Anatomy of Criticism*, 103.

59 Perloff, *The Radical Artifice*, 2.

60 Derrida, "Sending," 320.

61 Jay, *Downcast Eyes*, 508.
62 Friedlander, Reflections of Nazism: An Essay on Kitsch and Death, 27. Original emphasis.
63 Butler, *Frames of War*, 67.
64 Ibid., 64.
65 For a more extensive discussion on intellectual engagement and the role of the media, see chapter 5.
66 See Felman and Laub, *Testimony*, for an interdisciplinary overview of the genre of witness and testimonial texts.
67 Aleksandar Hemon's short story "A Coin" in *The Question of Bruno* exemplifies this technique very well.
68 See Perloff, *The Radical Artifice*, particularly the introductory chapter.
69 Perloff, *The Radical Artifice*, 19.
70 Bernstein, *Foregone Conclusions*, 11.
71 I am paraphrasing a line by P.N. Medvedev and M.M. Bakhtin: "One does not first see a given aspect of reality and then shape it to a given set of conventions [but] instead sees reality with the eyes of the genre." From *The Formal Method in Literary Scholarship*, 134.
72 Edkins, *Missing: Persons and Politics*, 7.
73 Foster Wallace, "E Unibus Pluram: Television and U.S. Fiction," in *A Supposedly Fun Thing I'll Never Do Again*, 34.
74 Ibid.
75 Sontag, *Regarding the Pain of Others*, 77.
76 Tester, *Humanitarianism and Modern Culture*, 52.
77 Even according to Edward Said's definition of an intellectual: "an individual endowed with a faculty for representing, embodying, articulating a message, a view, an attitude, philosophy or opinion to, as well as for, a public," there is an awareness that "not enough stock [has been] taken of the image, the signature, the actual intervention and performance." From Said, *The Representation of Intellectuals*, 9–10.
78 Tester, *Humanitarianism*, 43.
79 Mehmedinović, "Kompozitor," 78.
80 Translation into English changes matters somewhat. In Bosnian, the letter would be "b" for "Bog," the word for God.

3 The Phantasmagoria and Seduction of Kitsch

1 Norris, *Writing War*, 4.
2 Călinescu, *Five Faces of Modernity*, 235.
3 Ibid. Italics in the original.

4 Ugrešić, "State of the Art," 468.

5 *Batja* and *tata* are, respectively, the colloquial Russian and Croatian words for father. Ugrešić, *Kultura laži*, 70. All references to the text will henceforth appear in parentheses in the body of the text.

6 The Baška tablet is a stone monument believed to be the first example of an inscription in Croatian, dating to roughly 1100. It is written in the Glagolitic alphabet. The "wattle," an example of medieval Croatian art, is a metal ornament, in the shape of a ribbon, used for decoration in churches throughout Croatia from the ninth and eleventh centuries.

7 Greenberg, "Avant-garde and kitsch," in *Clement Greenberg*, 12.

8 Zoran Terzic has commented on the important role played by rural places in the discourse of urban elites, particularly in the Serbian context. See Terzic, "Between Destiny and Contingency," 223–61.

9 In English, the Homeland war is usually referred to as the Croatian War of Independence.

10 Baker, "War Memory and Musical Tradition," 1.

11 For an overview of HDZ and Tuđman's presidency, see Soberg, "Croatia Since 1989," 31–62.

12 For a documentation and analysis of this episode in Ugrešić's life, see Lukić, "Witches Fly High," 385–93.

13 The fact that the essay "Clean Croatian Air" was not published in Croatian is confirmed by Ugrešić in *Culture of Lies*: "Even though the text was not published in the local press, everyone immediately knew what was in it and its author found herself in the role of an isolated target for furious attacks by her countrymates" (85). Out of all the essays presented in *Culture of Lies*, only one was published in Croatian first: "Laku noć hrvatski pisci." It was published in the paper *Nedjeljna Dalmacija* on 25 November 1992.

14 Kesić, "Witch Hunt, Croatian Style," 16. Instrumental in instigating the media furore was an article in the weekly magazine *Globus* (an independent publication at a time when most media was government owned) that diagnosed these female writers as "a group of egotistical middle-aged women who have serious problems with their ethnic, moral, human, intellectual and political identity" ("Hrvatske feministice siluju Hrvatsku," *Globus*, 11 December 1992, quoted in Kesić, "Witch Hunt," 16). The tone of this anonymously authored piece was misogynistic, suggesting in no unclear terms that by being women, these writers were more likely to destabilize national goals and threaten the patriarchal order and values (the magazine published personal details about their marital status, education, and places of work). More recently, a literary scholar has pointed out that criticism of these women writers in the early 1990s also denounced them from the perspective of being

"literarily trivial" ("*kao književna trivijala*") given their naive, stereotypical, and clichéd portrayals of the political arena – or so their detractors claimed. See Mikulić, *Kroatorij Europe*, 139–40.

15 Lukić, "Pisanje kao antipolitika," 73–102.

16 My ideas here were informed by an essay on "offense" by J.M. Coetzee, who writes: "Taking offense is not confined to those in position of subordination or weakness. Nevertheless, the experience or premonition of being robbed of power seems to me intrinsic to all instances of taking offense. (It is tempting to suggest that the logic of provocative name-calling, when used as a tactic of the weak against the strong, is that if the strong can be made to take offense, they thereby put themselves at least momentarily on the same footing as the weak.)" Coetzee, "Taking Offense," in *Giving Offence*, 3.

17 The following is a list of some of the awards that Ugrešić has won: Prix Européen de l'essai Charles Veillon (Switzerland, 1996); SWF-Bestenliste Literaturpreis (Germany, 1998); Österreichische Staatspreis für europäische Literatur (Austria, 1999); Heinrich Mann Preis, Akademie der Künste Berlin (Germany, 2000); PEN Writers in Translation Award (UK, 2000). Ugrešić has been shortlisted for the Independent Foreign Fiction Prize (UK, 2006) and the Man Booker International Prize (2009). Most recently, she was awarded the Neustadt International Prize for Literature (2016).

18 Jelčić, *Povijest hrvatske književnosti*, 215.

19 Kuhlman, "The Culture of Lies."

20 Wachtel, *Remaining Relevant after Communism*, 153.

21 Šoljan, "Dubravka Cvek u raljama rata," 15. This is a review whose title ("Dubravka Cvek in the Jaws of War") is a reference to a book by Ugrešić titled *Steffie Cvek in the Jaws of Life*. The idiomatic "in the jaws of" casts Ugrešić in the role of her main character, Steffie Cvek. Šoljan's reading of Steffie is entirely negative – as a clueless young woman who tries to find love through schematic means – which are qualities he wishes to transpose onto Ugrešić the writer.

22 Wachtel, *Remaining Relevant after Communism*, 152.

23 Pisac, "Trusted Tales," 253.

24 Gordana Crnković, review of *The Culture of Lies: Antipolitical Essays*, by Dubravka Ugrešić, 545.

25 Ibid.

26 For more on this subject, see Obradović, "The Ironic Eternity of Objects," 415–41.

27 Good, *The Observing Self*, 7.

28 Some of these phrases had high been widely circulated. The slogan "HDZ – it is known!" has been ridiculed: What is known? And by whom? Milošević's

statement, now somewhat infamous, was first recorded at a meeting for mayors on 16 March 1991. All quotations are from *Culture of Lies*, page 778.

29 Vološinov, *Marxism and the Philosophy of Language*, 15.

30 Ibid., 10, 12.

31 Ibid., 19.

32 Buck Morss, "Aesthetics and Anaesthetics," 22–3.

33 NDH stands for Nezavisna Država Hrvatska (Independent State of Croatia), which existed between 1941 and 1945, first as the protectorate of Fascist Italy and later under the governance of Nazi Germany.

34 Vukovar was overrun by the JNA and Serbian paramilitary forces in September 1991. The army held the city's civilians hostage, until it was overrun by the Croatian army in November later that year.

35 Mark Thompson writes that "the HDZ [Croatian Democratic Union] was as determined to control the media as its predecessors [the Communist Party]: unlike those predecessors who had a functioning state, the HDZ took office when post-Communist disorder was magnified by the Yugoslav context of imploding federalism and the threat to Croatia posed very plainly by Serbia and imminently, by the JNA [Yugoslav People's Army]." In Thompson, *Forging War*, 135.

36 Crucially, the production of phantasmagoric forms, as gathered in the essays, often oversteps the boundary of centralized government control. Indeed, cultural forms – in all their diversity of genres and mediums, from commodities to oral Balkan epics – are equally instrumental in contributing to the total effect of the spectacle. They broaden the metaphors, metonyms, slogans, and images by which the same social ideas are represented; they extend the types of stimuli; and deepen the historical legacy.

37 Butler, *Frames of War*, 66.

38 Eagleton, *Ideology*, 151.

39 Turbo folk music refers to a distinct Balkan genre that combines the region's folk music with contemporary beats borrowed from – to name a few – pop, house, and techno music. It came to prominence in the early 1980s and is typically seen as the 1990s cultural counterpart to the national(ist) rhetoric of the political elites. Moreover, turbo folk music had a particular showbusiness identity: turbo folk singers promoted an image of a lavish, glamorous lifestyle that, in the war torn and economically impoverished region, were simply unattainable for the majority of the population. For more on turbo folk, see Ivana Kronja, "Turbo Folk and Dance Music in 1990s Serbia: Media, Ideology, and the Production of Spectacle," 103–14.

40 Nabokov, *Nikolai Gogol*, 54. Ugrešić herself quotes from this work to augment and justify her own arguments.

41 Viktor Žmegač, letter to the editor in section titled "Kroatische Kontroversen," 106.
42 Ibid.
43 Ibid.
44 Mikulić, "Zastave ili beskonačni manjak ideološke utjehe."
45 Ibid.
46 Ibid.
47 Jovanović, "Motiv tri žene u 'Muzeju bezuvjetne predaje' Dubravke Ugrešić," 123.
48 Ibid.
49 Assmann, "Beyond the Archive," 72.
50 Călinescu, *Five Faces of Modernity*, 226.
51 Ibid.
52 Huyssen, *After The Great Divide*, 198.
53 Eco, "The Structure of Bad Taste," in *The Open Work*, 183.
54 See Đekić, *Flagusova rukavica*.
55 Patterson, *Bought and Sold*, 1.
56 Ibid., 174.
57 Ugrešić, *Život je bajka*, 35–6.
58 Ibid., 51.
59 Modleski, "Femininity as Mas(s)querade," in *High Theory/Low Culture*, 38.
60 Ugrešić, *Štefica Cvek u raljama života*, 54, 56.
61 See Visković, *Mlada proza*; Đekić, *Flagusova rukavica*.
62 Huyssen, *After the Great Divide*, 46.
63 Ibid., 47.
64 Ibid.
65 Ugrešić, *Život je bajka*, 44, 48. In an earlier story from the collection *Poza za prozu* [*A Pose for Prose*], writing is a condition for the fulfilment of erotic desire.
66 Ugrešić, interview with Svetlana Boym, *Bomb* magazine.
67 Ibid.
68 Ugrešić, *Štefica Cvek*, 89.
69 His 1978 essay, "The Gingerbread Heart," is a model for Ugrešić's own work, both intellectually and stylistically. I discuss this essay and Ugrešić's debt to its technique later in this chapter.
70 Kiš, "Banalnost je neuništiva kao plastična boca," in *Homo poeticus*, 287.
71 Ibid. Italics in the original.
72 Binkley, "Kitsch as a Repetitive System," 132.
73 Zorić, "The Poetics of Legend," 161.
74 Kiš, "Buridanov magarac ili pisac u haosu sveta," in *Život, literatura*, 109–10.

75 Kiš, "Banalnost," in *Homo poeticus*, 285.

76 Kiš, "Radomir Reljić," in *Život, literatura*, 130.

77 Ugrešić writes: "In his book on Gogol, Vladimir Nabokov talks about *poshlost*. *Poshlost* is a Russian word which, on account of its richness of meaning, Nabokov presents with English adjectives such as *cheap, inferior, sorry, trashy, scurvy, tawdry*, and similar" (*Kultura laži*, 67).

78 Boym, *Future of Nostalgia*, 279.

79 Boym, *Common Places*, 41, 43.

80 Boym, *Future of Nostalgia*, 279.

81 Žižek, "Multiculturalism," 40.

82 Žižek, "The Military-Poetic Complex," 17.

83 Paul Fussell's classic work *The Great War and Modern Memory* demonstrates how medieval and classic legends were duplicated in the poetry of the First World War.

84 Žižek, "Multiculturalism," 38.

85 Ibid.

86 The overarching dilemma here is that modernism is archetypally male and possesses a masculine subjectivity in arts and literature. In fact, this brings us back full circle to Ugrešić's attempts to redefine the relationship between mass culture and women: the male (modernist) authority had marked women as consumers of trivial literature – a cultural form that was perceived as threatening to elite artistic expression.

87 See also Kaplan, *Reproductions of Banality*.

88 Lacoue-Labarthe, "The Aestheticization of Politics." in *Heidegger, Art and Politics*, 70, 61.

89 Chow, "The Fascist Longings," 37.

90 Sontag, "Fascinating Fascism," in *Under the Sign of Saturn*, 96.

91 Gingeras, "The Comeback of Sincerity," 85.

92 The advert in question is the work of the controversial Italian photographer Oliviero Toscani, who implemented Benetton's novel advertising campaign with its focus on social issues of international breadth. It was an unusual strategy insofar as it did not feature the company's own products but instead commodified moments of suffering and events of war. The most shocking of the images – images that have been equally lauded – include dying sufferers of AIDS, death row inmates, and a scene of wreckage of the explosion of a car bomb.

93 See Sigmund Freud, "Fetishism," in *The Standard Edition of the Complete Psychological Works of Sigmund Freud*, 152–5.

94 Mehmedinović, *Sarajevo blues*, 74.

95 Ibid.

96 The tie, it is believed, was popularized in the seventeenth century by Croatian soldiers who were in France during the Thirty Years' War (1618–48). The French word "cravate" comes from the word "Croata." The tie has become a source of pride in Croatia.
97 See Čolović, *Politika simbola*.
98 Stewart, *On Longing*, 138.
99 Ibid., 135.
100 Ibid., 135.
101 Chow, "The Fascist Longings," 26.
102 Jay, "'The Aesthetic Ideology' as Ideology," 45.
103 This autonomy of the aesthetic is a more recent phenomenon: Martin Jay and Susan Buck Morss both make this point.
104 For a discussion of aestheticized politics vis-à-vis avant-garde and Fascism, see Hewitt, *Fascist Modernism*.
105 Čolović, *Politika simbola*, 105.
106 Ibid., 105, 109.
107 Ugrešić, *Europa u sepiji*, 14.
108 Bošković, "Yugonostalgia and Yugoslav Cultural Memory, 54–78.
109 Ibid., 55.
110 Ibid., 75.
111 Ugrešić, *Europa u sepiji*, 12.
112 See Srećko Horvat and Igor Štiks, eds., *Dobro došli u pustinju postsocijalizma* (Zagreb: Fraktura, 2015).

4 The Search for a Language of the Historical Present

1 Albahari, *Pelerina i nove priče*, 149.
2 Albahari *Mamac*, 115.
3 Albahari, *Svetski putnik*, 40.
4 Albahari, "Ja sam prevejani postmodernista," 13.
5 Albahari, *Mamac*, 115.
6 Albahari, "Granice," in *Teret*, 136.
7 Albahari, "Srce na trpezi sveta," in *Prepisivanje sveta*, 123.
8 Albahari, *Mamac*,135.
9 Harootunian, "Remembering the Historical Present," 472.
10 Ibid.
11 Ibid., 475.
12 Jameson, *The Political Unconscious*, 20.
13 Albahari, "Balkan: književnost i istorija," in *Teret*, 8.
14 Albahari, "Moje viđenje književnosti," in *Prepisivanje sveta*, 42.

15 Albahari, "Balkan: književnost i istorija," 8.

16 Albahari, "Moje viđenje književnosti," 42.

17 Vladimir Tasić, "Snežni čovek i paralaksa," 88.

18 Albahari, "Granice," in *Teret*, 139.

19 Albahari, "Prvi jezik, druga zemlja," in *Teret* 39.

20 For a consideration of the "common cultural sphere," see Milutinović, "What Common Yugoslav Culture Was," 75–87.

21 Ribnikar, "Istorija i trauma u romanima Davida Albaharija," 619.

22 Albahari, "Moje viđenje književnosti," 45.

23 Albahari, *Snežni čovek*, 34.

24 Albahari, "Srce na trpezi sveta," 119, and "Iz dnevnika o nestajanju," *Prepisivanje sveta*, 114.

25 Albahari, "Balkan: književnost i istorija," 10.

26 Vološinov, *Marxism and the Philosophy of Language*, 116.

27 Albahari, "Prvi jezik, druga zemlja," 39.

28 Albahari, *Mamac*, 71.

29 Albahari, *Gec i Majer*, 68.

30 Albahari, *Snežni čovek*, 87.

31 See Ribnikar, "Istorija i trauma u romanima Davida Albaharija."

32 Milutinović, "The Demoniacism of History and Promise of Aesthetic Redemption in David Albahari's *Bait*," 18.

33 See Aleksić, "Grief Can only Be Written in One's Mother Tongue," in *Literature of Exile*, ed. Agnieszka Gutty (New York, Berlin: Peter Lang Publishing, 2009), 155–75.

34 According to *Voices of Yugoslav Jewry* by Paul Gordiejew, the Yugoslav Jewish population was broadly characterized by such a secular attitude. See Gordiejew, *Voices of Yugoslav Jewry* (New York: SUNY, 1999).

35 Albahari, *Snežni čovek*, 87.

36 Albahari, "Umetnik je izgnanik," 9.

37 Albahari, "Peter Handke," 58.

38 Albahari, "Umetnik je izgnanik," 13.

39 Albahar, "Ime stvari," in *Fras u šupi*, 46.

40 Jerkov, *Nova tekstualnost*, 99.

41 Albahari, "Koan od priče," in *Fras u šupi*, 56.

42 Albahari, "Fizika i jezik," in *Prepisivanje sveta*, 52.

43 Albahari, "Ujak Mihael kao sasvim mlad čovek," 20.

44 Albahari, "Tri stanice do kuće," in *Porodično vreme*, 12.

45 Albahari, "Nedovršeni rukopis," in *Opis smrti*, 68.

46 Ibid.

47 Nandrea and Ginsburg, "The Prose of the World," 244.

48 Hegel, *Aesthetics*, 150.
49 Ibid., 152.
50 *The Penguin Dictionary of Literary Terms and Literary Theory*, s.v "prose," 705.
51 Moretti, "History of the Novel, Theory of the Novel," 1.
52 Albahari, *Kratka knjiga*, 46.
53 Nandrea and Ginzburg, "The Prose of the World," 270.
54 Hegel: "This is the prose of the world, as it appears to the consciousness both of the individual himself and of others – a world of finitude and mutability, of entanglement in the relative, of the pressure of necessity from which the individual is in no position to withdraw" (Hegel, *Aesthetics*, 150).
55 Albahari, "Nedovršeni rukopis," *Opis smrti*, 71.
56 Albahari, "Alhemija," in *Porodično vreme*, 97.
57 Albahari, "U traganju za idealnom knjigom," 15.
58 Albahari, "Objašnjenje," in *Fras u šupi*, 86.
59 Nandrea and Ginsburg, "The Prose of the World," 272. They draw their conclusions based on a study of an Israeli novel entitled *Past Continuous*, by Ya'akov Shabtai. It has numerous similarities to Albahari's work.
60 Albahari, "Moje viđenje književnosti," 43.
61 The first time we see this is in *Kratka knjiga*, though Albahari makes use of the form in some of his short fiction, such as "Vlaga" ("Humidity") in *Opis smrti*.
62 Albahari, "Između buke i besa."
63 Jameson, "Postmodernism," 61.
64 Ibid., 71–2.
65 Ibid., 73.
66 Ibid.
67 Albahari, "Umetnik je izgnanik," 21.
68 Albahari, *Snežni čovek*, 83.
69 Ibid., 121.
70 Ibid., 143.
71 Ibid., 96.
72 Ibid., 33.
73 Ibid., 52.
74 Ibid., 136, 156.
75 Ibid., 21, 102.
76 Ibid., 124.
77 Ribnikar, "Istorija i trauma u romanima Davida Albaharija," 620.
78 Albahari, *Snežni čovek*, 24.
79 Ibid., 5 and 22.

 80 Eagleton, *The Illusions of Postmodernism*, 12.
 81 Albahari, *Snežni čovek*, 32.
 82 Ibid., 48.
 83 Ibid., 35.
 84 Ibid., 35–6.
 85 Ibid., 30.
 86 Ibid., 53.
 87 Ibid., 62.
 88 Ibid., 53.
 89 Ibid., 66.
 90 Albahari, "Iz dnevnika o nestajanju," in *Prepisivanje sveta*, 115.
 91 Ibid., 65.
 92 Ibid., 142, 139.
 93 Ibid., 43–4.
 94 Ibid., 59.
 95 Ibid., 68.
 96 Ibid., 115.
 97 Albahari, *Mamac*, 255.
 98 Ibid., 52
 99 Ibid., 27.
100 Fukuyama, "The End of History?" 3–18.
101 Albahari, *Snežni čovek*, 64.
102 Ibid., 77.
103 Tasić, "Snežni čovek i paralaksa," 93.
104 Albahari, *Snežni čovek*, 78.
105 Ibid., 62.
106 Albahari, *Svetski putnik*, 126.
107 Ibid., 127.
108 Albahari, *Snežni čovek*, 48.
109 Ibid., 49.
110 Ibid., 84.
111 Albahari, "Autorova beleška," in *Cink*, 128.
112 Albahari, *Snežni čovek*, 90.
113 For more on Albahari's reflections on anti-Semitism in the essay collection *Teret* as well as the 2005 novel *Leeches* (*Pijavice*).
114 A more comprehensive historical survey of the camp reveals that, in addition to the genocide of the Jews, a significant Roma population was incarcerated and subsequently executed at the camp. It is only with the publication of Milovan Pisari's monograph *Stradanje Roma u Srbiji za vreme Holokausta* (2014) that this dark chapter has been fully and historically explored. Furthermore,

after April 1942, the camp became an *Anhaltelager* – a detention camp – for tens of thousands of political prisoners (including partisans and nationalists). It is estimated that by September 1944, when the camp was disbanded, some forty thousand inmates had passed through its system, of whom ten thousand lost their lives. See Koljanin, *Nemački logor na Beogradskom sajmištu 1941–1944*). On the genocide of the Roma during the Holocaust, see Milovan Pisari, *Stradanje Roma u Srbiji za vreme Holokausta* (Belgrade: Forum za primenjenu istoriju, 2014).

115 Albahari, *Gec i Majer*, 33.

116 Two history books that Albahari acknowledges are the aforementioned work by Milan Koljanin and a study by Christopher R. Browning, titled *Fateful Months: Essays on the Emergence of the Final Solution.*

117 Albhari, *Gec i Majer*, 105.

118 Ibid., 87.

119 Sarah Horowitz, *Voicing the Void*, 17.

120 Albahari, *Gec i Majer*, 5. The witness, one presumes, is sourced form archival material.

121 Ibid.

122 Ibid., 21.

123 See Byford, *Staro sajmište.*

124 Susan Rubin Suleiman, "When the Perpetrator Becomes a Reliable Witness of the Holocaust, 2.

125 Albahari, *Gec i Majer*, 73.

126 Ribnikar, "Istorija i trauma u romanima Davida Albaharija," 636.

127 Ibid., 636.

128 Albahari, *Gec i Majer*, 103.

129 Ibid., 72

130 Ibid., 33.

131 For a theoretical exposition on how episodes of violence can illuminate other occurrences of oppression, even when they are not historically nor spatially related, see Michael Rothberg, *Multidirectional Memory* (Stanford, CA: Stanford University Press, 2009).

132 Mitrović, "*Gec i Majer* or Situational Education," *Serbian Studies*, 19:1 (2005), 83–93.

133 Albahari, *Gec i Majer*, 162.

134 Ibid., 165.

135 Ibid., 180.

136 Ibid., 79.

137 Both Mitrović and Ribnikar discuss this scene in their articles.

138 Ibid., 172.

139 Ibid., 159.

140 The Golem and the story of its creation is given explicit mention halfway
through the novel: "I resemble an old Prague rabbi who made a person-
monster from clay and breathed life into him, with the difference that
I am trying to create Götz and Meyer from imaginary souvenirs, fallible
memories" (*Gec i Majer*, 80). The evocation of the myth, inspired by the
sixteenth century Rabbi Loew of Prague, can be read as the framing device
that accounts for the novel's narrative strategy: that is, the means by which
the narrator gives life to the two signs, Götz and Meyer. The narrator's
interpretation of the myth focuses on the creator (himself) rather than
the clay beings (Götz and Meyer) that spring forth from the word. The
narrator understands the power he possesses, in his reconstructions,
to enact destruction and issues a warning about the creative potential
inherent with the act of creation.

141 Albahari, *Gec i Majer*, 142.

142 Ibid., 165.

143 Ibid., 108.

144 Ibid., 126.

145 Esh, "Words and Their Meanings," 134. See also Victor Klemperer's study
on the language of the Third Reich, *LTI – Lingua Tertii Imperii: A Philologist's
Notebook*. Klemperer's observations regarding the content and functions of
LTI attest to the ubiquity of the discourse that extends beyond its militaristic
use: "Following the Party's 'takeover *{Machtübernahme}*' in 1933 the language
of a clique became the language of the people, i.e., it seized hold of all
realms of public and private life: politics, the administration of justice, the
economy, the arts, the sciences, schools, sport, the family, playschools and
nurseries." Klemperer, *LTI*, 19 (original emphasis).

146 Albahari, *Gec i Majer*, 54.

147 For accounts of the functionalist paradigm, see Martin Broszat, "Hitler and
the Genesis of the 'Final Solution.'"

148 Bauman, *Modernity and the Holocaust*, 17.

149 Ibid., 149, 150.

150 Albahari, *Gec i Majer*, 6.

151 Ibid., 12.

152 Rousset, *L'univers concentrationnaire*.

153 Albahari, *Gec i Majer*, 91.

154 Ibid., 91.

155 Ibid., 55.

156 Ibid., 149.

157 Ibid., 92.

158 Ibid., 27.
159 Albahari, *Gec i Majer*, 154.
160 There are many parallels here with Hannah Arendt's presentation of Adolf Eichmann's language situation that she had the opportunity to observe during his trial in Israel. Arendt writes: "No communication was possible with him [Eichmann], not because he lied but because he was surrounded by the most reliable of all safeguards against the words and the presence of others, and hence against reality as such." Arendt, *Eichmann in Jerusalem*, 49.
161 Ibid., 149.

5 The Quickened Moral Pulse

1 Ugrešić, *Kultura laži*, 228.
2 Albahari, *Snežni čovek*, 33.
3 Ugrešić, *Kultura laži*, 229.
4 Rothberg, *Traumatic Realism*, 271.
5 Sontag, "Answers to a Questionnaire," in *Where the Stress Falls*, 296.
6 Bourdieu, *The Rules of Art*, 345.
7 King, "Stardom, Celebrity and the Money Form," 10. Barry King's phrase "the money form" refers to the process whereby the performance of a musician or an actor becomes "a process in which the aesthetic capacity of labor power is exchanged for cash through the consumption of a body image." One finds it easier to be cynical about stars like the members of the band U2: their musical contribution to the spirit of human perseverance and underground movements during the war with an album offering (called "Miss Sarajevo") was not so much an act of intervention as the propagation of their image as a commodity that continued to circulate after their initial expression of solidarity (through tours and album sales).
8 Bourdieu, *The Rules of Art*, 9.
9 Jaffe, *Modernism and the Culture of Celebrity*, 1.
10 This reference was first noticed by Jasmina Lukić. See her "Trivial Romance as an Archetypal Genre: The Fiction of Dubravka Ugrešić," *Ženske studije*, Women's Studies Journal Selected Papers, Anniversary Issue 1992–2000 (no page numbers).
11 Gilbert and Gubar, *Madwoman in the Attic*, 4.
12 Barthes, "The Death of the Author," 210.
13 Indeed, it would be interesting to pursue an enquiry into how these principles of authorship function in a society of real existing socialism with its insistence on the author's social role, of literature as a state project.

14 Burke, *The Ethics of Writing*, 23.

15 See Rieff, *Slaughterhouse: Bosnia and the Failure of the West*.

16 For more on this theme, see Tester, *Humanitarianism and Modern Culture*.

17 Garber, "Compassion," 19.

18 Moeller, *Compassion Fatigue*, 10.

19 See Sacco, *Safe Area Goražde: The War in Eastern Bosnia 1992–95* (Seattle: Fantagraphics Books, 2000).

20 Dominick LaCapra has written an extensive critique of the uncritical identification by the witness with the victim. See LaCapra, "Trauma, Absence, Loss," *Critical Inquiry* 25, no. 4 (1999): 696–727.

21 Baudrillard, "No Pity for Sarajevo," in *Screened Out*, 45.

22 Hammond, *Media, War and Postmodernity*, 50. The "West" is an undeniably broad brushstroke that disguises divisions manifest between American and European commentators, as well as the range of philosophical and intellectual traditions that underpin each individual's actions – not to mention their political loyalties.

23 Von Oppen, "Imagining the Balkans, Imagining Germany," 195, 198.

24 Duraković, "Pisac sagledava domovinu dok učeni postmodernist ulazi u njegov grad," 110.

25 Arsenijević, *Forgotten Future*, 142.

26 Castle, *The Professor*, 95.

27 Sontag, "Waiting for Godot in Sarajevo," in *Where the Stress Falls*, 304.

28 Ibid., 303.

29 Kalyvas, *The Logic of Violence in Civil War*, 39.

30 See Jestrović, *Performance, Space, Utopia*, and Ivana Maček, *Sarajevo under Siege: Anthropology in Wartime* (University of Pennsylvania Press, 2009).

31 Ibid., 220.

32 The film is entitled *Serbian Epics* (1992) and it is directed by by Pawel Pawlikowski and Lazar Stojanović.

33 Journalist Marc Bennetts writes the following in the *Observer*'s profile of Limonov: "He has been persona non grata in western literary circles since he was filmed shooting a machine gun into a besieged Sarajevo in the company of Bosnian Serb leader Radovan Karadzic. The incident, captured by Bafta award-winning director Pawel Pawlikowski in his *Serbian Epics* documentary and shown at Karadzic's trial at the Hague, cost Limonov publishing contracts in both Europe and the US. But he reacts furiously when I bring up the issue. 'That schmuck,' he says. 'I was shooting at a firing range, and that guy put in an extra frame to make it look like I was firing at buildings. I've been saying this for 15 years.' I'm unsure of how to react to this, as well as to his assertion that he was

'always a freelance journalist' during the conflict in Bosnia. I later dig up
an extract from his 2001 *Book of the Dead* where he appears to admit – the
sentence is ambiguously phrased – spraying the city with machine-gun fire.
I then come across an article where he explicitly states that he 'fought' in
Bosnia from 'February to May 1993.' I send him the quotes and call later
for a comment. He is beside himself with rage and barks down the phone
that he regrets having had anything to do with me. 'It wouldn't have
been a Limonov interview without a bit of shouting,' a fellow journalist
comments." See Bennetts, "Eduard Limonov Interview: Political Rebel and
Vladimir Putin's Worst Nightmare."

34 Mehmedinović, *Sarajevo blues*, 32.

35 Bourdieu, *The Rules of Art*, 141.

36 Casanova, *The World Republic of Letters*, xii.

37 Ugrešić, "Yugoslavia, an 'Almost Forbidden Word'," 303.

38 Klaus, "Essayists on the Essay," 172.

39 Oraić Tolić, *Teorija citatnosti*, 17.

40 A similar argument is made by Jacob Emery in his article "Guides to Berlin"
with regard to Ugrešić's 1997 novel *The Museum of Unconditional Surrender*.
The difference in genre takes our interpretations of citation in separate
directions. See Emery, "Guides to Berlin," *Comparative Literature* 54, no. 4
(Fall 2002): 291–306.

41 Miroslav Krleža is routinely regarded as the pre-eminent Croatian writer of
the twentieth century and a leading intellectual figure in Yugoslav cultural
life.

42 Ugrešić, *Kultural laži*, 238. Italics in the original.

43 Oraić Tolić stresses the importance of the "podtekst" (literal translation:
subtext) in her discussion of citation. In her definition of the word, there
is a particular valence to the meaning of "podtekst": it encompasses the
"former context from which the citation is taken" that often goes "uncited
but is taken into account" and functions like another text (Oraić Tolić,
Teorija citatnosti, 15). The "podtekst" affects whether we read citation
as referential or auto-referential. In the former scenario, a referential
mechanism points us to the role played by "the sense of the text" from
which the citation came from. In the latter, the citation points to the text
within which it is hosted. Starting with *Culture of Lies*, but also in *Zabranjeno
čitanje* (*Thank You for Not Reading*), Ugrešić leans more towards the
referential model of citation. See Oraić Tolić, *Teorija citatnosti*, 30–1.

44 Oraić Tolić, *Teorija citatnosti*, 14.

45 Hyland, *Disciplinary Discourses*, 29.

46 Karpinski, "Postcards from Europe," 50.

47 Also, it is important to state that her earlier corpus was immersed in Russian avant-garde writing and, while predominantly marked by references to male writers – among them Konstantin Vaginov and Danill Kharms – this is a disrupted and suppressed legacy.

48 Ugrešić, *Kultura laži*, 138.

49 Ibid, 243.

50 Ibid., 234.

51 Palavestra, *Istorija Srpskog PEN-a*, 95. Specifically, Palavestra details the controversy surrounding the 1981 publication of Gojko Đogo's poems in *Vunena vremena* (*Times of Wool*) which contain allusions to Tito, who had died that year. The book of poetry was withdrawn from sale and Đogo was detained by the police on the basis of having defamed Tito's image in his writing. PEN members – Albahari included – were vociferous in criticizing the actions of the Yugoslav elites on the grounds that the response to Đogo's work went against freedom of speech and publication. PEN members were particularly motivated to interefere in this case as Belgrade was scheduled to host the annual PEN congress some time in the near future. They were concerned with how participants and other representatives of PEN centres would react to the "Đogo affair" and were invested in putting as much political pressure on the Yugoslav elites to resolve the situation. Palavestra, 95–6.

52 Ibid., 134.

53 For more on the memorandum and analysis, see Jasna Dragović-Soso, *"Saviours of the Nation": Serbia's Intellectual Opposition and the Revival of Nationalism* (London: Hurts, 2002).

54 Marković, "Kako postati akademik."

55 Tomašević, "Novi Ždanovizam hic et nunc."

56 Ibid.

57 Bourdieu, *The Rules of Art*, 229. Italics are my own.

58 This section has been influenced by Tatjana Rosić's work in *Mit o savršenoj biografiji*, even when I do not make direct reference to it.

59 Though this collection appeared in 1997, the essays it collects date from the early 1980s through to the early and mid-1990s.

60 Foucault, "What Is an Author?" 180.

61 Albahari, *Prepisivanje sveta*, 53.

62 Jameson, *Marxism and Form*, 21.

63 Ibid., 109.

64 Albahari, "Iz dnevnika o nestajanju," in *Prepisivanje sveta*, 110.

65 Albahari, "Anđeli stižu prekasno," 51.

66 Ibid., 113.

67 Ibid.
68 Ibid., 112.
69 Albahari, "Prekasno," *Prepisivanje sveta,* 75.
70 Ibid., 112.
71 Albahari, "Prekasno," in *Prepisivanje sveta,* 74–5.
72 Ibid., 75.
73 Bourdieu, *The Rules of Art,* 291–2.
74 Albahari, "Anđeli stižu prekasno," 51.
75 Bourdieu, *The Rules of Art,* 291–2.
76 See Rosić, *Mit o savršenoj biografiji,* 182–4.
77 Ugrešić's return to a high modernist authorial position is more explicitly articulated in her essay "What is an author made of?" published in *Europe in Sepia,* in which she discusses new forms of authorship that have been enabled by contemporary digital technologies. Part of her argument is that the online medium, coupled with a "celebrity culture" of self-promotion, simply standardizes writing into a paint-by-numbers craft. As a result, affirmation of the author is about an affirmation of his or her image and not of the artistic form of expression. See Ugrešić, *Evropa u sepiji,* 242–6.
78 See Karpinski, "Postcards from Europe"; Nataša Kovačević, "Storming the EU Fortress: Communities of Disagreement in Dubravka Ugrešić," *Cultural Critique* 38 (Winter 2013): 63–86.

Conclusion

1 See, for example, Aleksandar Hemon, *Nowhere Man* (New York: Picador, 2002); Šehić, *Knjiga o Uni* (Sarajevo: Buybook, 2011); Saša Stanišić, *How the Soldier Repairs the Gramophone,* trans. Anthea Bell (London: Grove Press, 2009).
2 For more on this genre and its role in transitional justice, see Demiragić and Hodžić, "The Bleak Visions of *Literary Justice* for Survivors of Srebrenica: Examining the Fictional Narratives of Srebrenica in Light of the Insights from Transitional Justice," in *The Arts of Transitional Justice: Culture, Activism, and Memory After Atrocity,* edited by Peter D. Rush and Oliver Simić, 135–54 (New York: Springer, 2013).
3 For example, in 2010, the literary and cultural journal *Sarajevske sveske* (*Sarajevo notebooks*) published a special issue on the impact transition to a free market economy and neo-liberal society have had on the post-socialist cultural field.
4 Eagleton, *The Idea of Culture,* 7.
5 Ganguly, "Deathworlds, the World Novel, and the Human," 145.
6 Ibid., 145.

7 Tomsky, "From Sarajevo to 9/11," 52.
8 Ibid, 53.
9 Ibid.
10 Ibid.

Bibliography

Agamben, Giorgio. *Homo Sacer: Sovereign Power and Bare Life.* Translated by Daniel Heller-Roazen. Stanford, CA: Stanford University Press, 1998.

Ahmetagić, Jasmina. "Fantom postmoderne," *Novi izraz* 23 (2004): 1–34.

Albahari, David. "Anđeli stižu prekasno." By D. Savić, *Večernje novosti,* 12 June 1992, 51.

– *Cink.* Belgrade: Narodna Knjiga, 1996.

– *David Albahari.* Belgrade: Službeni glasnik, 2010.

– *Fras u šupi: proze.* Belgrade: Rad, 1984.

– *Gec i majer.* Belgrade: Stubovi kulture, 2008.

– "Između buke i besa." By Saša Ilić and Slobodan Georgijev. *Vreme* 724, 18 November 2004, http://www.vreme.com/cms/view.php?id=396807.

– "Ja sam prevejani postmodernista." By Slobodan Radović. *Reč po reč: književni razgovori,* ed. Slobodan Radović. Gornji Milanovac: Lio, 2001.

– *Kratka knjiga.* Belgrade: Narodna knjiga, 1997.

– *Mamac.* Belgrade: Stubovi kulture, 2011.

– *Opis smrti.* Belgrade: Rad, 1983.

– *Pelerina i nove priče.* Belgrade: Narodna knjiga, 1997.

– *Porodično vreme.* Belgrade: Narodna knjiga, 1996.

– *Prepisivanje sveta.* Vršac: Književna opština, 1997.

– *Snežni čovek.* Belgrade: Stubovi kulture, 2007.

– *Svetski putnik.* Belgrade: Stubovi kulture, 2004.

– *Teret: Eseji.* Belgrade: Forum Pisaca, 2004.

– "U traganju za idealnom knjigom." By Gojko Božović and Milovan Marčetić. *Reč* 23–4 (July/August 1996): 14–19.

– "Umetnik je izgnanik: razgovor Davida Albaharija i Mihajla Pantića." Interview by Mihajlo Pantić. *Gradac* 156 (2005): 6–24.

Aleksić, Tatjana. "National Definition through Postmodern Fragmentation: Milorad Pavić's *Dictionary of the Khazars.*" *Slavic and East European Journal* 53, no. 1 (2009): 86–104.

– *The Sacrificed Body: Balkan Community Building and the Fear of Freedom.* Pittsburgh, PA: University of Pittsburgh Press, 2013.

Andreas, Peter. *Blue Helmets and Black Markets.* Ithaca, NY: Cornell University Press, 2008.

Arendt, Hannah. *Eichmann in Jerusalem: A Report on the Banality of Evil.* New York: Viking, 1963.

Arsenijević, Damir. *Forgotten Future: The Politics of Poetry in Bosnia and Herzegovina.* Baden-Baden: Nomos, 2010.

Assmann, Aleida. "Beyond the Archive." In *Waste-Site Stories: The Recycling of Memories*, edited by Brian Nevile and Johanne Villeneuve, 71–84. Albany: State University of New York Press, 2002.

Baker, Catherine. *Sounds of the Borderland: Popular Music, War and Nationalism in Croatia since 1991.*Farnham, UK: Ashgate, 2010.

– "War Memory and Musical Tradition: Commemorating Croatia's Homeland War through Popular Music and Rap in Eastern Slavonia." *Journal of Contemporary European Studies*, 17, no. 1 (2009): 35–45.

Barthes, Roland "The Death of the Author." In *Theories of Authorship*, edited by John Caughie, 208–13. London: Routledge, 1996.

Bauman, Zygmunt. *Modernity and the Holocaust.* Polity Press, 1989.

Baudrillard, Jean. *Screened Out.* Translated by Chris Turner. London: Verso, 2002.

Benjamin, Walter. *Illuminations.* Translated by Harry Zohn. New York: Schocken Books, 1968.

– *The Origin of German Tragic Drama.* Translated by John Osborne. London: NLB, 1977.

Bennetts, Marc. "Eduard Limonov Interview: Political Rebel and Vladimir Putin's Worst Nightmare." *The Observer.* 12 December 2010. http://www.guardian.co.uk/world/2010/dec/12/eduard-limonov-interview-putin-nightmare.

Berman, Marshall. "Falling." In *Restless Cities*, edited by Matthew Beaumont and Gregory Dart, 123–38. London: Verso, 2010.

Bernstein, Michael André. *Foregone Conclusions: Against Apocalyptic History.* Berkeley: University of California Press, 1994.

Bertolino, Nikola. "Vreme inkubacije." *Sarajevske sveske* 4 (2003): 87–115.

Binder, David. "Anatomy of a Massacre." *Foreign Policy* 97 (1994–5): 70–8.

Binkley, Sam. "Kitsch as a Repetitive System: A Problem for the Theory of Taste Hierarchy." *Journal of Material Culture* 5, no.2 (July 2000): 131–52.

Blanchot, Maurice. *The Gaze of Orpheus and Other Essays.* Edited by P. Adams Sitney. Translated by Lydia Davis. New York: Station Hill Press, 1981.

Bošković, Aleksandar. "Yugonostalgia and Yugoslav Cultural Memory: *Lexicon of Yu Mythology.*" *Slavic Review* 72, no. 1 (Spring 2013): 54–78.

Bošković, Dragan B. "Politike srpskog postmodernizma." *Nasleđe* 8, no. 20 (2011): 9–22.

– *Zablude modernizma.* Belgrade: Službeni glasnik, 2010.

Bourdieu, Pierre. *The Rules of Art: Genesis and the Structure of the Literary Field.* Translated by Susan Emanuel. Stanford, CA: Stanford University Press, 1995.

Boym, Svetlana. *Common Places: Mythologies of Everyday Life in Russia.* Cambridge, MA: Harvard University Press, 1994.

– *Future of Nostalgia.* New York: Basic Books, 2001.

Brajović, Tihomir. *Komparativni identiteti: srpska književnost između evropskog i južnoslovenskog konteksta.* Belgrade: Službeni glasnik, 2012.

– "Kratka istorija preobilja: Zapažanja o srpskom romanu na prelazu stoleća." *Sarajevske sveske* 13 (2006): 187–214.

Broszat, Martin. "Hitler and the Genesis of the 'Final Solution': An Assessment of David Irving's Theses." In *Aspects of the Third Reich,* edited by H.W. Koch, 390–429. London: Macmillan, 1985.

Browning, Christopher R. *Fateful Months: Essays on the Emergence of the Final Solution.* London: Holmes and Meier, 1985.

Buck Morss, Susan. "Aesthetics and Anaesthetics: Walter Benjamin's Artwork Essay Reconsidered." *October* 62 (1992): 3–41.

– *Dreamworld and Catastrophe: The Passing of Mass Utopia in the East and West.* Cambridge, MA: Harvard University Press, 2000.

Burke, Sean. *The Ethics of Writing: Authorship and Legacy in Plato and Nietzsche.* Edinburgh: Edinburgh University Press, 2008.

Burt, Stephen. "Must Poets Write?" *London Review of Books* 34, no. 9 (10 May 2012): 33–4.

Butler, Judith. *Frames of War: When Is Life Grievable?* London: Verso, 2009.

Byford, Jovan. *Staro sajmište: Mesto sećanja, zaborava i sporenja.* Belgrade: Beogradski centar za ljudska prava, 2011.

Campbell, David. "Atrocity, Memory, Photography: Imaging the Concentration Camps of Bosnia – the Case of ITN versus *Living Marxism,* Part I." *Journal of Human Rights* 1, no. 1 (March 2002): 1–33.

Casanova, Pascale. *The World Republic of Letters.* Translated by M.B. Debevoise. Cambridge, MA: Harvard University Press, 2004.

Castle, Terry. *The Professor: A Sentimental Education.* New York: Harper, 2010.

Călinescu, Matei. *Five Faces of Modernity: Modernism, Avant-garde, Decadence, Kitsch, Postmodernism.* Durham, NC: Duke University Press, 1997.

Chow, Rey. "The Fascist Longings in Our Midst." *ARIEL* 26, no. 1 (January 1995): 23–50.

Crnković, Gordana. *Post Yugoslav Film and Literature: Fires, Foundations, Flourishes.* New York: Continuum, 2011.

– Review of *The Culture of Lies: Antipolitical Essays Culture of Lies: Antipolitical Essays,* by Dubravka Ugrešić. Translated by Celia Hawkesworth. *Slavic and East European Journal* 43, no. 3 (Autumn 1999): 544–6.

Coetzee, J.M. *Giving Offence: Essays on Censorship.* Chicago: Chicago University Press, 1996.

Čolović, Ivan. *Politika simbola: Ogledi o političkoj antropologiji.* Belgrade: Čigoja, 2000.

Dauphinee, Elizabeth. "The Politics of the Body in Pain: Readings the Ethics of Imagery." *Security in Dialogue* 38, no. 2 (2007): 139–55.

Denegri, Ješa. "Inside or Outside 'Socialist Modernism'? Radical Views on the Yugoslav Art Scene, 1950–1970." In *Impossible Histories: Historical Avant-Gardes, Neo-Avant-Gardes, and Post-Avant-Gardes in Yugoslavia, 1918–1991,* edited by Dubravka Djurić and Miško Šuvaković, 170–208. Cambridge, MA: MIT Press, 2003.

Denić Grabić, Amila. "Kraj dvadesteog stoljeća: Bosanskohercegovački roman između globalnog i lokalnog." *Sarajevske sveske* 27–8 (May 2010): 285–300.

Derrida, Jacques. "Sending: On Representation." *Social Research* 49, no. 2 (1982): 294–326.

Duraković, Ferida. "Pisac sagledava domovinu dok učeni postmodernist ulazi u njegov grad." In *Srce tame 1973–1993.* Sarajevo: Bosanska knjiga, 1994.

Đekić, Velid. *Flagusova rukavica: "originalnost prepisivanja" u prozi Dubravke Ugrešić.* Rijeka: Naklada Benja, 1995.

Đorđević, Mirko. "Književnost populističkog talasa." In *Srpska strana rata: trauma i katarza u istorijskom pamćenju,* edited by Nebojša Popov, 431–55. Belgrade: Samizdat B92, 2002.

Eagleton, Terry. "Capitalism, Modernism, Postmodernism." *New Left Review* 152 (July–August 1985): 60–73.

– *Ideology: An Introduction.* London: Verso, 1991.

– *The Idea of Culture.* Oxford: Blackwell, 2000.

– *The Ideology of the Aesthetic.* Oxford: Blackwell, 1990.

– *The Illusions of Postmodernism.* Oxford: Blackwell, 1996.

Eco, Umberto. *The Open Work.* Translated by Anna Cancogni. Cambridge, MA: Harvard University Press, 1989.

Edkins, Jenny. *Missing: Persons and Politics.* Ithaca, NY: Cornell University Press, 2011.

Erjavec, Aleš. "Filozofija kritičke teorije i postmodernizam." *Delo,* 35, nos. 4–5 (April/May 1989): 141–58.

– ed. *Postmodernism and the Postsocialist Condition: Politicized Art under Late Socialism.* Berkeley: University of California Press, 2003.

Esh, Shaul. "Words and Their Meanings: 25 Examples of Nazi Idiom." *Yad Vashem Studies* 5 (1963): 133–5.

Felman, Shoshana, and Dori Laub. *Testimony: Crisis of Witnessing in Literature, Psychoanalysis, and History.* New York and London: Routledge, 1992.

Fisk, Robert. "Waging War on History: In Former Yugoslavia, Whole Cultures are Being Obliterated." *The Independent*, 20 June 1994. http://www.independent.co.uk/voices/waging-war-on-history-in-former-yugoslavia-writes-robert-fisk-whole-cultures-are-being-obliterated-1423832.html.

Flaker, Aleksandar. *Proza u trapericama: prilog izgradnji modela prozne formacije na građi suvremenih književnosti srednjo- i istočnoevropske regije.* Zagreb: Liber, 1983.

Foster Wallace, David. *A Supposedly Fun Thing I'll Never Do Again.* New York: Back Bay Books. 1997.

Foucault, Michel. "What Is an Author?" In *Modern Criticism and Theory: A Reader,* edited by David Lodge and Nigel Wood, 174–87. Harlow, UK: Longman, 2000.

Freud, Sigmund. *The Standard Edition of the Complete Psychological Works of Sigmund Freud.* Vol. 21. Translated by James Strachey. London: Vintage, 2001.

Friedlander, Saul. *Reflections of Nazism: An Essay on Kitsch and Death.* Translated by Thomas Weyr. Bloomington: Indiana University Press, 1993.

Frye, Northrop. *Anatomy of Criticism: Four Essays.* Princeton, NJ: Princeton University Press, 1957.

Fussell, Paul. *The Great War and Memory.* Oxford: Oxford University Press, 1975.

Fukuyama, Francis. "The End of History?" *National Interest* 16 (Summer 1989): 3–18.

Ganguly, Debjani. "Deathworlds, the World Novel, and the Human." *Angelaki: Journal of Theoretical Humanities* 16, no. 4 (2011): 145–58.

Garber, Marjorie. "Compassion." In *Compassion: The Culture and Politics of an Emotion,* edited by Lauren Berlant, 15–27. New York and London: Routledge, 2004.

Genette, Gérard. *Seuils.* Paris: Seuil, 1987.

Gilbert, Sandra, and Susan Gubar. *Madwoman in the Attic: The Woman Writer and the Nineteenth Century Literary Imagination.* New Haven, CT: Yale University Press, 1979.

Gingeras, Alison. "The Comeback of Sincerity: Jeff Koons 1995–2001." In *Jeff Koons,* edited by Eckhard Schneider, 79–90. Cologne: Walther König, 2001.

Ginzburg, Lidia. *Blockade Diary.* Translated by Alan Meyers. London: Harvill Press, 1995.

Good, Graham. *The Observing Self: Rediscovering the Essay.* London: Routledge, 1988.

Gordy, Eric. *The Culture of Power in Serbia: Nationalism and the Destruction of Alternatives*. University Park: Pennsylvania State University Press, 1999.

Greenberg, Clement. *Clement Greenberg: The Collected Essays and Criticism*. Chicago: University of Chicago Press, 1986.

Hammond, Philip. *Media, War and Postmodernity*. London: Routledge, 2007.

Harootunian, Harry. "Remembering the Historical Present." *Critical Inquiry* 33, no. 3 (Spring 2007): 471–94.

Hebdige, Dick. "Postmodernism and the Other Side." In *Stuart Hall: Critical Dialogues in Cultural* Studies, edited by David Morley and Kuan-Hsing Chen, 174–201. London: Routledge, 1996.

Hegel, G.W.F. *Aesthetics: Lectures on Fine Art*. Translated by T.M. Knox. Vol. 1. Oxford: Clarendon Press, 1975.

Hell, Julia, and Andreas Schönle, eds. *Ruins of Modernity*. Durham, NC: Duke University Press, 2011.

Hemon, Aleksandar. *The Question of Bruno*. New York: Pan Macmillan, 2000.

Hewitt, Andrew. *Fascist Modernism: Aesthetics, Politics and the Avant-Garde*. Stanford, CA: Stanford University Press, 1993.

Horowitz, Sarah. *Voicing the Void: Muteness and Memory in Holocaust Fiction*. Albany: State University of New York Press, 1997.

Hutcheon, Linda. "The Politics of Postmodernism: Parody and History." *Cultural Critique* 5 (1986–7): 197–207.

Huyssen, Andreas. *After the Great Divide: Modernism, Mass Culture and Postmodernism*. Bloomington: Indiana University Press, 1986.

Hyland, Ken. *Disciplinary Discourses: Social Interactions in Academic Writing*. Harlow, UK: Pearson Education Ltd, 2000.

Iordanova, Dina. *Cinema of Flames: Balkan Film, Culture and Media*. London: British Film Institute, 2001.

Jaffe, Aaron. *Modernism and the Culture of Celebrity*. Cambridge: Cambridge University Press, 2005.

Jakovljević, Branislav. "Human Resources: June 1968, *Hair*, and the Beginning of Yugoslavia's End." *Grey Room* 30 (Winter 2008): 38–53.

– "Theatre of Atrocities: Toward a Disreality Principle." *PMLA* 124 (October 2009): 1813–19.

Jameson, Frederic. *Marxism and Form: Twentieth Century Dialectical Theories of Literature*. Princeton, NJ: Princeton University Press, 1971.

– *The Political Unconscious: Narrative as a Socially Symbolic Act*. Ithaca, NY: Cornell University Press, 1981.

– *Postmodernism, or, The Cultural Logic of Late Capitalism*. Durham, NC: Duke University Press, 1991.

– "Postmodernism, or, The Cultural Logic of Late Capitalism." *New Left Review* 146 (July–August 1984): 53–92.

– "Postmoderni prostor." By Mladen Kožul and Ivailo Dičev. *Quorum* 7, no. 1 (1991): 3–18.

– "Regarding Postmodernism: A Conversation with Frederic Jameson." By Anders Stephanson. In *Universal Abandon?: The Politics of Postmodernism,* edited by Andrew Ross, 3–30. Edinburgh: Edinburgh University Press, 1988.

Jay, Martin. "'The Aesthetic Ideology' as Ideology; or What Does It Mean to Aestheticize Politics?" *Cultural Critique* 21 (1992): 41–61.

– *Downcast Eyes: Denigration of Vision in French Thought.* Berkeley: University of California Press, 1994.

Jelčić, Dubravko. *Povijest hrvatske književnosti: tisućljece od Baščanske ploče do postmoderne.* Zagreb: Naklada Pavičić, 2004.

Jergović, Miljenko. "Sarajevski marketing." *Erasmus – časopis za kulturu demokracije* 4 (1994): 39–41.

Jerkov, Aleksandar. *Nova tekstualnost: ogledi o sprskoj prozi postmodernog doba.* Nikšić: Unireks, 1992.

Jestrović, Silvija. *Performance, Space, Utopia: Cities of War, Cities of Exile.* New York: Palgrave, 2012.

Jovanović, Nebojša. "Motiv tri žene u 'Muzeju bezuvjetne predaje' Dubravke Ugrešić." *Reč* 20, no. 74 (2006): 107–26.

Kalyvas, Stathis N. *The Logic of Violence in Civil War.* Cambridge: Cambridge University Press, 2006.

Kandić, Nataša, ed. "Škorpioni: od zločina do pravde." Belgrade: Fond za humanitarno pravo, 2012. http://www.hlc-rdc.org/wp-content/uploads/2012/06/Skorpioni.pdf . Accessed 11 September 2015.

Kant, Immanuel. *The Critique of Judgment.* Translated by J.H. Bernard. New York: Hafner Press, 1951.

Kaplan, Alice. *Reproductions of Banality: Fascism, Literature, and French Intellectual Life.* Minneapolis: University of Minnesota Press, 1986.

Karpinski, Eva C. "Postcards from Europe: Dubravka Ugrešić as a Transnational Public Intellectual, or Life Writing in Fragments." *European Journal of Life Writing* 2 (2013): 42–60.

Kazaz, Enver. "Mehmedinovićeva mistika emocija." *Sarajevske sveske* 3 (2003): 217–36.

– *Neprijatelj ili susjed u kući: interliterarna bosanskohercegovačka zajednica na prelazu milenija.* Sarajevo: Rabic, 2008.

– "Prizori uhodanog užasa." *Sarajevske sveske* 5 (2004): 137–65.

Kebo, Ozren. "Pismo iz Sarajeva." *Erasmus – časopis za kulturu demokracije* 11 (1995): 48–51.

Kermode, Frank. *The Sense of An Ending: Studies in the Theory of Fiction*. Oxford: Oxford University Press, 2000.

Kesić, Vesna. "Witch hunt, Croatian style." Translated by Vinka Lyubimir. *Women's Review of Books* 10, nos. 10/11 (July 1993): 16–17.

King, Barry. "Stardom, Celebrity and the Money Form." *Velvet Light Trap* 65 (Spring 2010): 7–19.

Kiš, Danilo. *Čas anatomije*. Belgrade: Nolit, 1981.

– *Homo poeticus*. Belgrade: Prosveta, 2006.

– *Život, literatura*. Belgrade: Prosveta, 2007.

Klaus, Carl. "Essayists on the Essay." In *Literary Nonfiction: Theory, Criticism, Pedagogy*, edited by Chris Anderson, 155–75. Carbondale: Southern Illinois Press, 1989.

Klemperer, Victor. *LTI – Lingua Tertii Imperii: A Philologist's Notebook*. Translated by Martin Brady. London: Continuum, 2002.

Ključanin, Zilhad. "Ushit ljepotom svijeta". In *Bošnjačka književnost u književnoj kritici: novija književnost – poezija*, edited by Enes Duraković, 744–8. Sarajevo: Alef, 1998.

Koljanin, Milan. *Nemački logor na Beogradskom sajmištu 1941–1944*. Belgrade: Institut za savremenu istoriju, 1992.

Kronja, Ivana. "Turbo Folk and Dance Music in 1990s Serbia: Media, Ideology, and the Production of Spectacle." *The Anthropology of East Europe Review* 22, no.1 (Spring 2004):103–14.

Kuhlman, Martha. "The Culture of Lies, the Museum of Unconditional Surrender: Dubravka Ugrešić's Recent Work." *ARTMargins Online*, 30 December 1999. http://www.artmargins.com/index.php/featured-articles-sp-829273831/473-the-culture-of-lies-the-museum-of-unconditional-surrender-dubravka-ugresics-recent-work. Accessed 3 October 2010.

Kulenović, Tvrtko. *Istorija bolesti*. Bosanska knjiga: Sarajevo, 1994.

Kundera, Milan. *The Unbearable Lightness of Being*. Translated by Michael Henry Heim. London: Harper Perennial, 1999.

Lacoue-Labarthe, Philippe. *Heidegger, Art and Politics*. Translated by Chris Turner. Oxford: Blackwell, 1990.

Lovrenović, Ivan. "The Hatred of Memory." *New York Times*, 28 May 1994, Y15, national edition.

– "Je li kasno za Bosnu?" *Erasmus: časopis za kulturu demokracije* 9 (1994): 2–4.

Lukács, Georg. *Soul and Form*. Translated by Anna Bostock. London: Merlin Press, 1974.

Lukić, Jasmina. "Witches Fly High: The Sweeping Broom of Dubravka Ugrešić." *European Journal of Women's Studies* 7, no. 3 (2000): 385–93.

Lydic, Lauren. "'Noseological' Parody, Gender Discourse, and Yugoslav Feminisms: Following Gogol's 'Nose' to Ugrešić's 'Hot Dog on a Warm Bun.'" *Comparative Literature* 62, no. 2 (2010): 161–78.

Lyotard, Jean-François. *The Postmodern Condition: A Report on Knowledge.*
Translated by Geoff Bennington and Brian Massumi. Minneapolis: University
of Minnesota Press, 1984.

Marković, Tomislav. "Kako postati akademik: Saveti mladom piscu." *Beton,* 20
June 2006. http://www.elektrobeton.net/strafta/kako-postati-akademik/.

Maass, Peter. *Love Thy Neighbor.* London: Papermac, 1996.

McLoughlin, Kate. *Authoring War: The Literary Representation of War from the Iliad
to Iraq.* Cambridge: Cambridge University Press, 2011.

Medvedev, P.N., and M.M. Bakhtin, *The Formal Method in Literary Scholarship.*
Translated by A.J. Wehrle. Baltimore: Johns Hopkins University Press, 1978.

Mehmedinović, Semezdin. "Izbaviteljska gesta poezije (Intervju sa Semezindom
Mehmedinovićem)." By Enver Kazaz. *Razlika/Différance* 12/13/14 (2006): 19–36.

– "Kompozitor." *Erasmus: Journal for Culture of Democracy* 9 (1994): 78.

– *Modrac.* Sarajevo: Svjetlost, 1984.

– *Sarajevo blues.* Sarajevo: Biblioteka Dani, 2004.

– *Sarajevo blues.* Translated by Ammiel Alcalay. San Francisco: City Light Books,
1998.

Mikulić, Boris. *Kroatorij Europe: Filosofistička kronika druge hrvatske tranzicije u 42
slike.* Zagreb: Demetra, 2006.

– "Zastave ili beskonačni manjak ideološke utjehe: povratak kritičkog diskursa
iz estetičke analiza kiča."http://arkzin.net/bastard/kultura.htm.

Milutinović, Zoran. "The Demoniacism of History and Promise of Aesthetic
Redemption in David Albahari's *Bait.*" *Serbian Studies* 19 (2005): 15–24.

– "What Common Yugoslav Culture Was, and How Everybody Benefited
from It." In *After Yugoslavia: The Cultural Spaces of a Vanished Land,* edited by
Radmila Gorup, 75–87. Stanford, CA: Stanford University Press, 2013.

Mitrović, Marija. "*Gec i Majer* or Situational Education." *Serbian Studies,* 19, no. 1
(2005): 83–93.

Modleski, Tania. "Femininity as Mas(s)querade: A Feminist Approach to Mass
Culture." In *High Theory/Low Culture: Analysing Popular Television and Film,* edited
by Colin MacCabe, 29–45. Manchester: Manchester University Press, 1986.

Moeller, Susan. *Compassion Fatigue: How the Media Sell Disease, Famine, War and
Death.* New York: Routledge, 1999.

Moranjak-Bamburać, Nirman. "Ima li rata u ratnom pismu?" *Sarajevske sveske* 5
(2004): 79–82.

– "Signature smrti i etičnost ženskog pisma." *Sarajevske sveske* 2 (2003): 113–22.

Moretti, Franco. "History of the Novel, Theory of the Novel." *Novel* 43, no. 1
(Spring 2010): 1–10.

– *Signs Taken For Wonders: Essays in the Sociology of Literary Forms.* Translated by
Susan Fischer, David Forgacs, and David Miller. London: Verso, 1983.

Nabokov, Vladimir. *Nikolai Gogol.* London: Penguin, 2011.

Nandrea, Lorri G., and Michal Peled Ginsburg. "The Prose of the World." In *The Novel Volume II: Forms and Themes,* edited by Franco Moretti, 244–73. Princeton, NJ: Princeton University Press, 2006.

Norris, Margot. *Writing War in the Twentieth Century.* Charlottesville: University Press of Virginia, 2000.

Novak Bajcar, Silvija. *Mape vremena: Srpska postmodernistička proza pred izazovima epohe.* Translated by Ljubica Rosić. Belgrade: Službeni glasnik, 2015.

– "Zašto je postmodernizam u Sribiji (ipak) moguć." *Nasleđe* 7, no. 16 (2010): 123–30.

Obradović, Dragana. "The Ironic Eternity of Objects in Dubravka Ugrešić's *The Museum of Unconditional Surrender.*" *Russian Literature* 70, no. 3 (October 2011): 415–41.

Oraić Tolić, Dubravka. "Citatnost u avangardi i postmoderni." *Umjetnost riječi,* 33, no. 23 (April–September 1989): 149–63.

– *Palindromska apokalipsa.* Zagreb: Durieux, 1993.

– *Paradigme dvadesetog stoljeća: avangarda i postmoderna.* Zagreb: Zavod za znanost o književnosti Filozofskoga fakulteta Sveučilišta u Zagrebu, 1997.

– *Teorija citatnosti.* Zagreb: Grafički zavod Hrvatske, 1990.

Ó Tuathail, Gearóid. *Critical Geopolitics: The Politics of Writing Global Space.* Minneapolis: University of Minnesota Press, 1996.

Palavestra, Predrag. *Istorija Srpskog PEN-a.* Belgrade: Serbian PEN Centre, 2006.

Pascoe, David. "The Cold War and 'The War on Terror.'" In *The Cambridge Companion to War Writing,* edited by Kate McLoughlin, 239–49. Cambridge: Cambridge University Press, 2009.

Patterson, Patrick Hyder. *Bought and Sold: Living and Losing the Good Life in Socialist Yugoslavia.* Ithaca, NY: Cornell University Press, 2011.

Pavičić, Jurica "Prošlo je vrijeme Sumatra i Javi." *Sarajevske sveske* 5 (2004): 125–35.

The Penguin Dictionary of Literary Terms and Literary Theory. Compiled by J.A. Cuddon. 4th ed., Harmondsworth: Penguin, 1997.

Peréz-Torres, Rafael. "Nomads and Migrants: Negotiating a Multicultural Postmodernism." *Cultural Critique* 26 (Winter 1993–4):161–89.

Perloff, Marjorie. *The Radical Artifice: Writing Poetry in the Age of Media.* Chicago: Chicago University Press, 1991.

Picard, Max. *The World of Silence.* Translated by Stanley Godman. South Bend, IN: Gateway, 1952.

Pisac, Andrea. "Trusted Tales: Creating Authenticity in Literary Representations from Ex-Yugoslavia." PhD diss., Goldsmiths, University of London, 2010, Goldsmiths Research Online.

Radhakrishnan, R. *Theory in an Uneven World.* Oxford: Blackwell, 2003.

Rem, Goran. *Slavonsko ratno pismo: monografija.* Osijek: Matica hrvatska, 1997.

Ribnikar, Vladislava. "Istorija i trauma u romanima Davida Albaharija." *Zbornik Matice srpske za književnost i jezik* 54, no. 3 (2006): 613–39.

Riedlmayer, András. *Destruction of Cultural Heritage in Bosnia-Herzegovina 1992–1996: A Post-War Survey of Selected Municipalities.* http://archnet.org/system/publications/contents/3481/original/DPC1420.pdf?1384775281.

Rieff, David. *Slaughterhouse: Bosnia and the Failure of the West.* New York: Simon and Schuster, 1995.

Rosić, Tatjana. *Mit o savršenoj biografiji.* Belgrade: Institut za književnost i umetnost, 2008.

– "Slepa mrlja realnog." *Sarajevske sveske,* 27–8 (2010): 149–76.

Rothberg, Michael. *Traumatic Realism: The Demands of Holocaust Representation.* Minneapolis: University of Minnesota Press, 2000.

Rousset, David. *L'univers concetrationnaire.* Paris: Hachette littératures, 1946.

Said, Edward. *The Representation of Intellectuals: The 1993 Reith Lectures.* London: Vintage, 1994.

Scarry, Elaine. *Body in Pain: The Making and the Unmaking of the World.* Oxford: Oxford University Press, 1985.

Shaw, Martin. "New Wars of the City: Relationships of 'Urbicide' and 'Genocide.'" In *Cities, War and Terrorism: Towards an Urban Geopolitics,* edited by Stephen Graham, 141–53. Malden, MA: Blackwell, 2004.

Simmel, Georg. *Essays on Sociology, Philosophy and Aesthetics.* New York: Harper and Row, 1965.

Slapšak, Svetlana. "Šta si radio u ratu, sine?" In *Srbija kao sprava: demilitarizacija nacionalne culture,* edited by Miloš Živanović et al., 159–64. Belgrade: Dan Graf, 2007.

Soberg, Marius. "Croatia Since 1989: The HDZ and the Politics of Transition in Croatia: Value Transformation, Education and Media." In *Democratic Transition in Croatia: Value, Transformation, Education and Media,* edited by Sabrina P. Ramet and Davorka Matić, 31–62. College Station: Texas A & M University Press, 2007.

Sokolović, Mirnes. "Susret sa odgođenim krajem dvadesetog vijeka: fakcija i angažman u postjugoslevnskom antiratnom pismu." *Polja,* 55, no. 463 (May–June 2010): 148–65.

Solar, Milivoj. "Obnova i kritika mitske svijesti o jeziku u romanu postmodernizma." In *Postmodernizam: Nova epoha ili zabluda?* edited by Ivan Kuvačić and Gvozden Flego, 9–15. Zagreb: Naprijed, 1989.

– *Retorika postmoderne: Ogledi i predavanja.* Zagreb: Matica hrvatska, 2005.

Sontag, Susan. *Regarding the Pain of Others.* New York: Picador, 2003.

– *Under the Sign of Saturn.* New York: Picador, 2002.

– *Where the Stress Falls: Essays.* London: Jonathan Cape, 2001.

Sretenović, Dejan. "A Journey Through the Pictures and Phantasms of the 1990s." In *On Normality: Art in Serbia,* 1989–2001, edited by Branislava Anđelković, translated by Novica Petrović, 131–216. Belgrade: Museum of Contemporary Art, 2006.

Stewart, Susan. *On Longing: Narratives of the Miniature, the Gigantic, the Souvenir, the Collection.* Baltimore: Johns Hopkins University Press, 1984.

Suleiman, Susan Rubin. "When the Perpetrator Becomes a Reliable Witness of the Holocaust: On Jonathan Littell's *Les bienveillantes.*" *New German Critique* 36, no. 106:1 (Winter 2009): 1–19.

Šoljan, Antun. "Dubravka Cvek u raljama rata." *Večernji list,* 11 November 1992, 15.

Šuvaković, Miško. *KFS: Kritične forme savremenosti i žudnja za demokratijom.* Novi Sad: Orpheus, 2007.

Tasić, Vladimir. "Snežni čovek i paralaksa." *Gradac* 156 (2005): 88–94.

Terzic, Zoran. "Between Destiny and Contingency: Variations on Historical Narratives in the Arts during the Break-Up of Yugoslavia". In *Myths and Boundaries in South-Eastern Europe,* edited by Pål Kolstø, 223–61. London: Hurst and Company, 2005.

Tester, Keith. *Humanitarianism and Modern Culture.* University Park: Pennsylvania State University Press, 2010.

Thompson, Mark. *Forging War: The Media in Serbia, Croatia, Bosnia and Hercegovina.* Luton: Luton University Press, 1999.

Tokača, Mirsad. *Bosanska knjiga mrtvih.* Sarajevo: Istraživačko dokumentacioni centar, 2012.

Tomašević, Boško. "Novi Ždanovism hic et nunc." *Beton* 11 February 2010. http://www.elektrobeton.net/beton-plus/novi-zdanovizam-hic-et-nunc/.

Tomsky, Terri. "From Sarajevo to 9/11: Travelling Memory and the Trauma Economy." *Parallax* 17, no. 4 (2011): 49–60.

Ugrešić, Dubravka. *Europa u sepiji.* Zagreb: Profil, 2014.

– *Kultura laži: antipolitički eseji.* Belgrade: Samizdat B92, 2002.

– Interview by Svetlana Boym. *Bomb* 80 (Summer 2002). http://bombmagazine.org/article/2498/.

– *Muzej bezuvjetne predaje.* Belgrade: Samizdat B92, 2002.

– "State of the Art: Constructing Identities, Crossing Borders." Translated by Celia Hawkesworth. *European Journal of Women's Studies* 10, no. 4 (2003): 465–71.

– *Štefica Cvek u raljama života.* Belgrade: Samizdat B92, 2001.

– *Zabranjeno čitanje.* Belgrade: Samizdat B92, 2002.

– *Život je bajka: métaterxies.* Belgrade: Samizdat B92, 2001.

– "Yugoslavia, an 'Almost Forbidden Word': Cultural Policy in Times of Nationalism – an Interview with Dubravka Ugrešić." By Natasa Kovacevic.

Women and Performance: A Journal of Feminist Theory 17, no. 3 (November 2007): 299–315.

Virilio, Paul. *A Landscape of Events.* Translated by Julie Rose. Cambridge, MA: MIT Press, 2000.

Visković, Velimir. *Mlada proza: eseji i kritike.* Zagreb: Znanje, 1983.

– *Umijeće pripovijedanja: Ogledi o hrvatskoj prozi.* Zagreb: Znanje, 2000.

Vogler, Thomas A. "Poetic Witness: Writing the Real." In *Witness and Memory: The Discourse of Trauma,* edited by Ana Douglass and Thomas A. Vogler, 173–205. London: Routledge, 2003.

Vološinov, V. N. *Marxism and the Philosophy of Language.* Translated by Ladislav Matejka and I.R. Titunik. Cambridge, MA: Harvard University Press, 1986.

Von Oppen, Karoline. "Imagining the Balkans, Imagining Germany: Intellectual Journeys to Former Yugoslavia in the 1990s." *German Quarterly* 79, no. 2 (Spring 2006): 192–210.

Wachtel, Andrew. "Postmodernism As Nightmare: Milorad Pavić's Literary Demolition of Yugoslavia." *Slavic and East European Journal* 41, no. 4 (Winter 1997): 627–44.

– *Remaining Relevant After Communism: The Role of the Writer in Eastern Europe.* Chicago: Chicago University Press, 2006.

White, Hayden. "Figural Realism in Witness Literature." *Parallax* 10, no. 1 (2004): 113–24.

Williams, Raymond. *Marxism and Literature.* Oxford: Oxford University Press, 1977.

Zorić, Vladimir. "The Poetics of Legend: The Paradigmatic Approach to Legend in Danilo Kiš's *A Tomb for Boris Davidovich.*" *Modern Languages Review* 100, no. 1 (January 2005): 161–84.

Žižek, Slavoj. "The Military-Poetic Complex." *London Review of Books* 30, no. 16. 14 August 2008.

– "Multiculturalism, or, the Cultural Logic of Multinational Capitalism," *New Left Review* 1:225 (September–October 1997): 28–51.

Žmegač, Viktor. *Povijesna poetika romana.* 3rd edition. Zagreb: Matica hrvatska, 2004.

– "Kroatische Kontroversen." *Literatur und Kritik* nos. 273–4 (April 1993): 105–6.

Internet Sources

– Croatian Constituion, http://www.sabor.hr/Default.aspx
– UN High Commissioner for Refugees (UNHCR), http://www.unhcr.org
– Internal Displacement Monitoring Centre, http://www.internal-displacement. org/

Index

aesthetic: definition, 95; of war literature, 4–5
aestheticization of politics, 79, 89, 95–6, 98
aesthetic judgment, 53–4
aesthetic pleasure of destruction, 39–40
Ahmetagić, Jasmina, 29, 172n45
Albahari, David: on boundaries of language, 110; career of, 18, 23; ethnic and cultural background of, 103, 107–8; on exceptionalism of the present, 100; form of writing, 114; as member of literary institutions, 152–3; practice of postmodernism, 23, 103; prosaic style, 111; on prose, 112–13; public and private life, 108, 109, 156; rejection of dissidence, 155; on representation of the past, 101–2; self-assessment of, 111–12; status in Serbian literature, 153–4; translations of American postmodernists, 109; travel to Santiago de Compostela, 152; understanding of time, 100–1; on value of art, 157; view of authorship, 154, 156–7, 158; on writers, 155
Albahari's prose: characteristics of, 100, 101, 102–4, 110–11, 112–14; *Cink*, 124; collective time, 115; comparison with prose of Dubravka Ugrešić, 105–6, 155–6; everyday life in, 112; impact of dissolution of Yugoslavia on, 136; Jewish motifs, 108, 111; *Kratka knjiga* (*Short Book*), 101; *Mamac* (*Bait*), 101; *Porodično vreme* (*Family Time*), 111; principle of silence, 154–5; quality of depthlessness, 22; *Rewriting the World*, 100, 154–5; role of history in, 17–18; "The Story of the Koan," 109; syntax of, 115; *World Traveller*, 123–4. See also *Götz and Meyer; Snow Man*
Aleksić, Tatjana, 31, 107, 167n24
Aralica, Ivan, 69, 173n62
Arapović, Ademir, 44
Arendt, Hannah, 190n160
Arsenijević, Damir, 175n18
Arsenijević, Vladimir, 159
art: aggressive desire for the real, 6; city under siege as object of, 3; Holocaust